Employing the Unemployed

EMPLOYING THE UNEMPLOYED

Eli Ginzberg

EDITOR

Basic Books, Inc., Publishers

NEW YORK

Library of Congress Cataloging in Publication Data

Main entry under title:
Employing the unemployed.
    Includes bibliographical references and index.
    1.   Manpower policy—United States—History—
Addresses, essays, lectures.   I.   Ginzberg, Eli,
1911-
HD5724.E43   331.11'0973   79-5352
ISBN: O-465-01957-9

For

Howard Rosen

Master-Builder of Manpower Research

Supporter of All Who Work in the Vineyard

CONTENTS

Contents

PREFACE

THIS VOLUME reflects the interest and support of my friend, Mr. Mitchell Sviridoff, vice president, national affairs, of the Ford Foundation, who contributed to the design and obtained the grant to turn the idea of assessing federal manpower programs into a reality. I am pleased to acknowledge his help and that of the Ford Foundation.

A word about the contributors. Care was taken not to invite any individual who had direct responsibility for operating a program under review. In the case of Dr. John Palmer, his acceptance occurred while he was still a senior fellow at The Brookings Institution, prior to his assuming the position of deputy assistant secretary for policy, research and evaluation, at the Department of Health, Education and Welfare.

Because of the tight schedule between initiation of the project and the release of the manuscript for publication, I am particularly grateful to my colleagues who made time to participate in this joint undertaking. My friend, Mr. William Hewitt of the U.S. Department of Labor, administrator, Office of Planning, Evaluation, Research (OPER), Employment and Training Administration (ETA), commented on my opening and closing chapters but I alone am responsible for the analysis and the conclusions. My wife, Ruth S. Ginzberg, improved their readability, for which I thank her.

As editor, I have taken some minor liberties to reduce the scholarly apparatus that supported some of the chapters. However, the Notes at the end of the volume provide the reader with the essential underpinnings.

Preface

The reader may be interested in knowing of two earlier, related assessment studies: *The Great Society: Lessons for the Future*, edited by Eli Ginzberg and Robert M. Solow (Basic Books, 1974) and *Jobs for Americans*, edited by Eli Ginzberg (Prentice Hall, 1977).

ELI GINZBERG
Columbia University
September 1979

Employing the Unemployed

1

ELI GINZBERG

Overview: The
$64 Billion Innovation

THIS CHAPTER has two interrelated objectives. First it will provide a summary of the federal government's employment and training policies and programs between 1962, when the Manpower Development and Training Act (MDTA) was passed, and the end of Fiscal Year 1979 (September 30), approximately one year after the reauthorization of the Comprehensive Employment and Training Act (CETA).

The second objective is to extract from this historical record a limited number of themes, some of which have been in the foreground of congressional debates and actions, and some of which have had a less exposed role in shaping and reshaping the nation's manpower policies during this period of rapid growth and redirection.

During this seventeen-year period, annual appropriations for employment and training, narrowly defined as programs under the jurisdiction of the U.S. Department of Labor, excluding the Employment Service, Unemployment Insurance, and federal administration, increased from approximately $81 million in 1963 to around $11 billion in fiscal year (FY) 1979, a more than 130-fold increase. The cumulative total is $64 billion.

3

Employing the Unemployed

PRESIDENTIAL ADMINISTRATIONS AND MANPOWER POLICIES

In recounting this evolution the following time periods should be distinguished: programs and policies put into place during the Kennedy-Johnson administrations, which coincided with the longest sustained expansion in the nation's economy from 1961 to 1969; the Nixon-Ford years, 1969 to 1976, which saw the establishment of CETA in December 1973, setting the stage for the decentralization and decategorization of manpower programs, and which included the antirecession efforts of late 1974; and the Carter years, 1976 to 1979, during which manpower programs were used for the first time to stimulate the economy, the Youth Act of 1977 was passed, and CETA was reauthorized in October 1978.

The Kennedy-Johnson Period

Kennedy had run on a platform of getting the country moving again, a reference to the economy's sluggish operations in the late 1950s and early 1960s. But once elected, Kennedy moved cautiously, more because of his personal inclinations and political instincts than his narrow victory, in my opinion.

Unemployment had almost pierced the 7 percent level in 1961, disturbingly high for an era in which the economists set the long-range target at 3 percent, the short-run target at 4 percent. To make matters worse, some influential authorities saw the cause of the high unemployment in an acceleration of technological change that went under the name of "automation" and concluded that many skilled workers, heads of families—the backbone of the U.S. labor force—might be permanently unemployed unless they were afforded an opportunity to be retrained.

With strong bipartisan support, MDTA was passed in March 1962, but appropriations were delayed until August because the chairmen of the respective appropriations committees of the House and the Senate could not agree in whose office to meet in to reconcile minor differences.

By the time Congress considered amendments to MDTA, in the summer of 1963, two issues had been clarified. The macroeconomists who had argued earlier that it was a softness in demand, not automation, that was responsible for the high unemployment were proved right; most skilled workers were back in jobs, mostly in their old jobs. But the initial training program had uncovered the existence of a considerable number of poorly educated, low-skilled workers with an erratic employment history. MDTA had discovered the hard-to-employ.

The following year, 1964, saw the inauguration of The Great Society

4

programs and the addition of amendments to MDTA as well as the enactment of the Equal Opportunity Act. Senator Humphrey, unsuccessful in
his efforts to establish a 1960s counterpart to the Youth Conservation Corps
(YCC) of the 1930s, came away with half a victory—the Job Corps, a
residential program for severely disadvantaged youth, and the Neighborhood Youth Corps (NYC), a program to provide work experience and
income for in- and out-of-school youth who might otherwise roam the
streets and cause trouble, especially during summer vacation.

Shortly thereafter, another proposal of the 1930s resurfaced, this one
relating to the federal government's role in direct job creation. In the words
of the chairman of the National Manpower Advisory Committee to the
secretary of labor:

> With respect to the desirability of the Government's initiating a program of direct
> employment, the Committee's preliminary response was favorable, contingent
> upon evidence that a substantial number of persons, in addition to those affected
> in the current unemployment figures, have persistent difficulty in finding and
> holding jobs; if the new program has a training facet built into the work
> experience; if special care is taken to deal with such matters as wages, supervision,
> etc., in a manner that would encourage movement of people from these programs
> back into the regular economy; and if the programs are responsive to the
> particular needs of particular groups of long-term unemployed persons.

The second half of the sixties was for MDTA, as for most other Great
Society programs, a period of holding the line. The budgetary crunch
resulting from our deepening involvement in Vietnam left little room for
expansion. In 1968 the president, through personal intervention with the
captains of industry, sought to enlist their active partipation in hiring the
hard-to-employ. President Johnson's strong personality, tight labor markets, and many industrialists' newly expressed concern with the plight of
the blacks, triggered by the urban riots, created the backdrop for a large-
scale national campaign under the National Alliance of Businessmen (NAB).

It has not been possible to reach a balanced judgment about the degree of
success that NAB achieved. To encourage their participation, businessmen
had not been required to submit regular reports on the numbers and
characteristics of their new employees. The end of the economic boom threw
a monkey wrench into this national effort which was just getting into full
stride. Seniority provisions governing layoffs resulted in the discharge of
many recent additions to the work force. It was impossible to sort out the
reasons for "voluntary" resignations, which reflected a host of causes from
conflict with supervisors to finding a job closer to home.

The score card for this initial period (1962 to 1969) of federal action on the training front follows: MDTA survived as a bipartisan program and together with the manpower programs funded under the Equal Opportunity Act of 1964 reached an annual level of around $1.5 billion in the late 1960s. It was directed primarily at assisting hard-to-employ persons and youth with work experience in obtaining institutional or on-the-job training, with the expectation that skills would enable them to get and hold jobs. Until the emergence of NAB in 1968 the federal government was the sole actor, the states having been relieved very early of their responsibility to make a modest contribution to the MDTA budget. President Johnson's intervention reflected his conviction that unless industry hired the hard-to-employ, training (most of which was of short duration) would prove ineffective, surely in placing the hard-to-employ in regular jobs.

The Nixon-Ford Years

The Nixon Administration also decided to tackle the excessive centralization of manpower programming in Washington, which involved the Department of Labor in executing and overseeing thousands of training contracts. In 1969 Secretary of Labor George Shultz developed decategorized and decentralized manpower legislation, including a provision for public service employment, which was not accepted by Congress. In 1970 Congress drafted its own new manpower act that aimed at alleviating these overly rigid aspects of the delivery system. At the same time, responding to a trade union initiative, Congress added a government job-creation program, an addition that had been recommended five years earlier but had been turned aside at that time because, among other reasons, of the rapid expansion of the economy. But now, with the country in a recession, the Democratic leadership, with strong urging from labor, insisted on a federal job-creation effort.

But President Nixon vetoed the bill and with his veto in December 1970 the long-established manpower coalition, which had become strained during the legislative session but had held together, was splintered. The president, in his veto message, said he wanted no part in reconstructing the leaf-raking jobs characteristic of the New Deal.

Six months later, faced with a determined Democratic majority that would pass no manpower reform legislation that did not contain a job-creation program, President Nixon signed into law a countercyclical public-service employment bill—the Emergency Employment Act of 1971 provided $2.2 billion over a two-year period for direct job creation to assist, among other priority groups, the large number of Vietnam veterans who were being released from active duty.

Overview: The $64 Billion Innovation

Once the Nixon Administration made a decision that it had to fight inflation, it looked for ways to reduce federal expenditures. In this effort it lighted upon manpower programs as a potential target for cutback if not elimination. The attack was led by Deputy Secretary of the Treasury Charls Walker, who argued that after the expenditure of $40 billion (a more reasonable estimate would have been less than half) the best that could be claimed for the manpower effort was a few tenths-of-a-percentage decline in the overall unemployment rate. The manpower community, lulled into security by the continuing bipartisan support in the Congress and the growing recognition that the urban areas contained large numbers of hard-to-employ persons, was taken by surprise by this attack. On its face remedial efforts to enhance the employability of the hard-to-employ appeared to be a worthwhile undertaking. George Shultz, first as secretary of labor, later as director of the office of management and budget, and finally as secretary of the treasury was helpful to Manpower advocates as they came under increasing attack.

In December 1973 at a time when the White House was increasingly embroiled in the Watergate scandal, Assistant Secretary of Labor William Kolberg, working with congressional supporters of manpower reform, succeeded in finding the middle ground; through the passage of the Comprehensive Employment and Training Act Congress and the Executive were able to take the major step toward decentralization and decategorization of the delivery system. Henceforth, principal responsibility for planning and operating manpower programs would be in the hands of about 500 prime sponsors, each representing communities with a population of at least 100,000.

The new structure was not really in place (prime sponsors took over management in July) when the severe recession of 1974–75 struck. In the fall of 1974, Congress, dissatisfied with the proposals advanced by President Ford, took the initiative to put in place a program that would help mitigate the plight of the large numbers of unemployed persons who had lost their jobs because of the recession.

Included in the antirecession response was a new Title VI of CETA, which provided about 300,000 public-service jobs for the cyclically unemployed. Eligibility for placement in such a job required only that a person be unemployed for seven days.

The recession of 1974, which got under way shortly after President Ford entered the White House, provided the backdrop for a recrudescence of congressional interest in and support for manpower programs with the reestablishment of a broad coalition. Manpower programs were viewed as a useful intervention to assist not only the hard-to-employ but also the regularly attached members of the work force who lost their jobs because of a cyclical downturn.

The Carter Period

Manpower policy, however, came into its own with the Carter Administration. Two personal policy references will help to make this clear. Secretary Marshall stated in the early days of the administration that the president would have agreed to an even larger Public Service Employment (PSE) program but that he, Marshall, decided that a 725,000 target would strain the CETA system. And as chairman of the National Commission for Manpower Policy (NCMP) I paid an early visit to Charles Schultze the chairman of the Council of Economic Advisers, to indicate the interest and concern of the NCMP with macropolicy now that the administration had placed half of its $20 billion stimulus package on manpower programs.

The results of the Carter Administration's manpower policy can be quickly delineated: the amendments to CETA in 1976 that targeted more of the funds on the structurally unemployed; a broad-based Youth Act in 1977; tax incentives in 1977 to stimulate total employment, and revised tax incentives in 1978 to stimulate the hiring of the structurally unemployed (that is, individuals who have experienced a long spell of unemployment and are members of a low-income family or welfare recipients); the reauthorization of CETA in October 1978; and the president's revised welfare-reform proposals of 1979 that propose 400,000 PSE jobs for the principal wage earner in welfare families with children.

The foregoing suggests that manpower programs got a second lease on life after the passage of CETA and surely with the coming into office of the Carter Administration. Having operated for more than a decade as a limited program to assist persons who had difficulty in obtaining regular employment, its scope was broadened to a point where it was being relied upon to serve as a powerful medium for stimulating the economy. But no sooner had the Congress responded to the new administration's enthusiasm than small doubts and then larger doubts began to surface in various quarters—in the White House, in Congress, among academicians, and in the press.

The skeptics and the critics called attention to a wide array of troublesome points: the Council of Economic Advisers early questioned whether federal expenditures for PSE jobs were not quickly dissipated by a withdrawal of equivalent sums by state and local governments (the substitution issue). As expenditures on manpower mounted rapidly, questions were raised as to whether the enrollees were being assisted in obtaining regular jobs, preferably in the private sector. It looked, from the inadequate reporting systems, as if many were not. Reports of mismanagement, corruption, and fraud surfaced with increasing frequency, which weakened if it did not erode the earlier strong support for manpower programs in Congress and in the public press. The continuing difficulties that the academic community faced in developing a rationale for manpower as an antirecession, antistructural, and/or anti-inflationary program added to the growing uncertainty and unease.

The budgetary resolution for Fiscal Year 1980 reflects in larger measure the current strength of opposition forces among doubters (against believers) in public-service employment, especially for countercyclical purposes. Prospective expenditures were cut about 10 percent from the 1978 level of approximately $11 billion. The widespread assumption of a late 1979–early 1980–recession probably kept the budget cutters from achieving a larger reduction.

FINDINGS TO DATE

This summary account of the evolution of manpower policies and programming during the seventeen years after the passage of MDTA points up the following:

- The federal government has developed a wide array of manpower programs—work experience, training, public-service employment, transitional services—to accomplish a variety of objectives, the most important of which is to improve the employability of hard-to-employ persons.
- The CETA system is highly decentralized with primary responsibility for operations resting with 500 or so "prime sponsors." The U.S. Department of Labor has continued to exercise relatively tight administrative and fiscal control over the primes, but it has been handicapped in this effort because of the continuing weaknesses in the management information system, which assesses the effectiveness of the programs as measured by the jobs and incomes that enrollees are later able to achieve.
- The principal beneficiaries of these manpower programs have been hard-to-employ persons, particularly in metropolitan areas, and they include a high proportion of minority group members. The intermediaries that gained the most from this large intergovernmental flow of manpower funding have been municipal governments, community-based organizations (CBOs), and other subcontractors that provide subsidized employment training opportunities for designated client groups. Because of the financial plight of such cities as Cleveland, Newark, and New York, CETA funding, particularly for PSE slots,

has come to play a critical role in enabling these urban communities to meet their basic service requirements, including police, sanitation, and education needs. This revenue-sharing aspect of federal manpower programs has created a powerful constituency among large city mayors who, finding it difficult to elicit broad financial assistance from the Congress, have pressed hard to hold on to their current levels of CETA funding. Future developments in the redesign of manpower programs must remain sensitive to the financial plight of these hard-pressed cities.

Against the background of this brief sketch of the evolution of federal manpower policies and programs we are now in a position to explore some of the important concerns that have engaged members of Congress as they shaped and reshaped the nation's manpower programs.

In recounting the history of MDTA and CETA, reference was made, if only in passing, to various goals of concern to legislators. To recall the more important: retraining unemployed skilled workers who were presumed to have lost their jobs because of automation; a perception that large numbers of persons with poor education and limited skills required assistance to improve their labor-market prospects; the importance of the federal government's direct involvement in job creation to assist those who needed the opportunity of a work experience before seeking a permanent job; the use of PSE jobs to assist the cyclically unemployed; the importance of concentrating a substantial effort on in-school and out-of-school youth who are poorly suited to make the transition into the world of work; helping people on welfare to secure training and jobs in the hope of speeding their removal from the public assistance rolls; and enabling minority youth to obtain badly needed income during summer vacation.

In addition to the explicit goals identified above, various leaders and groups looked to the new manpower programs to help them accomplish important ancillary objectives, which were often only loosely linked to critical considerations of enhancing employability and employment of disadvantaged members of the population. When Lyndon Johnson was vice-president, he played an important role in securing the support of the Southern senators for the passage of MDTA; he anticipated using a large portion of the new funds to help poorly educated and poorly trained blacks to improve their labor-market prospects. The critics of conventional education saw in the manpower legislation an opportunity to increase the flow of funds into vocational training, and the original MDTA legislation gave HEW and its vocational educator constituency a major role in the execution of this act. Shortly after the 1974 expansion of PSE, city and county executives recognized the importance of federal manpower funding in easing their budgetary difficulties. The involved academic community became enthusiastic supporters of the new manpower initiatives because, among other reasons, MDTA and later CETA provided funds for research and demonstration projects, which enabled them to explore important labor-market issues in depth. Community-based organizations, such as Opportunities Industrialization Centers (OIC), SER, the National Urban League, and many smaller social-welfare agencies found that they were able to enlarge and improve their staffs as well as to strengthen and diversify their training and employment projects. Governors who initially had little interest in manpower programs became more involved after the passage of CETA, which gave them funds to allocate to the "rest of state" (the small rural communities) and additional sums for planning and coordination. Certain business enterprises and trade unions learned to avail themselves of manpower funds to train a work force of neglected minority groups, which in the changed climate of opinion, and reinforced by EEO decisions, was seen as desirable. And finally, the members of Congress saw political gains in funding services attractive to many of their constituents.

The foregoing vastly expands the original limited list of goals but still falls considerably short of being inclusive. But the recapitulation clarifies the rapidly changing environment under which manpower programs were born, flourished, and, for some, died and the substantial gap between the aspirations of the sponsors and the capacity of the programs to meet them.

THEMES IN MANPOWER POLICY

Another approach to probing manpower policy with its admixture of successes, standoffs, and failures is to review the limited number of themes that were recognized, debated, and resolved; those that were recognized by the leadership but were finessed; and finally those that were not dealt with because of a lack of conviction, knowledge, and consensus. These several themes can be grouped under the following rubrics: scale, program elements, eligibility, delivery systems, federal oversight and control, and coordination.

Scale

With respect to scale, we noted earlier that between 1963 and 1979 the annual appropriations for manpower services increased 130-fold from around $81 million to $11 billion. With the advantage of hindsight we can see that until the expansion of PSE under the new title VI of CETA was precipitated by the recession of 1974, and more particularly until the economic-stimulus package introduced by the Carter Administration in 1977, the federal government had never viewed manpower as an important, not even a minor, front in macroeconomic policy. Our expenditures in manpower were at a level of .25 percent of GNP during the 1960s while the Swedish investment ran at the level of 3 to 5 percent, some twelve to twenty times greater.

There were only a few instances in the budgetary cycle where the two parties were in serious disagreement about the scale of next year's effort, the more surprising because during eight of the seventeen years, the president was a Republican and the Congress was Democratic. Only in 1974, when the Democratic leadership in Congress rejected out of hand the antirecession recommendations of President Ford and took the initiative to write the new legislation, were there serious differences over budgetary objectives. But this incident should not be exaggerated because of the speed with which the key executive departments—Treasury and Labor—moved rapidly toward the congressional proposals. There was considerable tension in reaching agreement on the FY 1980 budget, which reflected the growing disenchantment of the fiscal conservatives with CETA, particularly with the PSE effort in the face of a 5.7 percent unemployment rate.

The issues connected with scale are: modest but steady increases in appropriations during the 1960s; a contemplated but not serious or sustained attempt by Nixon to liquidate the manpower programs; renewed expansion during the first half of the 1970s, in response to enactment of CETA and higher levels of unemployment; a new effort by Carter (1977), who focused half of his stimulus package on manpower; some decline in appropriations in FY 1980, reflecting a growing disenchantment with the integrity and performance capabilities of CETA and the lower level of national unemployment.

Program Elements

The second major theme—program elements—can be described and assessed along the following axes. MDTA began in 1962 exclusively as a training effort. When I talked with Secretary Goldberg, early in the Kennedy Administration, prior to the passage of MDTA about the advisability of adding a job-creation dimension so that those who were trained would be assured employment at the completion of their course, he indicated sympathy with such an approach but explained it had been ruled out by both the White House and the congressional leadership. The early thrust of the training programs was almost exclusively on institutional training. On-the-job training never grew to be more than a small percentage of the total, with private sector O-J-T quite small except when NAB/JOBS was at its peak (1969).

Most training courses ran four to five months; a few approached a year's duration, such as the highly successful practical nurse training and the best of the automotive and electrical repair programs. Although it became clear early that many who had need for skill acquisition were unable to profit from the available courses until their reading and arithmetic abilities were improved, such remedial educational efforts were not broadly available. The principal barrier was the disinclination of the Labor Department to use its limited training monies for what it considered deficiencies that the educational system should respond to but seldom did.

The shape of the manpower programs was determined in the first instance by the desire of key parties, Congress and the Department of Labor, to make the federal appropriations stretch over the largest possible number of enrollees. Accordingly serious training was largely neglected. The Neighborhood Youth Corps and other programs financed under the poverty legislation sopped up more than half of the money on soft work experience.

From the earliest days of the manpower effort right down to today, a considerable portion of resources has been directed to work orientation, counseling, and testing of clients, sometimes in lieu of other services, but more often as an adjunct to training or placement assistance.

In the late 1960s the NAB's effort sought to hire the hard-to-employ first and train them once they were on the payroll. While many employers availed themselves of the federal subsidy, a substantial number, particularly the largest corporations, decided to respond to the president's request without seeking federal funds.

Introduction of subsidized "work experience" was the first major program change. The shift in favor of O-J-T in the late 1960s was the second. Government job creation under the Emergency Employment Act of 1971 was the third, followed by the PSE title in CETA in 1973, which provided the basis for the major expansions in PSE in 1974 and in 1977.

A low-level debate surfaced from time to time among selected employers, trade unions, and the federal establishment about the use of manpower funds for upgrading workers who were currently employed. The proponents argued that the use of manpower funds for the purpose of upgrading would act as a suction and provide openings at the bottom of the work force for the unemployed; the skeptics stressed that American employers had traditionally covered their training costs and it would be an error to relieve them of this responsibility by making public funds available. Moreover, they doubted that the openings would necessarily go to the hard-to-employ.

13

Employing the Unemployed

But only in the 1978 reauthorization of CETA did Congress authorize a small amount, not more than 5 percent, of training funds to be used for upgrading.

The Job Corps, the summer employment program (initially NYC, more recently SPEDY), and the multiple titles of the Youth Act of 1977 can be seen as one composite program involving youth or it can be viewed in terms of discrete elements. The two oldest components consisted of extended residential skill training in Job Corps centers for relatively small numbers of disadvantaged youth (who in addition to skill training and work experience were provided access to health services and remedial education) and the much larger summer program, which combined an income transfer objective—increasing the income available to poor people—with work experience. In the early 1970s, to respond to President Nixon's search for economies and rationalization, the number of residential Job Corps centers were radically reduced but provisions were made for opening some nonresidential Job Corps centers in urban areas.

The more ambitious youth initiatives were introduced in the Youth Act of 1977, which included conservation projects in the national parks, new efforts to link education and work for in-school youth, training and employment opportunities for out-of-school youth who were to be hired for jobs in neighborhood rehabilitation, and the imaginative and ambitious experimental entitlement project, which guaranteed in a limited number of competitively selected locations a part-time job during the school year and a full-time job during the summer for *all* young economically disadvantaged people who, within a designated area, stayed in or returned to school. The rationale for entitlement rests on the assumption that with employment and income opportunities, young people were more likely to try the program and earn their diploma, which in turn would aid them in their search for regular jobs.

In sum, the more important program elements have included institutional training, O-J-T, work experience, orientation and counseling, upgrading jobs, PSE, and various residential and nonresidential training efforts directed at youth. Those most important in terms of dollar expenditures have been in descending order: PSE, work experience, institutional training, youth programs, and O-J-T. An unsympathetic observer might conclude that since PSE never provided jobs for more than eight-tenths of 1 percent of the total work force, and that most training programs were not of sufficient length and depth to provide the enrollee with new skills, the justification for the manpower effort must lie elsewhere—in income transfers and work experience.

14

Eligibility

Over the years Congress had struggled with the issue of which groups in the population should be designated as eligible for manpower services. MDTA, it will be recalled, was initially focused on skilled members of the work force who had lost their jobs. In the CETA reauthorization of 1978 the principal thrust had shifted to the structurally unemployed. In the early years of MDTA a low ceiling was placed on the participation of young people in the belief that unemployed heads of families should receive preference. As the economy continued to expand in the middle and late 1960s and most job seekers were able to make their own way, the federal effort focused increasingly on the hard-to-employ with particular emphasis on members of minority groups.

Demobilization in the early 1970s brought the recently discharged veterans to center stage and they were to be given priority in filling the newly created public employment slots, or at a minimum, were to share this opportunity with the seriously disadvantaged who, it was hoped, after a spell in a PSE position could obtain permanent positions on the public or private payroll.

Youth selected for the Job Corps were drawn from among the seriously disadvantaged in terms of family income, living conditions, and educational deprivation. In contrast, those who entered the Neighborhood Youth Corps were drawn from a much wider base, skewed in the direction of low income families but by no means restricted to them.

In responding to the recession of 1974 Congress set a very short spell of unemployment (seven days) as qualification for a PSE job, with no reference to the family's total income. I testified in my capacity as chairman of the National Commission for Manpower Policy in favor of tying eligibility to family income, but Congress turned the suggestion aside, not wanting at that time to restrict prime sponsors from placing recently unemployed heads-of-households into these relatively high-paying jobs.

In the 1976 amendments to CETA, Congress took a major step toward targeting a considerable portion of Title VI (countercyclical) PSE jobs on the structurally unemployed and moved in this same general direction in the Youth Act (except for the conservation corps). In the reauthorization of CETA in 1978 Congress made a broad commitment to target manpower programs on the structurally unemployed. If President Carter's welfare-reform proposal of 1979 is passed more or less as submitted, it will further reinforce the recent trend in the direction of targeting training and job opportunities on the most disadvantaged segment of the population.

What we discover from this summary review is that starting as a training program to assist unemployed skilled workers, the manpower programs MDTA and CETA shifted a step at a time to focus more attention on youth, minorities, and, eventually, on the structurally unemployed. What the review did not reveal is that over time more and more women were afforded opportunities to participate. But such was not the case with respect to persons over forty-five.

The 1973 legislation that established CETA transferred operational responsibility from the federal government to the prime sponsors, except for a few groups of special clients. In these cases the federal government would continue to act as allocator and funder. Another deviation from the principle of all power to the primes was the explicit and implicit concern of the Congress that the major CBOs—OIC, the National Urban League, SER—should not be solely dependent on local funding. It was feared that in many cases they might suffer severe cutbacks or even fail to be selected as subcontractors. Although these fears proved exaggerated, the major CBOs continued to seek special consideration in subsequent legislation and to translate such favorable legislative attention into more funding and a more stabilized role as providers of manpower services.

Although a major objective of CETA was to decategorize as well as to decentralize—the former implying that the prime sponsors should decide which groups in their community were most in need of different types of manpower services—Congress never fully accomplished this goal. In the 1978 CETA reauthorization, for instance, it added a new group as worthy of special attention—single heads of households, including displaced homemakers. The latter consisted of women whose last ten or twenty years had been spent in homemaking and child-rearing and who were suddenly confronted with the need to enter or reenter the labor force to support themselves and their dependents.

The critical point to emphasize in assessing the changes in eligibility criteria is the large discrepancy between the funds available and the number of potential clients. In its *Fourth Annual Report* to the president and the Congress, the National Commission for Manpower Policy's staff estimated that for key titles in CETA the discrepancy was usually of the order of twenty to one and seldom less than ten to one.

In the face of such large discrepancies, prime sponsors have been able to "cream," that is, to select applicants more likely to succeed in a training program or in employment. This opportunity enabled the primes to assign different groups to different programs. At the NCMP's field hearings on PSE in 1978 a black speaker noted that in Boston everybody knew that PSE was for whites and Title I (work experience and training) was for blacks. This statement went unchallenged.

Overview: The $64 Billion Innovation

The law, and more particularly the regulations, stipulate that prime sponsors provide opportunities for groups in their community in relation to their numbers and their needs for services. But for the reasons previously noted this directive has been easier to write than to follow. There are well informed and friendly analysts of CETA who have begun to question whether the targeting effort might not prove counterproductive. They have pointed to the following: prime sponsors may balk at hiring the hard-to-employ if they estimate that the enrollees' productivity will be too low to justify the effort. They also point to the danger of having manpower programs viewed as directed primarily at the welfare population, a group that calls forth a negative image from the public. A third potential danger is the narrowing of the constituency base for manpower programs. The trade union movement and blue-collar workers are likely to lose interest if they have little or no opportunity to participate. All of these points have validity, but the obverse of targeting is creaming, and creaming is likely to result in the expenditure of large sums for relatively small social gains.

Delivery Systems

The next theme relates to the delivery system. During the first decade, under MDTA, the principal parties were the Department of Labor and the providers (as many as 10,000) that it negotiated and signed contracts with, running the gamut from a metropolis with a multimillion-dollar training effort to a small contractor with a program costing $70,000 and involving relatively few trainees.

The contracts for the operation of a Job Corps Center usually ran into several millions of dollars annually and were with private for-profit contractors, such as an aerospace company, or with a large nonprofit organization, such as a university. On-the-job training programs were written either with governmental or nonprofit organizations or with private employers. The bulk of the institutional-training grants went through the public vocational education authorities at state, county, and local levels. For a long time, the Department of Labor did not contract with for-profit vocational training institutions.

Various social welfare agencies, including some that were established to take advantage of the new manpower funds, became deliverers of services as the program shifted more to minorities and the seriously disadvantaged. Some of these organizations were better able to engage in outreach programs and to make contact with the groups on the periphery than was the federal-state employment service.

In the 1960s, and to a lesser degree after 1973 because of the freedom of choice that CETA allowed the prime sponsors in their selection of providers, the employment service performed a great many functions, particularly in helping to identify, screen, and refer eligible persons for training and to assist them in finding jobs once they had been trained. But the relations between the training agencies under MDTA, as well as those under CETA, and the employment service have often been strained. Representatives of minority groups in particular have argued that the employment service in most locations was poorly situated, poorly staffed, and poorly oriented to provide effective services to the target population. The principal source of friction was the quality of posttraining placement, which many constituencies found to be inadequate although they seldom were able to do better on their own.

After the establishment of CETA, prime sponsors moved rapidly to build up their administrative capability so as to be able to exercise effective control over the flow of manpower funds, which now came to them from the federal government and which they could use directly or use to pay subcontractors as they saw fit. In the case of cities in financial distress, the budget director or some other designated agent of the mayor made sure that the PSE funds in particular would be spent in such a manner as to ease the budgetary situation by, for instance, helping to provide basic services and thereby reducing the need to use local tax funds.

In many cities, financially distressed or not, well-established community-based organizations (CBOs) had sufficient political clout to retain, and even to expand, their roles as subcontractors. Secretary Marshall, early during the Carter Administration, moved to assure that CBOs would have a larger role in the operation of the PSE program, promising that they would receive at least 30 percent of all project monies. Current estimates refer to 100,000 subcontractors in a structure of about 500 prime sponsors.

What is striking has been the minor involvement of business and labor in the manpower programs, from planning to implementation. In the early days of MDTA it proved difficult in many states to persuade the governor to establish, as the federal legislation required, advisory committees that had to include representatives of business and labor. And the record in establishing local advisory committees with broad representation has also been spotty.

In California, the state AFL-CIO early insisted on screening all training projects to be certain that they did not contribute to the dilution of labor's control over the supply of skilled workers. Some local labor councils adopted similar stances and exercised a greater or lesser influence on the shape of the training effort.

The participation of businessmen was even more spotty until the NAB's effort in the late 1960s, and that went downhill once the recession set in and in most locations the involvement never recovered. A recent survey by the

U.S. Chamber of Commerce revealed that most firms replying to a question-naire indicated that they had little direct knowledge of and less experience with the MDTA-CETA systems. However, in South Carolina, the state economic-development authorities made good use of training funds to attract new business; and one can find other instances where business firms currently make constructive use of the training funds.

It is probably no exaggeration to say that the closest contacts between the business sector and the federal training programs came about when for-profit enterprises won contracts to operate multimillion-dollar Job Corps Centers.

The federal manpower effort has been from the start and still remains today a largely public-sector effort. In the early years of MDTA the principal channel was from Washington to the local vocational education establish-ment within the public school structure, which mounted and operated most of the institutional training efforts. With CETA, the channel changed and the responsibility shifted, and with it the funding, to the prime sponsors in the person of the chief elected official. The federal-state employment service under both MDTA and CETA played an active role in dealing with prospective enrollees and placing them once they had completed their training.

The most important nongovernmental participants have been CBOs, which of late have been aided and abetted by federal pressures so as to enable them to play more prominent roles as providers of services. If the Private Industry Councils (PICs) that are just now being put into place fulfill their promise, they will represent a new channel for active participa-tion by the business sector.

Although President Nixon floated a trial balloon to have manpower turned into a revenue-sharing program in which the federal government placed the funds on the stump and left its expenditure largely to the discretion of the states and local governments, the Democrats in Congress would have no part of his proposal. They favored decentralization but they also wanted a continuing federal involvement for, among other reasons, insuring that the primes did not reduce the funding for minorities.

In the years since the establishment of CETA in 1973, there has ben a continuing tug-and-pull among the primes, the regional offices of the Department of Labor, and the Labor Department in Washington, with the primes seeking more freedom and the department loath to grant it. The regional offices in-between serve as transmission belts, monitors, and eval-uators of the primes. In the big 1977–1978 push to expand PSE to 725,000 participants, more than a doubling within a nine-month period, the Labor Department in Washington was often in weekly and sometimes even more frequent contact with the primes, to pressure them to meet their interim and final quotas on time. The national goal was accomplished ahead of time but many primes argued with some justification—how much is hard to know— that almost all of their other manpower activities slipped because of the importance that Washington placed on achieving the rapid expansion of PSE.

Federal Oversight and Control

Congress, in pushing for decentralization and decategorization with the establishment of CETA, did not contemplate that the federal government would cease exercising oversight and control. Congress looked to the Department of Labor to insure that the money transferred to the primes and by the primes to their subcontractors was spent for the purposes outlined in the legislation and on behalf of priority groups of clients. At its simplest, departmental oversight could mean no more than the avoidance of fraud and graft in the expenditure of manpower funds; control could be limited to checking on the characteristics of the enrollees to be sure that they were eligible to receive manpower services. But oversight and control could be expanded to include matters of efficiency, equity, and stability concerned with the social value and costs of different programs for different client groups.

In 1978–79 Congress was alerted, largely by the press, to the fact that even minimum considerations of federal oversight and control had slipped to a point where an increasing number of cases of fraud, graft, mismanagement, and other fiscal shortcomings was surfacing with such frequency as to undermine the confidence of the public in the program as a whole. Secretary Marshall moved strongly to tighten controls by strengthening the field staff under an inspector general. While an enlarged and better-trained field staff reporting to the secretary of labor should be able to reduce gross abuses, we must ask if the primary responsibility for controlling the system should not rest with the prime sponsors. It is not practical for Washington to stay on top of the daily operations of some 100,000 subcontractors.

Matters of fraud and graft aside, the Labor Department must perform the critical task of monitoring the program in terms of costs and benefits, both in-program and more particularly postprogram outcomes. The crucial question that must be asked concerns the effectiveness of a manpower program: Is the cost to the taxpayer of running the program justified by the benefits that accrue in the first instance to the enrollee in terms of long-term additional employment and income, benefits realized because of his participation in the program? Of secondary consideration are the social benefits such as an enlarged pool of skills, lessened pressure on the wage structure, and less antisocial behavior.

Questions such as the foregoing are under the best circumstances difficult to answer because the environment in which manpower programs operate is constantly changing, sometimes rapidly. Furthermore, the programs themselves are altered in response to political, administrative, or technical considerations. Moreover, proper evaluation procedures require control samples that permit comparisons to be made between similar individuals, some of whom participate and others who do not. But the structuring of such demonstrations and experiments is difficult and costly. Even a well-structured research design still confronts difficulties when it comes to quantifying various benefits such as the gains to a society from fewer muggings because enrollees are engaged in training or employment.

But the federal manpower effort has until recently been seriously handicapped because of the lack of a management-information system that could have provided clues, if not definitive answers, as to how well the entire effort was proceeding. For many years we had no knowledge of the employment and income experience of persons who had participated in the manpower programs, but recently the Department of Labor has developed a mechanism to obtain follow-up information for a large sample.

Coordination

The last theme has been designated as "coordination," which involves several distinct dimensions: within the same federal department, among the federal agencies, between different levels of government, and between the government and nongovernmental sectors.

Note was taken earlier of the continuing tension between the federal manpower efforts directed at training and employment and the operations of the federal-state employment service, whose policy direction rests with the secretary of labor. Although there had been a long record of dissatisfaction with the effectiveness of the employment service, when MDTA was begun it was decided that the federal government had no option but to look at the employment service for operational assistance. Some years down the road the employment service found itself so heavily involved in the problems of the hard-to-employ that it was neglecting its basic labor-exchange mission, that is, to put job-ready persons and employers in search of workers together. In recent years the Department of Labor has instructed the employment service to give priority to its labor-exchange responsibilities.

The Department of Labor and HEW, which shared responsibility for

Employing the Unemployed

MDTA and which have also been closely associated in the operation of the Work Incentive Program (WIN) I and II, have been able to cooperate reasonably well in Washington; but vocational educators and manpower officials at state and local levels have encountered substantial difficulties in working together. The introduction and expansion of federal manpower programs did stimulate vocational educators to pay more attention to minorities and the hard-to-employ, but effective coordination has been difficult to achieve and maintain even though Congress tied certain conditions to its appropriation for vocational education and made certain incentives available to governors to encourage such coordination. The Youth Act of 1977 has contributed to improved coordination in the field.

Until recently, the Economic Development Administration of the U.S. Department of Commerce was directing most of its limited resources to stimulating the expansion of growth nodes, primarily in small cities and in the more rural regions of the country. In the last few years there has been a marked reorientation of EDA in the direction of assisting cities in distress. In this connection Commerce has been working with Labor and HUD to develop new mechanisms whereby federal funds for manpower could be put together synergistically with community and economic development funds in order to provide for a larger job-creation effort in urban centers experiencing high unemployment.

Although the employment problems of low-income urban populations have been recognized to be linked, often closely, to their difficulties in commuting to where the jobs are opening up, it has proved difficult for the U.S. Department of Transportation to play a constructive role in aiding them. Most subsidized bus lines such as in Watts, Los Angeles, have failed to attract a minimal ridership required for continuing operation.

The departments of Agriculture and Interior were given a major role to play in the Youth Act of 1977 since they are the responsible agencies overseeing the new young adult conservation corps, centered primarily in the West and dealing in water and land-reclamation projects.

The tax legislation of 1977 and 1978 providing substantial benefits for employers who expanded their total employment and, more recently, who offered jobs to the structurally unemployed has made the U.S. Treasury Department a collaborator in the expanded manpower efforts of the federal government. Those who have looked carefully at the use of tax incentives as an employment-stimulating device note that the U.S. Treasury is so concerned about the cost of the program that its rules and regulations interfere with the goal of encouraging employers to expand their hiring. In response, Treasury Department officials note that most of the hiring would occur without federal subsidy.

22

At state and local levels some progress has been made to improve human-resources planning, to bring manpower and vocational education into closer alignment, to establish consortia for planning and operating manpower program across one or more contiguous labor markets, in relating the educational system more closely to the manpower-training effort, and in working out sensible agreements between the employment service and the CETA primes and subcontractors.

But the principal challenge as seen by the Congress, the White House, and the Department of Labor is to improve the coordination mechanisms at the local level among government, education, employers, and labor. Title VII of the reauthorized CETA of 1978 looks forward to the establishment of Private Industry Councils aimed at encouraging the more active participation of business and labor in the design and execution of local manpower programs. Without their participation the proportion of CETA enrollees who will eventually find and retain private-sector jobs is likely to be very small. Whether this renewed effort to involve the private sector will, and to what extent, succeed cannot be determined at this time

CONCLUSION

We can now recapitulate the major lines of development of federal manpower policies and programs and note what emerged from the review of the six central themes. With respect to scale, the total federal involvement, narrowly defined as Department of Labor programs currently in the $10 billion range, represents something less than 2 percent of all federal expenditures, about one-half of one percent of the nation's gross national product. This is not an insignificant sum but clearly it is not of a scale to influence the general trend of economic activity.

With respect to program elements, there has been a relative downgrading of occupational training in favor of work experience and public-service employment. The establishment of the PICs looks to a prospective expansion of on-the-job training in the private sector. A focus on youth with the exploration of closer ties between education and work is also close to the top of the manpower agenda.

After many years of loose criteria for participation, which enabled job providers to cream the best among the applicants for training or employment, Congress in the 1978 reauthorization of CETA came out firmly in favor of targeting on the structurally unemployed. But there are some signs on the horizon that such targeting, sound as it is in principle, may result in lowering the level of participation on the part of certain primes, particularly with respect to filling PSE positions.

There is no way of reading the experience with decentralization after 1973 except as a success. The primes rose to the challenge and proved themselves able to operate the manpower programs in their respective communities at a level surely equal, and conceivably superior, to the previous centralized effort.

But this broad finding does not enable one to reach conclusions about the effectiveness and efficiency with which manpower programs are being run by the primes and their large number of subcontractors. The data base for such appraisals is simply not available, although the Department of Labor has recently begun to obtain critical follow-up results about the postprogram experience of enrollees. We know much less than we need to know about the long-term benefit from participating in a training program.

With respect to the sixth and final theme of coordination, the record is mixed. There have been some gains at the federal level and selected gain at state and local levels. But the critical issue of involving business and labor more actively in the planning and operation of these programs remains a promise, nothing more.

It would be a mistake to go beyond these discrete findings and search for an overall evaluation of the federal manpower effort during these first seventeen years. At least such an overall evaluation should wait upon a careful review of the chapters that follow, each one of which addresses a major dimension of the policy in depth. Only after these contributions have been received will an effort at generalization be justified.

2

MICHAEL E. BORUS

Assessing the Impact of Training Programs

THERE ARE many providers of training in our society, and training is provided in many forms. In this chapter we will be concerned with government-sponsored training programs for the unemployed, underemployed, and economically disadvantaged. Furthermore, we will examine only those programs that are provided outside the regular school system and that attempt to impart knowledge to increase the employability of program participants. We will not consider the training provided by vocational secondary or postsecondary schools, the military, or in avocational adult-education programs. Finally, because of the focus on government-sponsored programs, we will ignore the majority of employer-provided training.[20, 26]

Programs with which we are concerned are primarily remedial in nature, attempting to make up for a lack of the skills or knowledge that the majority of workers gain from other sources. Government training programs aimed at the unemployed, underemployed and economically disadvantaged usually offer instruction in how to perform a job. In addition, they often include an orientation to the world of work (information on finding and keeping a job) and remedial education (basic reading and writing skills, English as a second language, or preparation for a General Educational Development test—GED). The instruction can take place in a classroom, on a job, or in both settings. The training can be as short as two weeks or as long as two years. Because of the many dimensions of these government training programs, a variety of questions can be asked about which features are most effective and which forms of training are most efficient. Before turning to these questions, however, it is useful to review the rationale and history of government-sponsored training programs.

THE THEORY AND HISTORY OF TRAINING

Two hundred years ago Adam Smith noted in the *Wealth of Nations* (1776) that individuals would be paid higher amounts if they had received greater training and education. He argued that higher wage rates were required if society was to induce individuals to undertake the costs of such preparation for employment. Nearly one hundred years ago the British economist, Alfred Marshall (1890),[23] demonstrated that given perfect competition, each factor of production would receive, at the margin, an amount equal to the value of its output. Thus, in the case of labor, the last individual hired would be paid a wage equal to the value of his product. If the individual's productivity increased, his wage rate would also increase. Finally, approximately twenty years ago economists, unable to explain the growth that had occurred in the American economy solely in terms of increased capital equipment and improved technology, began to study what came to be known as investment in human capital. They found that higher earnings were associated with higher levels of education, greater amounts of on-the-job training, better health, geographic mobility, improved knowledge of the labor market, and greater training in vocational skills.

Unemployment was of limited concern to classical economists since it was assumed to be the transitory result of market imperfections that would not exist under conditions of perfect competition. Yet the original impetus for training programs under the Area Redevelopment Act of 1961 (ARA) and the Manpower Development and Training Act of 1962 (MDTA) was not concern with raising incomes but rather with reducing unemployment. The limited training efforts under the ARA were auxiliary to efforts to relocate business in depressed areas. The logic of the program was: (1) it is necessary to bring new industries into depressed areas in order to increase employment; (2) it may be difficult to entice industry into these areas because of a shortage of workers trained to perform tasks required by the new industries; (3) therefore, it is necessary to provide funds for training individuals in the depressed areas who are to be hired by the new industries. The MDTA was broader in scope, but it too was designed to combat a mismatch of demand and supply of labor. Its original intent was to provide new vocational skills to formerly employed persons displaced by automation. It was designed to provide classroom training that would allow the unemployed adult to develop the skills necessary to meet the requirements of industry.

With the expanding economy of the mid-1960s and the "discovery" of poverty, the emphasis of the training programs changed. Increasing attention was given to the training needs of the economically disadvantaged. However, it was realized that some individuals might be unemployed for long periods due not to depressed economies in their localities or obsolescence of their skills but rather because they might move repeatedly from employment to unemployment to employment, and while employed, they might earn low incomes because they lacked the knowledge necessary to get or perform higher-paying and stable jobs. To meet the needs of these workers, additional programs were provided, and new training techniques and subject matter were introduced. Beginning in 1964 the federal government signed contracts with employers to provide on-the-job training. It was argued that employers could more efficiently supply the training specifically needed in their plants or industries than could vocational education schools. Also, in reaction to perceived shortcomings of the institutional training being provided by the established vocational education agencies, skills centers were established in some areas to provide more flexible training designed to meet the needs of the unemployed and economically disadvantaged individuals (as opposed to the normal secondary school participants in vocational education).

The Economic Opportunity Act of 1964 began two training programs targeted on economically disadvantaged youth. The Neighborhood Youth Corps consisted primarily of work experience—the performance of low-level jobs for public and nonprofit agencies. The goal of work experience was to provide the youth with a work history and to acquaint them with general skills necessary to keep most jobs, such as getting to work on time, accepting supervision, and not having an excessive number of absences. Relatively little attention was paid to providing education or training in specific skills as part of this program since the work being performed was at a low level and demanded few, if any, skills. The second program was the Job Corps. Here, attention was placed on meeting educational and skill shortcomings of the participants. In particular, residential, rural camps dealt primarily with persons with low levels of functional literacy and attempted to remedy the educational deficiencies of the corpsmen. The camps where the functional ability of the participants was higher provided skills training and instruction that would lead to a GED test.

Employing the Unemployed

During the mid-1960s the composition of the persons being trained, both youth and adults, changed markedly. New programs—Model Cities, New Careers, Operation Mainstream, SER, Special Impact, and WIN—were introduced to aid the economically disadvantaged and the structurally unemployed, particularly minorities. For many of these groups the provision of basic skills training and/or remedical education was not sufficient. For example, Spanish-speaking persons also needed training in English as a second language. In the case of entrants and reentrants into the labor force, training in the basics of job search and job discipline—an orientation to the world of work—was often a prerequisite to skills training.

The late 1960s and the 1970s have seen many changes in existing programs and substantial creation of new ones. The basic forms of training, however, have not been altered. Under the Comprehensive Employment and Training Act (CETA), as amended, persons are provided with: (1) job-search assistance, including orientation and counseling; (2) education and skill training provided in an institutional setting to prepare them to enter the labor market or to qualify them for more productive job opportunities and increased earnings; (3) on-the-job training and training leading to self-employment in small businesses; (4) work-experience programs providing employment opportunities for eligible individuals unable to attain employment with public- or private-sector employers, designed to increase the employability of the participants through the development of work habits, occupational skills, and linkages with other training programs; and (5) for persons of limited English-speaking ability, the teaching of occupational skills in their primary language for jobs that do not require a high proficiency in English, and programs designed to increase their English-speaking ability.

While the types of training have not changed substantially in the last ten years, the providers of such training have increased greatly in number and diversity. Under the ARA and MDTA, skills training was provided by local vocational education agencies, primarily vocational secondary schools. Today classes are still provided in these institutions; however, many organizations outside of the regular school systems now provide training. Proprietary schools may contract with local prime sponsors under CETA to provide skills training. Community-based organizations, such as affiliates of the Urban League, Opportunities Industrialization Centers (OIC), and former community-action agencies, may now provide both skills training and orientation to the world of work. Because of the decentralization of responsibility for training under CETA, it is impossible to list all of the agencies that may be providing such training or the range of services provided. They are, however, many and varied.

WHAT WE SHOULD KNOW ABOUT TRAINING PROGRAMS

A series of questions should be asked about the value of government-sponsored training programs for the unemployed, underemployed, and economically disadvantaged. In this section, we will lay out these questions. In the next section, we will discuss the evidence available to answer the questions, and in the final section of this chapter we will discuss the implications of this evidence for policy and for future research.

Does training work? The purpose of the government-sponsored training programs we have discussed is to increase the employability and earnings of the participants. Consequently, each type of training definitely should be evaluated in terms of whether or not it has increased the participants' earnings. Other measures of program success may also be used.[7] Each program should be examined using all relevant criteria (the choice of criteria may determine whether or not the program is judged a success) and the benefits measured by these criteria should be compared to the program's cost. The amended CETA, however, makes it clear that increased earnings of participants is the primary goal of government-sponsored training.

Who should be trained? Persons eligible to receive government-sponsored training are quite heterogenous. They range from fourteen-year-olds in junior high school to men and women beyond the age of retirement. They include groups who face substantial labor-market discrimination because of their race, ethnic background, or minority status, as well as members of the majority. Persons who are totally illiterate and those with advanced college degrees are eligible.

Training cannot be provided for all these individuals so choices must be made to decide who will receive the training. These decisions can be made on the basis of several criteria. One possible criterion is efficiency, whereby training would be provided to those individuals who would show the greatest increase in earnings for each dollar of the program's expenditure. Another criterion is need; training would be provided to persons having the lowest expected earnings if they did not participate in the program. Finally, training could be provided on the basis of politics, that is, training either would be supplied to those groups of individuals with the greatest political power or would be spread among the greatest number of individuals in order to maximize the number of persons benefiting.

What type of training should be provided? As discussed earlier, the two major settings for providing training are in classrooms and on the job. Obviously we would like to know whether one setting is more appropriate for certain groups of participants. For which groups are skills training, remedial education, orientation to the world of work, or some combination of these most appropriate? Who should provide the training—which training agencies will do the best job?

We also can question how the training should be scheduled, in concentrated doses or spread out over a number of weeks. For what occupations should skills be taught? Finally, how much training should be provided? Should only enough be given to meet minimal requirements for hiring by employers, or should it be of sufficient duration to produce workers who are above average in their productive abilities when the training has been completed?

When is training most appropriate? Training can be provided under different economic conditions. Arguments can be made that major training efforts should be undertaken when the economy is approaching full employment so that training can be used to reduce skill shortages that contribute to inflation. On the other hand, training undertaken during periods of high unemployment will have low "opportunity costs" since little production is foregone.

Obviously, these four questions are highly interrelated. The value of training must be dependent upon who is being trained, the nature of the training they receive, and the economic climate in which it is offered. If individuals who are not in need receive training, or if individuals in need are trained improperly, the benefits to society, the government, and the individual will not be sufficient to justify the costs involved. Likewise, who should be trained depends, in part, upon the benefits the trainees can derive from instruction. It makes little sense to train persons who may not benefit from it because of their lack of preparation or because of the unsuitability of the program, even if these individuals are the ones most in need or with the most political clout. Finally, training must be tailored to the individuals who are to receive it. It is a safe assumption that some settings, types, and lengths of training will be more appropriate for some groups of participants than for others. For example, it makes little sense to provide skills training in English to a group of Indochina refugees who have no knowledge of the language and therefore cannot understand the instruction. Nor will skills training be useful for occupations where there are no job openings.

To untangle these questions requires a relatively sophisticated evaluation design, one which has many cells representing settings, types of training, client groups, economic conditions, and agencies providing training. Cells would then be compared, for example, the effectiveness of on-the-job training for black female Aid to Families with Dependent Children (AFDC) recipients in a recession versus that of classroom training for these women under identical economic conditions. Studies approaching this level of sophistication, however, are rare and incomplete. Therefore, we must treat each of the four questions separately.

ANSWERS TO THE QUESTIONS

There is surprisingly little evidence on the relative merits of different types of training programs.[3, 12, 37] Much of what is available is, in the opinion of this author, fallacious. The majority of evaluations of training programs that have been conducted to date measure changes that have occurred in the lives of the participants from some period immediately prior to the training program to some postprogram period. These studies are almost unanimous in finding gains in earnings for the program participants.[24] They do not take into account, however, that one should expect gains even in the absence of training. Maturation can be expected to increase the employment and earnings of the younger enrollees regardless of the effects of the program. Inflation also can be expected to cause higher earnings, particularly when the training program is long and the preprogram to postprogram measurement covers a substantial period of time. Most important, however, eligibility requirements for the government-sponsored training programs are such that individuals must be at low levels of earnings and employment in order to enter the programs, often they are at low points in their careers. What we may thus observe is *regression toward the mean*. Individuals participating in government-sponsored training—the unemployed and economically disadvantaged—are unlikely to have their positions become worse. In effect, if there is any change, it has to be positive. If one is unemployed, he cannot be more unemployed; but if he is engaged in job search, there is a possibility that he will find a job and become employed. Furthermore, if even one of a group of unemployed trainees becomes employed, the mean earnings for that group will be increased since none will have had the opportunity to earn less. It is for these reasons that before and after studies estimating the impact of training are deemed invalid. And to the extent that the individuals selected for different types of training vary in their personal and economic characteristics, one expects differences in the extent that maturation, inflation, and regression toward the mean influence their earnings. This will invalidate evaluations that compare before and after measurements across different types of training.

What remain are evaluations that use control or comparison groups, that is, persons thought to be similar in every respect to the trainees except for participation in the program. In practice, with one or two exceptions the comparison groups have been found to differ from the trainees in measurable characteristics, and oftentimes are thought to be different in unmeasured characteristics too. In a review of a number of studies, Director has shown that there seems to be a direct relationship between the inferiority or superiority of the comparison group, and the evaluation's conclusions about the success or failure of the training program.[12] Statistical controls on measurable variables are apparently insufficient to account for all of the differences between trainees and comparison group members. Even so, however, it is this author's view that evaluations using comparison groups are superior to before and after studies. Therefore, only studies with comparison groups will be reviewed in answering the questions asked in the preceding section.

Does training work? Earnings gains for participants is the major goal of government-sponsored training, as previously noted. Table 2–1 presents twenty-five sets of estimates of first-year increases in earnings associated with participation in various training programs. Because the types of participants differ, each training setting is examined separately. Also presented are estimates of society's cost per trainee for these programs. As can be seen in the table, the range of estimated increased earnings resulting from government-sponsored training programs is wide. The findings may be summarized as follows:

- Institutional vocational training increases the earnings of participants by approximately $300 to $400 in the year following the program. Of the twelve sets of studies reviewed, only two showed earnings increases of less than $100 for female trainees[8] and for male trainees.[18] The estimates of impact of on-the-job training on participant earnings in the year after participation were on the order of $600. Almost all of the findings were statistically significant, but the range of estimates was quite broad, from reductions in earnings to gains of over $2,000.
- The Job Corps did not yield substantial gains in earnings among corpsmen during the first year following enrollment. It appears that average gains in earnings probably did not exceed $200 and may have been even lower.
- Work-experience programs, for both in-school and out-of-school youth, appear to raise the earnings of their male participants by about $600. For women participants the earnings gains are less clear and are in the neighborhood of $100 to $200.

TABLE 2-1

The Change in Earnings for the Year after Program Participation and Program Cost per Person (in Current Dollars)

	Impact on Earnings/Trainee	Costs/Trainee
CLASSROOM TRAINING		
Ashenfelter[1,2]†		
Black Males	$318* to $470*	
White Males	139* to 322*	
Black Females	441* to 552*	
White Females	354* to 572*	
Borus[4]		
Males	305*	$218
Borus and Prescott[8]		
Males	516*	
Females	38	
Cooley, McGuire and Prescott[11]		
Males	71* to 234*	
Females	168* to 291*	
Hardin and Borus[16]**	251‡	1,272
Ketron[17]†		
Minority Females	184	1,368
White Females	701*	1,368
Kiefer[18,19]**		
Black Males	(−742) to (−355)	
White Males	(−644) to (−375)	
Black Females	591*	
White Females	639*	
Main[21]	409‡	
Page[28]; Gooding[14]	446‡	698
Prescott and Cooley[30]§		
Males	652*	
Sewell[32]		
Males	432*	2,530
Stromsdorfer[36]§		
Cain and Stromsdorfer[10]		
White Males	828*	789
White Females	336*	401
ON-THE-JOB TRAINING		
Cooley, McGuire and Prescott[11]**		
Males	(−38)* to 59*	
Females	30* to 226*	

TABLE 2–1 Continued

	Impact on Earnings/Trainee	Costs/Trainee
ON-THE-JOB TRAINING		
Ketron[17]§		
Minority Males	$1,984*	$2,799
White Males	2,181*	2,799
Minority Females	884*	1,974
White Females	926*	1,974
Kiefer[18]**		
Black Males	(−160)	
White Males	(−61)	
Black Females	386*	
White Females	926*	
Prescott and Cooley[30]§		
Males	796*	
Sewell[32]§		
Males	375*	1,233
Females	754*	1,187
JOB CORPS		
Kiefer[18]**		
Black Males	(−179)	
White Males	(− 74)	
Black Females	(−188)	
White Females	(−780)	
Mallar[22]		
Males	187‡	4,987
Females without Children	565‡	
Females with Children	(−206)‡	
YOUTH WORK-EXPERIENCE PROGRAMS		
Borus, Brennan, and Rosen[6]		
Males	554‡	562
Females	74‡	562
Kiefer[18]**		
Black Males	101	
White Males	(−1,298)*	
Black Females	(−40)	
White Females	(−419)	
Somers and Stromsdorfer[35]		
Black Males	1,245*	393
White Males	795	393
Black Females	1,031*	393
White Females	187	393

Assessing the Impact of Training Programs

	Impact on Earnings/Trainee	Costs/Trainee
ADULT BASIC EDUCATION		
Brazzie [9]		
Males	$2,368‡	
Roomkin [31]		
Males	318	$1,414
Females	12	1,120
ADULT WORK EXPERIENCE		
Ketron [17]§		
Minority Females	367*	912
White Females	629*	912

* Significantly different from zero at $P \geq .10$.
† See Notes for full title of study.
‡ Significance level not presented in original study or cannot be applied to calculation method used in this study.
§ Director [12] found trainee group superior to the comparison group members in preprogram characteristics likely to affect subsequent earnings.
** Director [12] found trainee group inferior to the comparison group members in preprogram characteristics likely to affect subsequent earnings.

- Adult basic education appears to increase the earnings of its participants by approximately $300 per year for males. For females the results appear to be negligible.
- Women on welfare seem to gain approximately $500 in the first year after completing an adult work-experience program.

When reviewed in relationship to their costs, classroom training, on-the-job training, and work-experience programs appear to yield benefits sufficient to justify the programs if the first-year benefits continue relatively intact for five or more years. The evidence of the continuation of benefits, however, is not clear.[2, 11, 34] These results, while far from universal or definitive, would seem to indicate that programs that do not have relatively high immediate payoffs and programs with lower completion rates are less likely to be justifiable when examined in terms of increments in participants' earnings. Thus, programs such as the Job Corps, which have a relatively high cost and a low immediate payoff in terms of increased earnings of participants, must be justified on other bases, such as reductions in crime or on equity grounds, that is reducing the gap between poor and rich.[22]

Who should be trained? Table 2–1 presents the increment in earnings by sex and race where information is available. Unfortunately, the studies are contradictory and no patterns emerge. Among the classroom training studies, females increased their earnings more than males in three of the studies, and in two, males have higher earnings gains. On-the-job training yields higher earnings increases for females according to three studies and for males according to one study. In the Job Corps study, women without children have the highest gain in earnings, and women with children have the lowest gain when compared with males. Among the youth work-experience programs, males generally have the higher earnings gains. The only conclusion that can be reached from this evidence is that none of the programs result in distinctly superior gains for one sex rather than the other.

The same conclusion can be reached with regard to the race of the participants. Blacks had higher earnings gains than whites in one institutional training study and lower earnings gains in two. In training programs that reported gains by race, whites had slightly higher earnings gains in t two on-the-job training studies, while blacks had higher earnings gains in the two youth work-experience programs. Although there does appear to be some predominance in the earnings gains evidence for blacks or whites in several of the programs, it is not clear that the differences by race are statistically significant. Furthermore, five studies[6, 8, 11, 16, 30] for which separate black and white estimates are not presented in Table 2–1 found no statistically significant differences between the two groups. We conclude that none of the programs studied was superior for either racial group.

The effect of training on other groups is also unclear. One study[11] found that the increase in earnings caused by training increased with age, and another[32] found higher benefits from training persons over forty-five. On the other hand, yet another study[8] found substantially lower increments in earnings for women over forty-five and, contrary to the findings above,[32] no benefits for training of persons under twenty-one. This last study found higher benefits for women under twenty than for other women.

The effect of education is also unclear. One group of researchers[11] found higher returns to training men with high school diplomas although this was not true for women. On the other hand, there are studies[16] that found higher returns for training persons with less education, including one[6] that reported that school dropouts gained the most from out-of-school work-experience programs. A recent study[17] of AFDC recipients found higher increments in earnings among women in work-experience and vocational training programs and among men in on-the-job training programs if they had previously completed high school.

It is obvious that there is no conclusive evidence upon which to base an answer to the question, "Who should be trained?" The individuals assigned to different programs vary markedly in their characteristics, due to both the program and self-selection. For example, most comparisons note higher before-training earnings for on-the-job training participants than for those with classroom training. And within the classroom-training category, there is broad variation in the characteristics of individuals participating in programs for different occupations. This helps to explain the otherwise contradictory results discussed previously. The white male with a high school education examined in one study may differ noticeably from a person with those same three characteristics examined in another study. In addition, as noted earlier, there is substantial variation in the types of training provided comparable individuals and this too probably accounts for some of the differences in results. We are forced to conclude, therefore, that the evidence to date does not indicate that training is more appropriate for one group than for another. Consequently, one could argue that training should be distributed on an equity or political basis since the evidence is not clear that there are any differences with respect to the efficiency criterion of outcomes

What type of training should be provided? There is a temptation to make inter-program comparisons based on Table 2–1, to say, for example, that on-the-job training and classroom training are preferable to adult basic education or the Job Corps. Such inferences should *not* be made. The programs enroll individuals from different groups. The participants decide whether or not to enter the programs and the programs themselves have different eligibility standards. There is no reason to believe that if the enrollees of one program were placed in another, the benefits would be constant. Therefore, judgments as to whether on-the-job or classroom training is preferable cannot be made on the basis of available data. Nor is there evidence to indicate when skills training, remedial education, or orientation to the world of work is most appropriate.

None of the studies detail who should provide the training. Most of the studies, it should be noted, are based on training that occurred during the 1960s, when classroom training was more likely to be conducted by educational agencies and work experience was provided primarily by and in public agencies. This should not be interpreted, however as indicating that if the training had been provided by other agencies the increase in earnings might have been either higher or lower.

A study in which I collaborated[16] found that short courses offered in institutional settings yielded higher gains in earnings than did longer courses. There are several possible explanations for this finding, including our inability to assure full comparability between the participants and the comparison groups.[12] However, the implication of this finding for the design of institutional training is considerable; training should be provided in short rather than long courses. Only two other studies have examined the effect of course length on classroom training, and their results differ. In another study in which I collaborated,[8] no significant effect of course length on subsequent earnings gains was ascertainable, but another study published at about the same time[11] found a positive association between course length and the impact on earnings of those who had participated in either institutional or on-the-job training. The average increase in earnings in the latter study was approximately equal to the estimate of the earnings foregone by the trainees while participating in the program. This suggests that additional earnings resulting from longer course length must be weighed against the additional costs. Much will depend on the pattern of earnings in the years subsequent to training. Under the circumstances, it would appear wise to avoid training programs of extended length.

Many studies differentiate between persons who complete training and those who drop out. Almost all found greater earnings gains for those who complete training. Two studies of youth work-experience programs,[6, 35] one of which I collaborated in, found that the longer individuals participated the greater was their gain in future earnings. These findings argue for greater efforts to increase the completion rates of participants and favor programs with higher completion rates.

Limitations to these recommendations stem from the fact that it is not clear whether persons who remain in training the longest and complete the program are identical or differ from those who drop out, or whether the differences that exist between the two groups have been adequately controlled in developing the recommendation. It is likely that the dropouts consist of the less able trainees as well as the less motivated. However, without direct measures of ability and motivation, we cannot determine the extent of or control for the biases caused by noncomparability.

With the exception of Job Corps, all the training programs studied have been relatively inexpensive and have yielded increments in earnings measured in hundreds rather than thousands of dollars. Thus, we cannot say whether or not expensive, intensive training programs would increase participant earnings sufficiently to justify their greater cost. We can say, however, that the apparently common strategy under CETA of providing relatively short, inexpensive training to many people, a politically favored decision, may have been efficient. On the other hand, it should be clear that government-sponsored training of the types reviewed here will not substantially reduce the number of persons in poverty. The investments in training are marginal and the increments in earnings likewise tend to be marginal.

When is training most appropriate? The evaluation studies reviewed here do not provide any guidance about the economic conditions best suited for conducting different types of training programs. The studies, with one exception, look at only a single cohort of trainees, so that the only way to examine the effects of changing economic climates on program impacts is to compare the results of studies conducted at different times. Unfortunately, when this is done, no pattern is discernable among the findings presented in Table 2–1. Studies conducted in the early 1970s, a period of relatively high unemployment, do not differ systematically in their results from those undertaken in the late 1960s, when unemployment was low.

The sole study[11] that examined persons trained in more than one year looked at those who were in training in 1969, 1970, and 1971. The authors found somewhat higher earnings gains for the 1969 and 1971 cohort than for the 1970 group, but it would be presumptuous to generalize this finding and say that training provides higher rewards when unemployment is low. This is particularly true in light of another finding in the same study, that the local unemployment rate was not related significantly to the first-year gains in posttraining earnings. Moreover, the same study found no relationship between the growth in employment and the gains resulting from participation in the training program.

Based on this empirical information, training programs seem equally appropriate for periods and areas of high and low unemployment. Theoretical arguments support undertaking training regardless of the level of unemployment (that is, the opportunity costs are lowest in periods and places of high unemployment, and the opportunities to meet skill bottlenecks are best in locations and times of low unemployment). The unemployment level should not be a criterion for determining the degree of training effort.

SUMMARY AND IMPLICATIONS

We know much less about the impact of government-sponsored training programs than we should. Four major questions were asked: Does training work? Who should be trained? What type of training should be provided? When is training most appropriate? Fully reliable answers to any of these questions could not be developed.

What we do know, based on gains in participants' earnings as the major criterion of success, is:

- Classroom, on-the-job, and work-experience training programs appear to justify their costs.
- Training is not distinctly superior for either sex or racial group. Nor does the evidence indicate that the impact of training is higher for any educational, age, or other grouping.
- Short classroom training courses and training programs with high completion rates appear to yield significant gains in earnings.

- Economic climate does not clearly affect the success of training.

What we still need to know is:

- Are there differences in the effects of training by type of trainee, type of program, and economic climate examined together?
- What types of programs are preferable and most appropriate for specific groups of trainees?
- Who can best provide training?
- Does increasing the length and intensity of training sufficiently increase the benefits to justify the higher costs of such programs?
- Are particular programs more effective in areas and times of high or low unemployment?
- How long do the benefits from training programs continue and at what rate do they decay or grow?

The implications of these findings for government policy point in the following directions:

- Government-sponsored training programs should be continued for all groups of the unemployed, underemployed, and economically disadvantaged, and under all economic conditions.
- At the same time, training, at least as it currently exists, should not be viewed as the major weapon for fighting poverty. The gains in participants' earnings are measured in the hundreds of dollars and are unlikely to move many people out of poverty. Small investments yield small returns.
- The choice of trainees should be on the basis of equity considerations, so as to give training to those most in need or to provide it to the greatest number of eligible persons.
- Course length in institutional training should be limited in order to reduce costs and contribute to high completion rates.
- All programs should encourage participation for the full period of the training.
- Additional evaluations should be conducted to answer the open questions.

3

BERNARD E. ANDERSON

How Much Did the Programs Help Minorities and Youth?

INTRODUCTION

EMPLOYMENT and training programs have been characterized by continuously changing objectives. At the time of their inception, during the early 1960s, such programs were developed to provide new job skills to help reduce long-term unemployment among experienced members of the work force who had lost their jobs as a result of automation and technological change. In recent years, however, such programs have assumed increasing importance as instruments to help reduce racial inequality in economic life. This chapter will attempt to explain how much employment and training programs have contributed to improvement in the relative labor-market status of minorites and youth, and why, despite large expenditures on manpower programs, minorities and youth continue to occupy an unfavorable position in the labor market.

This discussion is based on a review of policy-development and program-implementation experience and the evaluation literature that measures the

41

impact of manpower programs on minorities and youth. Although programs developed and implemented during the 1960s will be discussed, most emphasis will be placed on the experience during the last decade.

The scope of the topic is broad and it is difficult to distill from the vast literature the information specific to only a segment of the participant population. For this reason, the discussion will focus on the most general themes and the most clear-cut results.

Furthermore, because of serious limitations in the availability of data on Hispanics and other non-black minority groups, many comments concerning "minorities" will refer primarily to blacks. Hispanic minorities face some problems, such as language difficulties and the influence of recent immigration, which make their labor-market experiences different than those of other minorities. When viewed in broad perspective, however, the labor-market experiences of the black and Hispanic minority groups are similar, that is, each is characterized by relatively high unemployment, lower incomes, and less favorable occupational status than that among majority-group workers.

Based on a review of the evidence, several major conclusions can be stated:

- Selective employment and training programs are now widely recognized, and accepted, as important social policy instruments for helping achieve the objective of full employment. While fiscal and monetary policies still play the major role in determining overall economic performance, employment and training programs are seen as necessary for achieving efficiency in labor-market operations and equity in the distribution of employment opportunities
- Minorities and youth have emerged as major target groups for participation in government employment and training programs. In the last several years, significant efforts have been made to direct an increasing flow of employment and training resources toward the employment problems of minorities and youth.
- Government employment and training programs have helped improve the economic status of many minority adults and youth, but how much such programs have contributed to the improved economic status of these groups relative to others in the labor market is less clear. Still, the consensus of most carefully designed and executed studies is that program benefits exceed costs, suggesting that employment and training policy is a useful social investment.

The discussion below will provide support for these assertions. It might be useful, however, to comment upon some of the major trends and institutional forces that influence the perception of racial inequality in economic life and to set the framework for identifying "appropriate ways" of dealing with the problem through labor-market policy. These features of the policy-formulation and program-implementation environment have special significance in understanding the government's response to the labor-market difficulties of minorities and youth.

POLICY FRAMEWORK FOR MINORITIES AND YOUTH

First, the rate of unemployment among minorities and youth significantly exceeds that of other groups. In both good times and bad, the unemployment rate among blacks has been about twice that of whites. A similar disparity is evident in the unemployment experience of Hispanics, for whom the statistical evidence is not as complete as for blacks, but who are gaining increasing attention from policymakers because of, among other reasons, their rapid increase in numbers. Minority-youth unemployment rates are now and have for many years been very high relative to both adults and other youth. In addition, the withdrawal from participation in the labor market is a serious problem among a significant proportion of minority-group youth, thereby making the reported unemployment rate an understatement of wasted human resources.

Second, the minority and youth unemployment experience is substantially affected by structural barriers in labor markets, as compared with deficiencies in the aggregate demand for labor. To a considerable extent, minorities and youth are jobless because (1) they are disproportionately concentrated in areas where job opportunities have declined as a result of outmigration of industry and technological change; (2) their educational attainment and job skills are incompatible with employer hiring requirements; and (3) they are the victims of racial, and often age, discrimination. These and still other factors contribute to structural unemployment, that is, unemployment that tends to be long-term and persistent. Such unemployment is more likely to be responsive to selective remedial approaches than to generalized economic stimulus, especially when the latter policy is inhibited because of high inflation.

Third, a widely accepted approach to dealing with problems of racial inequality in economic life is to improve the opportunities for minorities to compete in the marketplace. One alternative to this strategy, of course, might be to compensate minorities for past discrimination and to give them a monetary payment sufficient to equalize their income and that of other persons of similar age, education, work experience, and family responsibilities. The strategy of income equalization through monetary transfers, however, has never been accepted as a legitimate approach for reducing racial disparities in income distribution. Large income transfers, moreover, might have to be continued for a very long period before minorities would be able to compete effectively for their share of the good jobs.

The preferred approach is to improve the investment in the human capital of disadvantaged minorities in order to enable them to compete on more equal terms in the labor market. This strategy is broad enough to encompass a wide range of specific program approaches. The common feature of such programs, however, is their focus on improving the labor supply.

In recent years direct job-creation programs have become a major component of employment and training policy. Such programs provide for hiring the unemployed in temporary jobs in state and local governments. The jobs created by the programs can affect the minority and youth unemployment rate, but only if the programs are heavily targeted toward areas in which the minority and youth unemployed are concentrated. Experience has shown the difficulty in targeting job-creation programs in ways that would have a major impact on minority and youth unemployment.

Fourth, almost since the beginning of major federal initiatives in the employment and training field, minorities have been heavily concentrated in programs of short duration characterized by little substantive training content. For example, during the 1960s the vast majority of minority youth who participated in manpower programs were in work-experience programs, such as the Neighborhood Youth Corps. The training content of such programs was very limited, or often nonexistent, and as a result, many youth failed to acquire skills that would improve their labor-market position. This experience reduced the potential for program participation to contribute significantly to improvements in employment and earnings of minorities.

Finally, a major development affecting labor markets during the past two decades was the rapid growth in labor-force participation among women, especially married women. In 1962, the year in which the first major manpower-training effort was initiated, somewhat more than one-third of the female population was in the work force. Less than two decades later, that proportion had increased to about one-half. During that period 18 million women entered the labor force, and by 1979, 16 million had joined the ranks of the employed.

Although the evidence on labor-market competition between women, minorities, and youth is far from conclusive, it is likely that efforts to expand the job opportunities of minorities and youth have been affected by the rapid growth in female labor-force participation. Specifically, labor markets were experiencing major adjustments to accommodate the increased participation of women at the same time employment and training programs were turning toward a focus on minorities and youth. This development undoubtedly made more difficult the task of improving the relative labor-market position of minorities and youth.

SHIFTING PROGRAM GOALS AND STRUCTURE

The Manpower Development and Training Act of 1962 (MDTA), the foundation of selective-employment policy, provided for training opportunities and labor-market services for the long-term unemployed, administered largely through skills centers operating in cooperation with local offices of the U.S. Employment Service. Relatively few minorities and youth participated in the programs at that time, in large part because the unemployment problems of these groups had not yet become an issue of major national priority.

Civil Rights and the War on Poverty

The shift toward greater concern about the employment problems of minorities and youth occurred in the wake of the civil-rights movement and the increased interest during the mid-1960s in reducing poverty. Increasingly, the MDTA programs were adjusted to be more responsive to the national goal of equal employment opportunity, and new legislation, the Economic Opportunity Act of 1964, was enacted to speed the reduction in poverty. These policy developments made available more resources for attacking joblessness among minorities, but the scale of effort, and the nature of training and job programs, were generally unequal to the task.

For example, between 1965 and 1972, there were about 1.8 million participants in the MDTA institutional and on-the-job training programs. These were programs that placed the greatest emphasis on training for the development of marketable job skills. Minorities represented about one-third, and youth (that is, persons under age twenty two) about two-fifths of the participants in such programs.

In comparison, during the same period, there were about 5 million participants in the in-school and out-of-school components of the Neighborhood Youth Corps (NYC), a part-time work-experience program developed under the Economic Opportunity Act. In addition, each year during this period approximately 500,000 youth participated in the summer NYC programs with the number of youth and programs increasing each year from 1965 to 1972. These programs were more and more concentrated on urban minority youth, especially after civil disorders erupted in 1966 and 1967. The universe of need, however, exceeded by several times the number of training opportunities available in manpower programs.

As employment and training policy turned more toward the employment problems of the disadvantaged, the content of the programs gradually changed. Relatively less emphasis was placed on institutional training of the type most prevalent when experienced workers were being retrained for new occupational careers. A much broader range of services, including outreach, basic education, prevocational training, counseling, job development, and supportive services was offered. The more diverse service mix was developed in response to the special problems of the disadvantaged, many of whom had no previous work experience and often had inadequate basic educational skills and little motivation for participation in manpower programs. The panoply of programs developed varied widely in service, quality, and content, and many did not emphasize the acquisition of marketable job skills.

The Job Corps

The Job Corps was the first program with training content that was strongly focused on minorities. This program, created under the Economic Opportunity Act, was intended to provide training opportunities for the most disadvantaged low-income youth, who were in serious need of basic education, vocational training, work experience, and counseling. The early Job Corps program emphasized residential skills centers where youth would have the opportunity to receive training away from their community. The residential centers, however, proved to be expensive to maintain and somewhat controversial when located in communities that were apprehensive about the presence of large numbers of urban disadvantaged youths. Because of these difficulties, the U.S. Department of Labor shifted toward greater emphasis on nonresidential centers during the early 1970s.

From its inception through 1972, the Job Corps had a 60 percent black enrollment, with other minorities accounting for about 10 percent of the participants. Program enrollment has continued to reflect similar minority participation, even through the doubling in size of the Job Corps from 22,000 to about 44,000 available positions in 1978.

Did the Programs Help Minorities and Youth?

Other Programs with Substantial Minority Enrollment

In addition to their prominent participation in NYC and the Job Corps, minorities also represented a sizable proportion of enrollees in the Concentrated Employment Program (CEP) (73 percent), National Alliance of Businessmen/Business Sector (NAB/JOBS) (69 percent), and the Work Incentive Program (WIN) (44 percent) before 1973. These programs were conceived in an environment of heightened national attention to the problems of unemployment and poverty among the disadvantaged and concern about ways to reduce welfare dependency.

The CEP program was designed to focus manpower training and employment services on disadvantaged persons located in areas with a high incidence of poverty. It was heavily concentrated in sections of cities where minorities represented a large proportion of the total population. The objective was to improve the coordination among manpower service delivery agencies in such communities in order to maximize the impact of available resources on persons in greatest need.

Similarly, the NAB/JOBS program was stimulated by the federal government to persuade the private-sector employers to hire more disadvantaged persons. The program, like CEP, was focused strongly on cities with serious problems of minority and youth unemployment. Employers were encouraged to "hire, train, and retain" the disadvantaged unemployed, with financial subsidies from the federal government if necessary.

Likewise, the WIN program, authorized by an amendment to the Social Security Act of 1967, provided opportunities for job training, counseling, and job placement for persons receiving aid to families with dependent children. The goal of the program was to reduce welfare dependency by increasing the employability of welfare recipients. Although most welfare recipients were not members of minority groups, a disproportionate number of minorities experienced welfare dependency. As a result, almost from its inception, the WIN program included large numbers of minority women.

Finally, in 1968, the U.S. Department of Labor organized the Apprenticeship Outreach Program to increase the participation of minorities in the apprenticeable skilled trades, especially in the construction industry. Studies by F. Ray Marshall and Vernon M. Briggs analyzed the major barriers to full participation of minority youth in the apprentice occupations, and they also identified several program approaches that seemed useful in expanding job opportunities for minorities. The major feature of AOP was the effort by selected local community organizations to seek out interested and potentially qualified minority youth and to help them meet the requirements for admission into apprentice programs. From the inception of AOP through

1972, about 22,000 minorities, mostly under age twenty-two, participated in the program. In all, about 700,000 black and other minorities participated in CEP, WIN, and NAB/JOBS as of 1973. Hispanics also participated in these programs, but reliable data on their enrollment is not available.

Community-based Organizations

Another approach pursued in an effort to reach minorities was federal government support of training and employability-development services provided by community-based organizations. Such organizations typically served a predominantly minority clientele, and, for that reason, could help achieve the program targeting objectives, which increased in importance during the late 1960s and the 1970s.

Some community-based organizations, such as the National Urban League, had been in the employment service field for some time. Others, such as the Opportunities Industrialization Centers, SER, and Recruitment Program, were organized during the 1960s as expressions of the desire by minority groups to play a larger role in designing and implementing programs to improve the status of their members. The role of such organizations in the service-delivery system steadily increased, and today, the CBOs are among the major providers of employment and training services for minority participants.

Comprehensive Employment and Training Act (CETA)

In 1973, the Congress enacted a new employment and training policy that reversed the previous emphasis on categorical programs and moved toward a decentralized system. Under CETA, state and local jurisdiction (prime sponsors) gained the authority and responsibility to design employment- and training-service plans for their communities. When approved by the federal government, the plans were expected to be implemented through services provided by the prime sponsor or by other agencies and organizations operating under contract with the prime sponsors. The central purpose of the new policy was to make local political leaders more responsible and accountable for the expenditure of employment-training funds in their communities.

Program Mix

Although the administrative arrangements for implementing employment and training policy changed under CETA, a major change in the content of programs occurred only in the job-creation component of the new policy. Shortly after the new act was adopted, the nation entered a serious recession that led to a sharp rise in unemployment. In response to this development, the Congress passed the Emergency Jobs and Unemployment Assistance Act of 1974, authorizing expenditures for 300,000 public service jobs. The jobs were distributed among areas experiencing high unemployment due to the recession and not to the joblessness that emerged from structural imbalances in labor markets.

Comprehensive manpower services under CETA bore close similarity to previous programs. There was a mixture of classroom training, outreach, counseling, remedial education, and supportive services. On-the-job training programs were less visible in comparison with pre-CETA practice, but in general, the early CETA programs largely continued old practices in a new administrative setting.

Most important for our purposes, the participation of minorities in CETA programs continued at levels similar to previous experience. (See Table 3-1.)

Minorities accounted for about two-fifths of enrollees in comprehensive manpower services. Likewise, minority participation (black and Hispanic) in the Job Corps was about two-thirds, and in the counterstructural public service employment program, about one-fourth—both proportions similar to minority enrollment in such programs before CETA.

Youth Employment Programs

In 1977, the Congress enacted the Youth Employment and Demonstration Projects Act (YEDPA), authorizing the expenditure of $1.5 billion for programs to serve about 200,000 unemployed youth. Under YEDPA, several different approaches to youth employment problems were followed:

1. Youth Incentive Entitlement Pilot Projects (YIEPP), an experimental program in seventeen communities throughout the nation to test the feasibility of increasing school retention through guaranteed jobs.
2. Youth Community Conservation and Improvement Projects (YCCIP), to provide disadvantaged, mainly out-of-school youth with opportunities for job training through work or community-betterment projects.
3. Young Adult Conservation Corps (YACC), for youth to perform conservation on public lands, and
4. Youth Employment and Training Program (YETP), to provide comprehensive employability development services, mainly to school youth.

The purpose of YEDPA is to test the effectiveness of the alternative approaches to youth employment problems in order to determine what works best for whom. The act is being implemented primarily by prime sponsors, but there is also a large experimental and demonstration component funded out of the secretary of labor discretionary funds. In addition to

TABLE 3-1

Selected Enrollee Characteristics in Major Employment and Training Programs, Fiscal Year 1977

| | | Minorities | | Sex | Percent Youth | Education | On Public |
Program	Total Enrolled	Black	Other	Women	Under 22 Yrs.	Under 22 Yrs.	Assistance
1. CETA							
Title I — Comprehensive Manpower Services	1,416	34.7	5.2	48.5	51.7	49.8	26.5
Title II — PSE	353	22.9	3.5	40.0	20.3	22.5	13.8
Title III — Migrants	260	46.6	20.3	43.9	48.8	88.6	NA
Indians	50	0.1	3.9	48.8	22.4	49.8	17.0
Summer Programs	907	48.0	4.3	46.4	100.0	83.3	47.5
Title IV — Job Corps	41	53.6	1.8	31.3	100.0	85.4	26.5
Title V — Emergency Jobs Program	593	25.9	3.3	35.9	20.3	27.1	18.4
2. WIN	272	38.7	2.8	72.5	15.7	59.0	100.0
3. Apprenticeships	255	9.4	2.5	1.7	NA	NA	NA
4. Employment Service	15,817[a]	28.6[b]	NA	44.7	26.9	NA	NA

a. Applications taken
b. Minorities

SOURCES:
National Commission for Manpower Policy, CETA: An Analysis of the Issues. Special Report No. 23 (Washington, D.C.: May 1978). Table 3.
U.S. Department of Labor and the U.S. Department of Health, Education and Welfare, Employment and Training Report of the President (Washington, D.C.: 1978).

the development of the new programs listed above, the U.S Department of Labor was authorized to double the size of the Job Corps.

As of mid-1979, program enrollment data revealed that blacks accounted for about half of all persons participating in YEDPA programs. Black and other minority enrollment was especially high in YIEPP and YCCIP. Relatively fewer minorities participated in YACC, but the proportion was still higher than the minority youth proportion of all unemployed youth. In addition, programs funded under the secretary's discretionary funds were heavily targeted toward black and Hispanic youth.

ASSESSING PROGRAM IMPACT ON MINORITIES AND YOUTH

Two factors are most important in assessing the impact of employment and training programs on minorities and youth: (1) general trends in the economy at large, especially labor demand, and (2) the experiences of minorities and youth enrollees compared with similar persons who did not participate in such programs. Limited information about both factors make it difficult to draw firm conclusions about how much labor-market programs helped minorities and youth.

Economic Conditions

Employment and training programs operated in somewhat different labor market environments during the pre-CETA and CETA periods. Between 1966 and 1973, the period when increased concern with minority and youth labor-market problems emerged, the rate of unemployment for the work force at large averaged 4.5 percent; employment grew at an average of 1.9 million jobs per year; and the labor force grew by 17.1 percent. In comparison, from 1973 through 1977, the unemployment rate averaged 7.2 percent, total employment grew by 1.5 million per year, and the labor force increased by 9.8 percent. Thus, during the CETA years, the national economy has had a relatively high rate of unemployment, but has also shown both vigorous job-creation and labor-force growth. The dilemma in labor markets during recent years has been the rapid growth in the number of persons who want jobs (including minorities and youth), together with rapid growth in job opportunities, but only modest improvement in the wide gap between the unemployment experience of minorities and youth groups. During 1977, for example, the economy produced slightly more than 3 million additional

51

jobs. In that year, the black unemployment rate remained at 13.1 percent, while unemployment among whites fell from 7.0 to 6.2 percent. Similarly, unemployment among black youth showed little change despite the vigorous job growth.

To a considerable degree, the persistence of unemployment among minorities, and especially among minority youth, in an environment of rapid job creation reflects the seriousness of structural barriers to greater employment opportunity for the disadvantaged. The stickiness at a high level of the minority and youth unemployment rate also reflects labor-force growth among these groups that exceeds their rate of employment growth. Minority youth, for example, had vigorous employment growth during 1978, but their unemployment rate remained much higher than that of other youth. Employment and training programs are likely to benefit such groups primarily by targeting heavily upon them and improving their competitive position for opportunities in the labor market relative to that of other claimants.

One aspect of the problem that deserves increased attention is the location of employment growth. Increasingly, studies of minority and youth employment problems have identified the limited job availability in inner city areas as a major factor contributing to persistent unemployment among such groups. Employment and training programs that have job-creation features, such as part-time work experience and public service employment, can help ease minority and youth unemployment if they are aimed at areas where such unemployment is concentrated. Indeed, some observers have suggested that the YEDPA and summer youth employment programs accounted for the entire net growth in minority youth employment during 1978. One need not accept such estimates uncritically to recognize the value of careful targeting of employment and training opportunities as a device for improving the employment prospects for minorities and youth.

The Evaluation Evidence

In order to determine the unique contribution of employment and training programs toward improving the labor-market status of any group, it is necesssary to compare program enrollees in that group with similar persons who did not participate in the programs. Unfortunately, only limited evidence of this type is available on minority and youth enrollees. Many studies of employment and training programs either included no comparison group or included too few minorities and youth to permit a separate evaluation of their relative benefits.

Most of the evidence on programs in operation before CETA has been summarized in detail elsewhere and need not be reviewed here. The general conclusion about the pre-CETA programs, however, is that those offering skills training (institutional and O-J-T) showed some beneficial impacts for minorities and Apprentice Outreach Programs showed significant earnings gains.

Evidence from an analysis of program operating statistics showed that, on average, blacks earned less than whites, and women less than men, when posttraining hourly wages are considered. On the other hand, both blacks and women experienced larger gains in hourly earnings over their pretraining level than did white males, with the largest relative gain recorded by black women in CEP, WIN, and the Job Corps. Still, even after program participation, black women, as a group, had the lowest earnings of either race or sex group.

Furthermore, the evidence on pre-CETA programs suggests that employment and training programs had a limited positive effect in reducing some of the labor-market barriers facing minorities. For MDTA, AOP, Job Corps, WIN, and NAB/JOBS, however, incomplete and often anecdotal data, while not conclusive, still suggest that some minorities gained access to better-paying, more stable jobs as a result of participation in these programs. The full magnitude of these benefits, however, cannot be estimated because no program operated with a carefully designed information system that would make postprogram evaluation possible.

Recent Evidence on Program Impact

In recent years, evaluation studies have been improved, both by including larger samples and by using more appropriate benefit-measurement techniques. These studies provide additional evidence about the impact on minorities and youth of a small number of programs.

A review of evaluation studies summarizing recent research on MDTA and other pre-CETA programs concluded that adult black males generally gained less than others from institutional retraining programs. Yet minority earnings, as reflected in social security data, did improve as a result of training, especially among minority females. Review of the literature also revealed gains for black males who participated in vocational education programs. Because the analysis, however, included a very small sample of black youth, the estimated effects have a low level of reliability.

Studies of WIN, CETA, and an experimental program, the National Supported-Work Demonstration, generally show improved labor-market experiences by participants but very mixed findings when adjusted for program and enrollee characteristics. Most studies of the postprogram labor-market experiences, for example, show a decline in program effects over time and significant variation in outcomes among those who completed

TABLE 3–2

Net Effects Estimated for Four Employment and Training Programs: Program-Control Group Differentials

Program and Measurement Dates	Earnings Changes				Employment Changes			
SUPPORTED WORK 1975 to 1978	Monthly Earnings Increase ($)				Percent Employed			
	AFDC	Ex-Addict	Ex-Offenders	Youth	AFDC	Ex-Addict	Ex-Offenders	Youth
1 to 9 months (in-program)	351	201	205	240	62.9	47.9	38.9	48.4
16 to 18 months (postprogram)	78	–1	29	–2	10.4	–2.6	3.6	–5.3

JOB CORPS 1977 to 1978	Weekly Earnings Increase ($)				Percent Change in Employment			
	Males	Females without Children			Males	Females without Children		
Overall Change	31.31	20.55			.141	.096		
Black	26.08	19.90			.119	.078		
White	44.84	28.46			.175	.168		
Hispanic	37.61	14.91			.252	.111		
American Indian	12.17	10.28			–.023	–.107		

WIN 1974 to 1976	Annual Earnings Increase ($)			
	Males		Females	
	White	Black	White	Black
Job Search	12	– 373	514	33
Education	–720	–1667	–145	8
Training	1024	– 390	537	451
Subsidized Employment	2225	753	1641	1357
All Services	580	270	634	255

Sources:
WIN: B. Schiller, "The Pay-Off to Training for Blacks: The WIN Experience," *Review of Black Political Economy* (Winter 1978). Table 2, p. 216.
SUPPORTED WORK: R. Maynard, R. Brown, J. Schore, et al. *The National Supported Work Demonstration: Effects During the First 18 Months After Enrollment.* Report prepared by Mathematica Policy Research, Inc., Princeton, N.J., for the Manpower Demonstration Research Corporation (April 1979), Table 1, p. xi.
JOB CORPS: C. Mallar, *Evaluation of the Economic Impact of the Job Corps Program. First Follow-up Report,* prepared by the Mathematica Policy Research, Inc., Princeton, N.J., for the Office of Program Evaluation, Employment and Training Administration, U.S. Department of Labor, Washington, D.C. (December 1978), Tables V.5 and V.6, pp. 81 and 82.

TABLE 3–3

Absolute Earnings Outcomes for CETA Twelve-month Terminees

	Absolute Annualized Earnings Increase[a]			
	Males		Females	
	White	Black	White	Black
Postprogram Earnings[b]	$5,808	$4,699	$3,376	$3,142
Changes in Earnings[c]	1,981	1,683	1,637	1,640
	(52%)	(56%)	(94%)	(109%)
CLASSROOM TRAINING				
Postprogram Earnings[b]	$5,915	$4,353	$2,718	$2,653
Change in Earnings	2,484	1,703	1,346	1,485
	(72%)	(64%)	(85%)	(127%)
PUBLIC SERVICE EMPLOYMENT				
Postprogram Earnings[b]	$5,951	$4,856	$4,117	$3,861
Change in Earnings	1,758	1,781	1,868	1,715
	(42%)	(58%)	(83%)	(80%)
ADULT WORK EXPERIENCE				
Postprogram Earnings[b]	$4,401	$3,835	$2,892	$3,347
Change in Earnings	1,127	603	1,454	1,592
	(34%)	(19%)	(101%)	(91%)
ON-THE-JOB TRAINING				
Postprogram Earnings[b]	$6,612	$6,088	$3,725	$3,552
Change in Earnings	2,686	2,495	2,313	1,989
	(68%)	(69%)	(164%)	(127%)

a. No control group.
b. Mean annualized earnings in fourth quarter after termination.
c. Annualized earnings change, where preprogram earnings are measured by the fourth quarter before program entry.
NOTE: Percentage increases are shown in parentheses.

SOURCE: David H. Finifter, "A Longitudinal Analysis of CETA Participants' Earnings: Initial Evidence from Six CLMS Cohorts," Office of Program Evaluation, Employment and Training Administration, U.S. Department of Labor (June 1979), Table IV, p. 17.

the program compared with others who did not. Only those who completed Job Corps programs have significantly higher postprogram earnings; partial or early dropouts reported no increases in earnings or employment status (Table 3–2). Similarly, recent estimates of earnings increases among CETA enrollees vary from the 19 to 164 percent spread to the 151 to 448 percent spread, depending on the time period assumed to represent the preprogram earnings (Table 3–3).

Job Corps

The studies reveal important race, sex, and program variations in postprogram impact. Postprogram earnings experiences among Job Corps enrollees showed black males ($26) somewhat below the average for all males ($31) in weekly earnings gains relative to similar nonparticipants. White males reported the highest weekly earnings increase ($45), about double the increase among blacks. Black female Job Corps enrollees ($20) were close to all childless female participants ($21) in earnings gains. Hispanic males showed earnings improvement ($38) greater than that among black men, but still lower than that for whites. In contrast, Hispanic females ($15) lagged behind both black and white female enrollees in earnings gains relative to the control group. The earnings differentials for females, however, while numerically measurable, are not statistically significant.

A study of WIN estimated negligible returns for blacks from programs designed to improve job search skills and education but significant returns for them in subsidized employment. Gains for whites, however, were almost double that of blacks overall. regardless of sex. A study of the Job Corps program found similar racial differences. Preliminary analysis of CETA participants suggests some racial differences in earnings outcomes but until further analysis is conducted, which takes into account control group behavior, these findings should be regarded as inconclusive. Overall, black males report similar earnings increase rates to that of white males (56 percent versus 52 percent) but the raw data suggest significant racial variations may be occurring by program. The National Supported-Work Demonstration, on the other hand, utilizing randomized control groups, discerned no significant postprogram earnings or employment effects among youth, the great majority of whom were minorities.

A major conclusion which can be gleaned from a comparative review of the major studies, is the need for strengthened evaluation, both in control group analysis and longitudinal perspective. During the past ten years, sophisticated studies have been undertaken to provide answers to the question of program impact. The studies suggest disparate program effects that are not conclusive, but which, on balance, suggest that minorities and youth gain from some programs, while deriving little benefit from others.

Some Lessons from Past Experience

In addition to the conclusion drawn from the assessment of the evaluation literature, several lessons can be drawn from past experience of minorities and youth in employment and training programs. First, it is clear that targeting on such groups, although difficult, can have beneficial effects in helping larger numbers gain a foothold in the labor market. Greater targeting, however, is limited by the reluctance of policymakers to tilt too far in the direction of one population group at the expense of others in need of assistance. For example, while minority youth have the highest unemployment rates, there is also concern about the employment problems of majority-group youth, many of whom also experience difficulties in making a satisfactory entry into the world of work. The dilemma for policymakers is how to strike a reasonable balance between limited resources available for employment and training programs and the serious needs of different youth groups, all of whom require labor-market services.

However the question of equity is resolved, it is important to recognize that allocation formulas that emphasize labor-market difficulties (that is, the incidence and duration of unemployment and the employment/population ratio) are likely to direct more funds to minorities and youth than are formulas that emphasize personal income variations. Also, experience with past programs has shown that direct support of nongovernmental community-based organizations contribute significantly to greater targeting toward disadvantaged minorities.

Second, studies of the experience under YEDPA have illustrated the need for greater efforts to enlist the services of school systems in improving the labor-market preparation of youth. Improved quality of basic education, together with school-based labor-market counseling and cooperative work experience can help reduce the employment problems of minority youth. The recently concluded American Assembly on Youth Employment recommended a major role for the schools in better preparing youth for the world of work. In particular, the assembly recognized the need for closer linkages between schools, employers, and unions. Employability development can be enhanced through active involvement of private-sector employers in planning and implementing vocational education and cooperative education programs for youth.

Finally, the experience of the recent past and the projections for the immediate years ahead suggest continued competition among minorities, youth, and others in the labor market. Most forecasts of economic activity during the next several years are not optimistic about the growth of the American economy. It is expected, however, that additional numbers of women, youth, and minorities will seek employment. Although the increase in the number of majority-group youth will decline somewhat by 1985, the number of minority youth aged sixteen to twenty-four will continue to grow rapidly and will become a larger proportion of the youth workforce.

These projections will influence the potential for employment and training programs to help improve the relative status of minorities and youth. If past experience is a guide, the programs will be under strong pressures imposed by trends in the national economy, and only modest improvement from the programs can be expected. At the same time, the projections offer no support for efforts to diminish the role of employment and training programs within the policy mix designed to achieve full employment. Continued support for employment and training services, including both skill enhancement and job-creation programs targeted toward minorities and youth with serious labor-market problems, will undoubtedly contribute to a reduction in joblessness that would otherwise result from slow economic growth and labor-market competition among different population groups.

CONCLUDING REMARKS

Minorities and youth are groups with serious employment problems, and the federal government has increasingly attempted to respond to such problems through the development and implementation of employment and training programs. The level of expenditures has risen dramatically during the past decade, although in real terms, the available dollars may purchase less than in earlier years. The programs have broadened in their scope of services and in the range of service-delivery agents. By any measure, employment and training policy must be judged a major form of social policy directed toward improving the relative economic status of minorities and youth.

The scale of effort in the employment and training field insures a wide panoply of effects on individual participants and in local labor markets. In general, however, the evidence about the impact of such programs on the position of minorities relative to others, and youth relative to adults, is not conclusive. Some programs such as the Job Corps and other programs emphasizing skills training seem to contribute relative gains of reasonable value to minorities and youth. On the other hand, less specific training programs, like work experience seem to offer little comparative advantage to their participants in relation to similar nonparticipants. This conclusion, however, must be tempered by the limitations of evaluation data, which all too often are not adequate for assessing the postprogram experience of participants.

What is clear is that employment and training programs as a whole provide returns to society that exceed their cost. Moreover, the prevailing view of policymakers, and of the community at large, is that measures to improve the earnings and employment opportunities of the disadvantaged are much preferred over other strategies for reducing economic inequality among racial groups. As long as that view prevails, there will be a major role for employment and training programs in the social-policy mix.

4

R I C H A R D P. N A T H A N

Public-Service Employment

PUBLIC-SERVICE EMPLOYMENT[1] was first used by the Roosevelt Administration with the establishment in 1935 of the Works Progress Administration (WPA) to relieve unemployment. The WPA employed over 3 million workers at its peak (at a time when more than 9 million were unemployed) and averaged about $1.4 billion annually in wage payments from 1935 to its termination in 1943.

Public-service employment appeared on the domestic policy scene again in the early seventies, though in this period its purpose was twofold: to reduce unemployment and to provide jobs for disadvantaged and structurally unemployed workers. In 1971 President Nixon, having vetoed a public-service employment bill a year earlier, signed the Emergency Employment Act, which authorized a two-year public-employment program (PEP). The PEP program peaked at $1.25 billion in 1973. Spending for public-service job programs trailed off after 1973, but was revived under the Comprehensive Employment and Training Act (CETA), which went into effect in July 1974.

The story of the growth of the public-service employment (PSE) component of CETA under the Carter Administration is well known. Authorized at $370 million for 1974, PSE spending grew to over $6 billion in fiscal year 1978, at which time it was by far the largest of three components of the Carter Administration's economic-stimulus package enacted in 1977. (The stimulus package also included local public-works funding and emergency revenue-sharing payments.)

The Carter Administration's 1978 goal for the CETA-PSE program (a goal that was exceeded) was 725,000 participants, equivalent to approximately 10 percent of all unemployed persons in the labor force in 1978. This was the highwater mark for CETA-PSE. Enrollment has been declining since then, amid a political environment of challenge and controversy. This is not surprising when one considers two key points about the history of the CETA-PSE program. Its crest of activity coincided almost exactly with the adoption of Proposition 13 in California and the rapid eastward movement of the taxpayers' revolt. By the time the taxpayers' revolt got to Washington (and it traveled very fast), the CETA program as a whole, and PSE in particular, were among the biggest and fastest growing of all domestic grant-in-aid programs. For many localities in this period, the largest source of grant-in-aid funds from Washington was the CETA program. The growth and prominence of this program in the midst of the taxpayer revolt made it an obvious target for budget cuts. Important changes were made in the PSE program in the fall of 1978, limiting its size and shifting its objectives.

THE OBJECTIVES OF PSE

The point referring to changes made in the objectives of the PSE program in 1978 raises an important aspect about all public-service employment programs in the United States: *the multiple and constantly shifting character of their objectives.* Two of the basic purposes of public-service employment programs have already been identified: *countercyclical* measures (to reduce aggregate unemployment in times of recession) and *structural* measures (to provide employability, jobs, and income assistance to the disadvantaged). There is a third major category of objectives involving the local *services* provided by PSE participants to fulfill unmet public needs. These three main objectives—countercyclical measures, structural measures, and community service—have swirled around in the debate over public-employment programs throughout their entire history.

In its most ambitious form a public-employment program has been urged as a "guaranteed job" or "employer-of-last-resort" strategy to aid the structurally unemployed. In this form it is often portrayed as an alternative to the dole—jobs instead of welfare for the poor. While every important politically salable welfare-reform plan advanced in recent years has included a job component, few have gone the full mile and embraced the idea of a comprehensive guaranteed-job program. The reasons for caution are obvious. Simple calculations demonstrate that a *bona fide* "employer-of-last-resort" program would require between 15 and 20 million jobs, depending on the assumptions made about eligibility and labor-force participation rates. A primary reason for this high estimate is the effect that such a guarantee would have in drawing people from outside of the labor force into the new program. The cost of such a program would be in the range of $100 billion annually.

The recent history (since 1971) of public-employment programs is best understood in terms of the relative standing of its three principal objectives. Most recently, in enacting the 1976 CETA amendments and when debate was conducted in 1977 on the Carter Administration's expansion of PSE as a countercyclical tool, its job-creation potential, as would be expected, was hotly debated. Senator Henry Bellmon Republican, Oklahoma, successfully offered a Senate amendment requiring the National Commission for Manpower Policy (now the National Commission for Employment Policy) to conduct a study of the "net employment effects" of the CETA-PSE program. Bellmon's concern was job displacement, spurred on by the contention of many observers that additional PSE funds would be used, to a significant degree, as a substitute for wage and salary payments, which would otherwise be made from other sources by the recipient state and local governmental jurisdictions. In response to the Bellmon amendment, the National Commission for Manpower Policy initiated a series of parallel research efforts, including a national monitoring study of the CETA-PSE program to be conducted by the Brookings Institution.

The Brookings study is the basis of much of the information about the CETA-PSE program presented in this chapter.[2] Two sets of field observations have now been made in forty-one recipient jurisdictions by twenty-six field associates. Two more rounds of field research are planned for the extension phase of this research, to be carried out by the Woodrow Wilson School of Public and International Affairs of Princeton University. Briefly, the monitoring methodology involves the establishment of a network of independent social science researchers who report on a regular basis, using a uniform analytical framework, on what they interpret to be the effects of a particular grant-in-aid program on a representative sample of recipient jurisdictions. These analyses by the field research "associates" are then compiled and summarized as the basis for presenting a longitudinal account of the most policy-relevant effects of the particular program under examination. The product is distinctly a *group* product: the associates typically include an equal number of economists and political scientists. Although the monitoring study of the CETA-PSE was initiated to investigate the displacement issue, it has from the outset included other aspects of the program.

PSE AS A POLITICAL BARGAIN

In essence and at its roots, the PSE program is the product of a political bargaining process at two levels. At the national level, its three principal policy objectives must be balanced out, one against the other. The program's implementation also involves a bargaining process between the national government and the state and local jurisdictions that carry out the program. This two-dimensional policy bargain was not consciously planned. Congress and the administration have never made fully explicit the relative weights and interrelationships of the objectives of PSE. In describing its purposes, some policymakers stress its countercylical rationale, others highlight its structural goals. Even among those who concentrate on structural goals, there are differences. Some observers stress training for the disadvantaged; others emphasize the transition of PSE employees to regular, unsubsidized positions; still others stress the importance of targeting on the relatively least employable workers as a way of avoiding the possible inflationary effects of the increased labor demand generated by PSE spending.

Previous studies of public-service job programs have often ignored the interactions among objectives, focusing on one issue without giving sufficient attention to others. Most frequently overlooked is the public-service objective of local officials, which on the basis of the Brookings monitoring research was found to be an especially important purpose of the program for officials of the recipient state and local governments.

Until very recently, the central topic in most academic writing about federally aided job-creation programs has been the tension between the federal objective of job creation and the presumed goal of state and local officials under a flexible program like CETA, to obtain fiscal relief—to substitute Federal funds for local funds that would have been spent anyway. The results of the Brookings monitoring research cast doubt on this standard way of thinking about the policy trade-offs of the PSE program. The two rounds of field observations conducted so far (in July and December of 1977) indicate a job displacement rate for retained positions (those kept by the recipient governments and not farmed out by them to other governments or community-based organizations) of between 20 and 25 percent. This is by no means inconsequential, but it is much less than had previously been assumed. We found several reasons why local officials may not want to use PSE funds for substitution purposes. Some are influenced by the explicit legal prohibition against doing so, although such federal requirements are hard to enforce in the real world of state and local finance. Others have pragmatic concerns about the PSE program because of the uncertainty surrounding the future funding and the rules for its use. Federal spending levels and regulations in this area have been in a constant state of flux. Officials of the recipient governments of PSE positions may for this reason decide that they should avoid mixing PSE funds with their regular funds for operating purposes in a way that creates a commitment to continue the aided spending on a long-term basis. There is still a third major reason why local officials may wish to avoid displacement under the PSE program; they may indeed share the national objectives of reducing unemployment and aiding the disadvantaged. Whatever the reason, the essential finding is that national policymakers and state and local officials may not be as divided on the job-creation objective of PSE as is often assumed.

One way of looking at the net employment effects of PSE is to think in terms of three classes of effects of the PSE program—job displacement, job creation, and the maintenance of positions that would have been cut otherwise. The last category (program maintenance) was found to be important in both rounds of the field research. It was noted above that the PSE program crested with the taxpayers revolt; however, even before Proposition 13, we found, as did other researchers, that local governments were cutting back their employment in the mid-seventies. It is not surprising therefore that some PSE positions—which end up having a job-creation effect—were used to continue programs and activities that would otherwise have been cut back or eliminated. Fifteen percent of the positions studied in December 1977 were so classified, the great bulk of them being PSE jobs of the most fiscally hard-pressed governments in the sample.

The discussion so far has concentrated on the job-creation or countercyclical objective of the CETA-PSE program. The tension between the two other objectives of the PSE program—the provision of local public services and the program's structural aims—has received relatively little attention. Our research indicates that the use of PSE funds to expand and improve government services is a very strong interest of state and local officials. In the second round of PSE field observations, those of December 1977, we found that "primary" or basic services accounted for three-fifths of all PSE positions retained by the large cities in the sample and two-thirds of all PSE positions retained by the two other main groups of sample jurisdictions, small cities and suburban and rural jurisdictions. The analyses provided by the field-research associates indicate that many local government officials emphasize the service aspect of PSE in planning their programs. They see PSE as an opportunity to provide "extra" local services (clean up a park, add hall monitors in the schools, establish new arts and cultural programs). In exchange, they must be willing to use workers to provide these services who face labor-market barriers that make them less productive than the workers who would normally be hired. Thus the program can be seen as an intergovernmental policy bargain.

This state and local emphasis on community service often results in considerable policy tension between the structural and the local public-service aims of the program. The field-research associates frequently noted concern on the part of local officials that the federal government was "pushing too hard" on the targeting requirements. This pressure was seen as reducing the opportunity of local officials to carry out projects and activities of "value" to the community.

This discussion highlights the federal dimension of the policy bargain of PSE. State and local officials cannot be expected to hire hunderds of thousands of hard-to-employ workers unless there is some benefit to them and to their jurisdictions to offset the costs of the extra responsibility and supervision involved. Some local benefit derives from job displacement and the resultant local fiscal relief, but there are many recipient jurisdictions where our data suggest little or no job displacement. The major benefit of PSE to state and local officials in these jurisdictions is the added service that can be provided, and a major cost is compliance with federal requirements that this service be provided by persons who are disadvantaged.

Does the Bargaining Process Yield a Workable Program?

The most striking conclusion of the Brookings monitoring research to date is the degree to which the balancing of the goal at all government levels has produced a workable bargain, one that has allowed the PSE program to function reasonably smoothly and to build up rapidly in 1977 and 1978. A total of 424,000 jobs were added nationally between May 1977 and 1978. Overall we found a large stimulus effect. The jurisdictions in the Brookings sample spent all but 3.5 percent of what they planned to spend in the month of December 1977. Eighty-six percent of this funding had a direct expenditure effect; another 8 percent had an effect similar to a tax reduction.

Returning to the trade-off between the public-service and the structural goals of PSE, the data for the field sites are generally reassuring. Of the positions retained by large cities in the sample in December 1977, 68 percent went to persons unemployed for fifteen or more of the previous twenty weeks; 71 percent went to participants who were classified as economically disadvantaged. Of positions retained by suburban and rural jurisdictions, 57 percent went to the unemployed and 61 percent to the economically disadvantaged. The proportions were higher for nongovernmental sponsors—community-based organizations, or CBOs in the parlance of CETA. The figures for school districts and for other local governments to which

PSE positions are subcontracted were generally in line with those for the sample governments.

Admittedly, the definition of economic disadvantage in Labor Department regulations is a general one. Some long-term unemployed persons are not disadvantaged. Although some observers may not feel that the targeting impact of PSE is strong enough, on the whole the targeting objectives appear to be taken seriously, producing a "delicate balance" between skimming the top and scraping the bottom of the pool of eligible participants.

This delicate balance is also pertinent to training and transition, which are necessary steps in reaching the structural goal of the PSE program. Training and transition are more easily achieved if participants are not at the polar ends of what might be considered the continuum of disadvantage—if they are neither well-qualified workers who could be placed immediately nor the most severely disadvantaged for whom on-the-job training and transition are very difficult to provide.

The data on PSE-related job training from the monitoring research and official reports are limited. As of December 1977 very little formal training was found. The new law passed in 1978 requires earmarking some PSE funds for training. Hence we may find a different picture in the third and fourth rounds of the monitoring research.

Records on PSE job transition are especially scarce. The associates generally reported that, despite a requirement for transition planning, recipient local jurisdictions gave low priority to setting and meeting specific transition goals. Transition occurred and was encouraged but was not likely to be a conscious and planned program element; rather, it was the result of a reasonably good "fit" between a PSE participant and the availability of a position. The first two observation periods for the monitoring research occurred in the period of rapid build-up of the PSE program. Recipient governments had all they could do, we were told, to keep up with the flow of new positions. Planning for placement and transition is a task that appeared to suffer as a consequence.

The Bargain Under Pressure

If one views PSE as a bargaining process between the levels of government, there are then important questions about the possible future effects on it by the new policies of the federal government embodied in the 1978 CETA amendments. The new law tightens the targeting requirements by requiring both income and labor-market status requirements to apply to *all* PSE participants. All new participants must be classified as disadvantaged (that is, earn less than a certain income limit or be Aid to Families with Dependent Children [AFDC] recipients) and must have been unemployed for at least ten of the previous twelve weeks. The new law also sets limits on the wages of PSE participants (both average and maximum). It also puts an eighteen-month limit on the tenure of PSE participants and, as noted above, requires the earmarking of funds for training.

Obviously these changes put pressure on the PSE policy bargain. This is especially so for the requirement restricting average wages to no more than $7,200 per year. The average PSE wage in most jurisdictions in December 1977 was close to or above $7,200, which translates into $3.46 per hour on a forty-hour week basis.

The effect of these new requirements will be observed in the extension phase of the Brookings monitoring study of the CETA-PSE program. Field observations were made in December 1979, by which time the new law was in effect for three months, and one year later in December 1980.

The monitoring study of the CETA-PSE program has been a longitudinal study, but not necessarily a study of one program; it has been more a study of several different programs as its size and purpose have shifted. To complicate the picture still further, PSE is not just a different program from year to year; it is also a different program from place to place. This point is worth some elaboration as it has not been treated yet in the reports issued on the monitoring research.

POLITICAL BEHAVIOR UNDER THE PSE PROGRAM

The monitoring study of the CETA-PSE program has from the outset been designed to consider three basic kinds of effects of the PSE program—its fiscal and labor-market effects (does it create jobs?), its programmatic effects (what services are provided?), and its political/institutional effects (how does it work?). It is the merging of the analysis in three areas that produces a full picture.

This point can be illustrated by considering the political/institutional effects of PSE. The PSE program is a curious animal. In some ways it is like a general-purpose grant, providing funds for wages to implement a wide variety of local public services. It is also like a block grant; it is part of a system of broad formula allocations for manpower purposes—job creation, training, and placement. And in other ways it is like a categorical grant in that funds must be used for a specific purpose, jobs for disadvantaged persons.

Over the past year we have devoted research attention to a set of questions

67

involving the way in which the PSE program affects the politics and institutional setting of the recipient jurisdictions. There are three ways, as suggested above, in which local jurisdictions can treat PSE funds: (1) as revenue-sharing funds, fungible resources to be used to help relieve fiscal pressures and service deficiencies, (2) as a block grant to be operated, in effect, as an extension of the original CETA block grant for job training and related manpower activities, and (3) as a categorical-grant program in the mold of antipoverty programs of the mid-sixties: funds to aid the poor, often administered by quasi-governmental entities established for this purpose.

A second conceptual trilogy used in this analysis involves decision makers: (1) generalist officials, that is, elected chief executives and various cross-cutting staff officials like budget, planning, and finance directors, (2) manpower staff specialists, the "professionals" who run the block-grant training program and other job placement, training, and related programs, and (3) employing organizations, here referred to as agencies—both public and non-profit—which receive and use allocations of PSE positions.

Still a third set of definitions that needs to be introduced involves dimensions of PSE program execution. It includes: (1) organization—deciding who should run the PSE program and then setting up the local apparatus for carrying it out, (2) allocation—distributing PSE positions to the various employing agencies, and (3) implementation—referring to the process of carrying out the program once an organizational framework is in place and positions have been allocated.

As we have noted, there are three ways in which local jurisdictions can treat PSE funds: as revenue-sharing behavior, as block-grant behavior, and as categorical-grant behavior. For the first type of behavior, it is the generalist officials who dominate; for the second, it is the manpower specialists; for the third, it is the sponsoring organizations. By "dominate" we mean that a certain group of actors in the decision process has the greatest influence for two out of three dimensions of the PSE execution process. If in a particular jurisdiction generalist officials dominate two out of three dimensions of PSE execution (organization, allocation, implementation), then that jurisdiction is classified as demonstrating revenue-sharing behavior in its treatment of PSE funds.

The revenue-sharing behavioral group includes cases in which generalist officials concerned about rising fiscal pressures see PSE as a way to use federal funds to displace local funds, to continue programs that would otherwise have to be cut, or to provide basic public services that are of high priority but that could not be provided unless external fiscal flow were to be increased. Revenue-sharing behavior was found to be most prevalent for the most fiscally hard-pressed jurisdictions in the sample, though there were exceptions. The exceptions generally relate to attitudes on a liberal-conservative dimension. Some hard-pressed governments with a strong social orientation regard PSE primarily as a program to aid the disadvantaged. Their emphasis is on the structural objectives and they judicially avoid job displacement effects even though it means keeping the pressure on the local fisc to find new locally raised or external revenue. Other recipient governments that are not fiscally hard pressed, but that are controlled by persons and groups with a fiscally conservative orientation, resent having the federal government pressure them into undertaking new and additional program expenditures and hence regard PSE as a way to hold down local taxes.

Continuing the explanation of how the definitions used here come together, we define block-grant behavior as involving cases in which manpower specialists principally influence two out of three dimensions of PSE program execution. Categorical-grant behavior involves cases in which user organizations (that is, the sponsoring agencies) control two out of three dimensions of PSE program execution. The important questions, of course, relate to the reasons why a certain behavioral response occurs (what are the factors that explain it?) and the kinds of program effects associated with different behavioral responses to the PSE program. For example, is successful transition to unsubsidized employment under the PSE program more likely to occur for the revenue-sharing behavioral group? Is training more likely to be provided for jurisdictions manifesting block-grant behavior in their approach to the PSE program?

The basic point is: "What you see is what you get under the PSE program," referring here to the way in which the conception of the program and the viewpoint toward it on the part of the recipient jurisdiction determine the form of PSE as a grant-in-aid instrument of domestic policy. This situation especially applies to the CETA-PSE program because of the shifting nature of its objectives and the amorphous nature of its characteristics, having at the same time features of a revenue-sharing, block-grant, and categorical grant-in-aid program.

Having developed this descriptive framework, we plan in the third and fourth rounds of field research to ask associates to use this approach as a basis for studying the political/institutional effects of the PSE program. In the meantime, using the data from the second round of field monitoring (as of December 1977), thirty-one local recipient jurisdictions of PSE funds were classified on a preliminary basis according to this three-part conceptual framework. Just under half of this group (fifteen jurisdictions) were found to have manifested revenue-sharing behavior in their treatment of PSE funds. Nine jurisdictions were classified in the block-grant behavioral group, and seven units were grouped as evidencing categorical-grant behavior in their treatment of PSE funds. The last group is the least clear-cut of the three in terms of the type of actors who dominate.

It must be reiterated that these classifications are preliminary. Moreover, they are presented here in a summary form that results in making them appear simpler and more straightforward than is in fact the case. For these reasons, as well as for possible effects of the changes in the 1978 law, one should avoid drawing policy conclusions at this stage of the analysis. Special caution should be urged about adopting regulations that attempt to change recipient-government behavior under the PSE program. Such requirements often fail and sometimes backfire. Furthermore, it appears at this stage of the analysis that no one behavior pattern is best for all seasons. There are advantages and disadvantages to each.

WHAT IS PSE GOOD FOR?

As the research group involved in the monitoring study of the PSE program has gained experience, we have increasingly asked ourselves the bottom-line question, what is PSE good for? The program has evolved into a two-part program with a countercyclical component that presumably contracts in good times and a structural component that operates permanently. Both components are to be more specifically targeted under the new law. Reference was made earlier to "the delicate balance" of the PSE program. The program does not focus on the most severely disadvantaged group of workers who are extremely difficult to employ, and at the same time it does not recruit from the very top of the unemployed pool, which would aid workers who are transitionally unemployed and do not need such expensive employment assistance.

These findings need to be viewed in the larger context of employment and training policy. One can think in terms of layers of the labor market which, while they cannot be rigorously defined, are important concepts for purposes of thinking about social policy. There is a top layer of people who are or can be employed on a permanent and continuing basis without recourse to special employment aids. Next there is a group of workers who in good times can find stable employment but need help to tide them over periods of temporary joblessness. Unemployment compensation and labor-exchange programs in the public sector may be all that this group needs, although in periods of severe economic decline a public-sector job-creation program may be needed to absorb some of these workers, in order to avoid what society would regard as an unacceptably high level of aggregate unemployment. Farther down the line is a group of workers who face serious barriers to employment, are hard to employ, and need training and work experience. They face problems in good times and bad. Nevertheless, the workers in this group can overcome these barriers by acquiring experience and some training (often on-the-job training) and with such help can move up to the layer of transitionally or frictionally unemployed workers. Finally, there is the bottom of the labor pool, workers with very serious problems that take a long time to solve and perhaps can never be fully solved. These are workers with severe emotional, aptitude, and perhaps physical problems for whom highly structured employment assistance programs are required. One might argue that the PSE program is a good vehicle for aiding the two middle groups but not as effective for the bottom group. The bottom group requires more specialized programs, like supported work, sheltered workshops, and intensive remedial education and training.

Perhaps this delicate balance is what makes the PSE program work. Local governments take on the federal structural objective, but only on a basis that yields something of value in the way of local public services that can be provided, not necessarily easily, but in any event with a carefully designed PSE allocation and placement system. It can be argued that if one were to push this policy bargain to the top of the job ladder, the cost per person in relation to the service needed would be too high. Such a shift, in addition, could cause pressure on the labor market and be inflationary. Likewise, if one were to push very hard to have local jurisdictions serve the bottom group in the labor market—that is, serve them primarily or exclusively—then there is the chance that local jurisdictions would alter their behavior in ways that would reduce the usefulness of the program, both to participants and to the local community. For participants, the result could be a shunting-off effect, putting PSE participants in jobs with little or no training or transition opportunity.

As of December 1977, which is the date of the most recent monitoring-research observations, we were struck by the workability and speed of implementation of the PSE program. It needs to be added that many of the people involved in the monitoring study of the CETA-PSE program had substantial doubts at the outset about the program and were surprised by the findings of the first two rounds of field research. This is not to say that we have studied all of the issues one would want to examine. We have devoted little systematic research attention to the management of the PSE program, though we intend in the third round of study to examine this subject.

The PSE program is not a stable program. It has changed nationally with new laws and regulations. We have not been studying one program, but rather several programs. It is not only a different program from year to year, it is also a different program from place to place. The two types of change are related. As the rules change nationally, the program changes locally. The PSE program, like any large and complex program, is the result of constant shifts in rules, attitudes, and interpretations. All of this suggests that managing such a program requires much more than looking at the results of a policy review or research project at any one point in time and making changes that will apply for a very long period. A constant process of observation and iteration is needed.

There is a final point to be made about the limits of PSE. Such a program can only be built up so far before it begins to show signs of pressure on the federalism bargain so necessary to its execution. Moreover, within the public sector, there are distinct advantages to the bifurcated structure of the current PSE program. It is essential that the countercyclical component (now Title VI) contract in good times. This is necessary in order to avoid the absorption of PSE jobs into the regular work force of recipient governments. There is in this respect utility to the uncertainty associated with the PSE program; it tends to discourage dependency on PSE as a regular fiscal subvention. The second tier of the PSE program—the structural component—needs to have (as it now does) limitations on the tenure and wages of participants and requirements for targeting on the disadvantaged. This is necessary in order to avoid a permanent wage-push effect of the PSE program in the economy as a whole. This conclusion that there are limits to the size and scope of job-creation programs in the public sector means that if the need for job-related manpower services exceeds its given level (which would appear to be the case), the private sector, too, must have a role in the pursuit of employment-policy goals. Employment policy, in short, is not a job for just one sector.

5

JUDY GUERON

The Supported-Work Experiment

IN LATE 1973, a consensus emerged at a number of federal agencies and a private foundation on the importance of funding a major experiment to test the potential of a specific work-experience program.[1] The program was directed toward a part of our population that has traditionally had severe difficulty obtaining or holding regular jobs. Several factors contributed to this commitment. First, there had been growing national concern with the problems of central cities, as reflected in high rates of criminal activities and drug abuse, extensive unemployment, large numbers of discouraged workers, and increasing welfare dependency. While general policies to stimulate the economy might yield some improvement, it appeared that there was a group of people largely outside of the regular economy who were at once the chief source of social disintegration and its major victims. Moreover, previous service programs and intervention strategies seemed to have been largely ineffective in reaching or benefiting this group.

Second, the individuals involved in creating the supported-work experiment shared a perception of the value of work as an integrating force in people's lives. They argued that stable employment would offer this group an opportunity and a reason to change.

Third, the experiment's planners had been close to the employment initiatives of the sixties and had been impressed both with the potential of the programs and the paucity of hard facts about their actual impact, despite the large number of evaluation studies. In addition, they had observed the roller coaster sequence of policy development prevalent during that period, where a bright idea was quickly transformed into a national program and just as rapidly discredited. A new approach seemed warranted. The planners wanted to demonstrate the feasibility and utility of a more cautious method, moving from a small-scale demonstration to a slightly larger test and only then, if warranted, replication of the program on a national scale.

A program called supported work appeared to answer the three concerns: it addressed the population of concern with a program stressing work; it had already been the subject of a promising pilot test in one city and a limited expansion with a rigorous research design seemed feasible. The program model had several objectives. In the short run, supported work offered twelve to eighteen months of subsidized employment in an environment intended to attract and hold people who had previously been unable to secure more than sporadic employment. In the process, it was hoped that supported-work employees would move from being recipients of welfare payments to being producers of goods and services of value to their local communities. For the longer term, moreover, the program sought to develop the work habits, attitudes, skills, and credentials necessary to increase future unsubsidized employment and thereby reduce welfare dependency. In addition, for those with a history of criminal activities or drug abuse, it was hoped that steady employment during and after the program would reduce recidivism. In combination, the goal was a reduction in poverty and an improvement in the quality of life for the people employed in the program and living in the communities that the program served.

In 1972, the Vera Institute of Justice pioneered the first supported-work program for a group of ex-addicts in New York City. The early positive evaluation of that program prompted representatives of the Ford Foundation and five federal agencies, led by the Employment and Training Administration of the U.S. Department of Labor, to propose that an expanded demonstation be undertaken, with a built-in research component that would provide more reliable information than had been obtained from studies of earlier employment programs. The resulting National Supported-Work Demonstration became one of the country's largest social experiments, employing a total of 10,000 individuals at fifteen different locations across the country over a four-year period, starting in 1975.

In keeping with the lessons drawn from the experience of the sixties, the project's sponsors had a circumscribed yet ambitious agenda. They did not view the demonstration as a dry run of welfare reform, as a way to get definitive answers about the utility of all employment programs, as a test of a guaranteed job program, or even necessarily as a trial run of a large-scale national supported work program. Rather, they were interested in obtaining conclusive evidence on the usefulness of one particular employment program, including whether or not it had an impact on welfare expenditures, criminal activities, and subsequent employment of its participants, and how program benefits compared to costs. In an effort to test the replicabilty of the supported-work model, the program was run under varying conditions in different locations. To find out which populations would benefit most, the experiment included four target groups: unemployed ex-offenders, former drug addicts, women who were long-term recipients of welfare benefits, and young school dropouts. To get firm answers on the program's effectiveness, the research design, for the first time in a large-scale employment program, adopted an experimental methodology, including a control group obtained by random assignment. As a result, the supported work experiment tested both the potential of the program model and the utility and feasibility of a new research approach to the evaluation of employment programs. This chapter contains a preliminary assessment of the experiment's findings, which will be examined in full in a series of reports scheduled for publication in early 1980.

THE SUPPORTED-WORK PROGRAM AND ITS PARTICIPANTS

The national supported-work demonstration was implemented at the local level by fifteen legally distinct nonprofit corporations, which were established to provide supported employment under the auspices of the demonstration. At the national level, the demonstration was administered by the Manpower Demonstration Research Corporation (MDRC), which had responsibility for monitoring, for providing technical assistance and operating funds to the local programs, and for the development and implementation of the research plan.

Supported work is a transitional work experience program in which several special features are added to the work environment to assist its employees in gaining experience with the realities of the work place and in preparing them for subsequent, unsubsidized employment. The program's emphasis is on work, and only a limited amount of paid time may be spent in services such as formal training, counseling, and job-search assistance.

A participant is the employee of one of the local supported-work sites that assigns him or her to a job, pays a salary either slightly above or at the minimum wage, and promotes, fires, or suspends the person depending on his or her performance. At the end of the maximum twelve or eighteen months of employment, the local program personnel assist the participant in finding a permanent job. While there is an attempt to re-create a real-world environment, several features contribute to the structured, supportive environment: peer support, graduated stress, and close supervision.

The first element, peer support, is based on the theory that the target individual will work better and learn more in the company of his or her peers than if placed directly into a regular work environment. The second, graduated stress, is a conscious effort to adapt the demands of work to the worker, attempting not to overwhelm him or her at the beginning and yet eventually creating a demanding work environment that will prepare the person for a regular job. These concepts were implemented in a number of different ways, usually including the grouping of workers into crews. Finally, for the third element of close supervision, the programs made an effort to hire skilled supervisors who would be sensitive to the experiences of the target populations, with the ratio of supervisors to participants at about 1 to 12.

In order to focus the demonstration on a group of individuals who were particularly in need of assistance and not typically served by other programs, the local supported-work programs recruited only people meeting detailed eligibility criteria (summarized in Table 5–2, page 81). As a result, as indicated in Table 5–1, supported workers are primarily black or Hispanic, usually have not completed high school, and have very limited recent work experience and earnings (with the extreme range reached by the Aid to Families with Dependent Children [AFDC] group, of which fully three-fourths have either never worked or have not worked for at least two years prior to supported work). A comparison of the characteristics of supported workers with those of adults working in positions funded under the Comprehensive Employment and Training Act (CETA) and served by the Work Incentive Program (WIN) shows that supported work succeeded in reaching a population with distinctly greater employment problems than is typical among enrollees of these other programs.

At the supported-work sites, the actual types of jobs, customers, and funding arrangements varied greatly, with each program establishing a number of different and often unrelated activities to provide work for its 50 to 300 participants. As expected, over half of the total hours worked by the participants was in the broad area of general services, (for example, working in a day-care center, performing general clerical duties, or serving as a nurse's aide). Almost a third of the work was in the construction industry, ranging from the winterization of homes for the disadvantaged elderly to the cleaning and sealing of abandoned houses to the painting of public

TABLE 5-1

Selected Characteristics of the Supported-Work Sample at Enrollment,
by Target Group

Characteristic	AFDC	Ex-Addicts	Ex-Offenders	Youth
Male (%)	0.0	80.1	94.3	86.4
Average age (years)	33.6	27.8	25.3	18.3
Race/ethnicity (%)				
black, non-Hispanic	83.2	78.0	83.8	78.4
Hispanic	12.1	8.2	8.8	15.6
white, non-Hispanic	4.6	13.8	7.4	5.9
12 or more years of education (%)	30.4	28.5	26.7	0.7
Currently married (%)	3.0	23.1	11.8	3.7
Number of dependents in household	2.2	0.9	0.4	0.2
Months since last full-time job (%)				
Now working or unemployed less than 2 months	3.4	11.6	7.4	12.1
2–12	11.9	31.1	20.4	37.7
13–24	9.9	20.0	22.3	19.6
25 or more	60.7	32.4	38.9	8.6
Never worked	14.2	4.9	11.0	21.9
Weeks worked during previous 12 months	3.4	10.0	5.5	9.3
Earnings, previous 12 months ($)	240	1227	580	827
Average number of years received welfare	8.6	NA	NA	NA
Received welfare during previous month (%)	99.8	39.2	17.1	12.5
Used heroin regularly (%)[a]	NA	85.4	31.3	2.6
Ever used heroin (%)	NA	94.3	44.5	7.8
In drug treatment during previous 6 months	NA	88.6	12.2	1.7
Ever arrested	NA	89.6	99.6	54.2
Average number of arrests	NA	8.3	9.2	2.2
Average number of convictions	NA	2.9	3.0	0.6
Average number of weeks ever incarcerated[b]	NA	137	201	21
Number in sample	1351	974	1479	861

SOURCE: Interviews administered to experimental and control group members at the time of their enrollment in the research sample. The data are for a sample of individuals who completed baseline nine-month and eighteen-month interviews.
NOTES: Distribution may not add up to 100 percent as a result of rounding. Averages are calculated including all members of the sample. The notation "NA" means the data are not available.
a. "Regular" use of heroin refers to those individuals who reported using the drug at least once a day for at least two months.
b. For the full baseline sample.

housing projects and hospitals. Supported workers also engaged in other activities, from manufacturing (for example, building furniture, making concrete products, and recapping tires) to transportation (for example, delivering school breakfasts to disadvantaged children and running a small moving service for disadvantaged families). About three-quarters of the work was performed for public or nonprofit customers, with the remainder split between private firms and individuals. Most of the work was performed under the direct supervision of employees of the supported-work program, often in its own small shops or factories. Finally, in contrast to the usual CETA procedure, the supported-work corporations charged their public- or private-sector customers for the services or products.

Overall, the four-year demonstration and five-year research effort cost a total of $82.4 million, with $49.5 million coming from federal and Ford Foundation sources and $32.9 million from funds raised by the local programs from the sale of goods and services and from locally generated grants. A total of $66.4 million was spent on local program operations, with the remaining expenditures covering research activities, monitoring and technical assistance, and the operation of the demonstration's fiscal- and management-information systems.

The average net subsidy cost (total expenditures minus sales revenue) of employing a supported worker for a full year was $13,000 during the first start-up year of the demonstration, but it declined to $10,280 during the last two years of the demonstration. Because of the varying lengths of time workers spent in the program, this translated into an average per person cost during the latter period ranging from $4,450 for the ex-offender group to $8,140 for AFDC participants (an average of $5,740 per person for the four target groups). Per year of employment, supported work appears more expensive than CETA public-service employment (at $8,560 per person per year in 1978) and close to the Job Corps (at $10,180 per person per year in 1977). (However, this difference may be more a reflection of variations in accounting practices than real costs, since supported-work estimates cover the full cost of overhead, supervision, and materials which, in CETA-PSE, are usually incurred by the host agencies and not counted as program costs.) Moreover, because people stay in the various programs for different lengths of time, on a per person basis, supported work compares favorably to CETA (at $8,000 in 1978) and costs slightly more than the Job Corps.

THE RESEARCH DESIGN

The evaluation strategy formulated by MDRC's board of directors and the funding agencies sought to answer several basic questions:

1. How effective is supported work in increasing the long-term employment and earnings of participants and in reducing welfare dependency, criminal activities, or drug abuse?
2. What target populations benefit most from the program?
3. What does the program cost? To what extent does it produce valuable goods and services? How do the program's costs compare to its measurable benefits?
4. What local conditions, administrative auspices, and implementation strategies seem to be the most conducive to program success?
5. What particular characteristics of the program model have the greatest impact on individual performance and behavior?

This list reflected an interest both in getting hard answers on program effectiveness and in exploring the usefulness of a variety of approaches to program implementation. Thus, while the major resources went by far toward an evaluation using an experimental design, there was also a more qualitative analysis, focusing on questions of program variety and replicability.

There were four major components of the research: (1) the behavioral or impact analysis, which would measure short- and long-term impacts through interviews; (2) the benefit-cost analysis, which would assess net program benefits to the participants and society in general; (3) the documentation, which would report on the less quantifiable elements of program operation, such as variations in the implementation of the program model; and (4) the process analysis, which was aimed at assessing the effects of different program features. While MDRC had overall responsibility for the management of the demonstration and for all the research, the evaluation of program impact and cost was conducted by researchers at Mathematica Policy Research and the Institute for Research on Poverty of the University of Wisconsin. The group included individuals who had participated in the design and analysis of a number of negative income-tax experiments, and they therefore brought to the supported-work project a familiarity with the challenges of social experimentation that was critical to all aspects of the development and implementation of the research design.

In developing a strategy to address the question of supported work, the researchers and planners sought to avoid a repetition of the features of earlier evaluation studies—the absence of an independent evaluation, the lack of an appropriate comparison group, the small size of the sample, the insufficient length of follow-up, the atypicality of the program under examination, and the absence of accurate and complete cost information—which had caused them to be rejected as inconclusive or unreliable. This resulted in the adoption of a structure and design with a number of unusual features.

Employing the Unemployed

Impact and Cost Analysis. The first step in determining whether a program has an effect on its participants is obtaining a measure of what would have happened to them in the absence of the program. In all large-scale studies of employment programs prior to supported work, such estimates were at best obtained by contrasting participants to a comparison group selected for its similarity (for example, people in the same neighborhood or program applicants who were not enrolled). While this approach was faulted as containing a variety of unmeasurable biases, there was a widespread belief that the preferable random procedure would encounter such adamant opposition from program operators as to jeopardize the project and its evaluation.

The supported-work demonstration tested the accuracy of that belief: individuals were randomly assigned to a participant group (offered a supported-work job) or a control group (not offered a job). Once the participant and control samples were obtained, program impacts could be measured by a comparison of the behavior of the two groups (as determined through personal interviews), and because of the random assignment procedure, any observed differences could be attributed with known levels of statistical confidence to the impact of participation in supported work. While there was initial resistance by some of the referral agencies and operators, the process eventually worked uneventfully for over 6,500 individuals at ten locations.

In deciding on the size of the sample for random assignment and follow-up interviews, the designers sought both a sample sufficiently large to provide a good prospect of detecting the anticipated postprogram effects at statistically significant levels, and a follow-up period adequate to provide some information on the duration of program impacts. A rigid budget constraint resulted in the adoption of a procedure whereby early enrollees were followed for thirty-six months after random assignment, but later enrollees for only eighteen months. The combination of this policy and of an expected number of individuals who could not be located for reinterviews resulted in the sample sizes shown in Table 5-2.

The aim of social experimentation is to generate findings that are relevant to the larger target populations. One criticism of prior social experiments has been that they have not done this because of their exclusive focus on a very small number of sites. Despite efforts to model or simulate national conditions, there has been a suspicion that the findings might be idiosyncratic. The designers of supported work decided to use a broader approach, gathering the research sample from a sufficient number of sites so that it would approximate the variety in operating experience and local conditions likely to be encountered in an expanded program. Data from ten of the

TABLE 5–2
Key Features of the Experimental Design and Its Implementation

Design Feature	Criteria or Outcome
Target groups and eligibility criteria (at enrollment)	AFDC: women on AFDC for 30 out of past 36 months, with no children under 6. Ex-addicts: enrolled in a drug-treatment program currently or within the past 6 months. Ex-offenders: incarcerated as a result of a conviction within the last 6 months. Youth: 17 to 20 years old, no high school degree, delinquency record (for at least 50%). All: currently unemployed, spent no more than 3 months in a job during the past 6 months.
Sites with random assignment	AFDC: Atlanta, Chicago, Hartford, Newark, New York, Oakland, Wisconsin (Fond du Lac) Ex-addicts: Chicago, Jersey City, Oakland, Philadelphia Ex-offenders: Chicago, Hartford, Jersey City, Newark, Oakland, Philadelphia, San Francisco Youth: Atlanta, Hartford, Jersey City, New York, Philadelphia
Initial sample and control group strategy	Random assignment of 6,616 eligible program applicants to participant (3,214) and control (3,402) groups.
Data-collection strategy	In-person interviews conducted at time of random assignment and 9-month intervals thereafter for up to 36 months. Data validated by comparison with social security, welfare, and arrest records.

		AFDC	Ex-Addicts	Ex-Offenders	Youth
	Baseline	1597 (98.6)[a]	1394 (97.3)	2268 (98.4)	1241 (99.1)
Final sample sizes and completion rates by length of follow-up	9-month	1440 (88.9)	1111 (77.5)	1682 (72.8)	1001 (80.0)
	18-month	1362 (84.1)	987 (68.9)	1539 (66.6)	924 (73.8)
	27-month	620 (79.2)	885 (72.5)	995 (62.9)	506 (70.4)
	36-month	[b]	317 (67.2)	302 (59.8)	155 (76.7)

a. Figures in parentheses are completion rates, calculated as a percent of the number of assigned interviews. (All individuals were scheduled for baseline, nine-month and eighteen-month interviews and those due for reinterview before March 30, 1979 were scheduled for twenty-seven-month or thirty-six-month interviews.)

b. No thirty-six-month interviews were scheduled for the AFDC sample as a result of a delay in program start-up for that group.

program sites could thus be combined to determine the impact of the overall demonstration. To make this strategy work, the different supported-work programs had to share a core of common features.

The extent of standardization was determined by a balance between this pressure for uniformity and a concern that a "hot house" environment of excessive definition or constraint might both compromise the local projects' success and limit the generalizability of the research findings to a postexperiment environment. In contrast to several prior social experiments—such as the negative income tax, health insurance, or housing-demand projects—the operational component of the supported-work experiment was more complex. Going beyond the administration of a payment policy to the establishment of an employment program, it was dependent on local economic conditions and had to be responsive to the particular needs of the supported-work employees and the communities they served.

The supported-work experience suggests that some program features are amenable to rigid specification (for example, eligibility criteria, wage levels, maximum program duration), some defy uniform definition but can be controlled by detailed guidelines (for example, the method for implementing peer support or graduated stress), and others are so dependent on local conditions that they cannot be rigidly limited without seriously jeopardizing the program's viability (for example, the type of work or the source of local funds).

The key features of the experimental design for the assessment of the behavioral effects of supported-work participation are summarized in Table 5–2. The research design also called for a study of the program's costs and benefits. Prior cost-benefit studies had been criticized for many of the reasons discussed above (inadequate comparison groups and follow-up), as well as for their incomplete and poor quality data or because of confusion about who received the benefits and who paid the costs. The supported-work study sought to avoid some of these problems through (1) a comprehensive and uniform fiscal and information system in operation at all of the sites; (2) the early articulation of the possible program benefits and costs; (3) an effort to obtain estimates of the magnitude and value of the different items (for example, an extensive study of the value of goods and services produced by supported work-crews); and (4) the early and persistent accounting of which items were costs and which were benefits from the perspectives of society as a whole, the program participants, and the program nonparticipants.

Process Analysis and Documentation. The supported-work evaluation contained a substantial effort to determine what particular characteristics of the program or the local environment and administrative structure had the greatest effect on performance and behavior. Two nonexperimental strategies were followed: a qualitative documentation effort, drawing on observations of the program, interviews with program staff and other interested parties, and data from the program's information system; and a statistical process analysis, which sought to determine if in-program or postprogram performance was statistically related to different features of the program treatment. Studies from the documentation analysis have already been published. They analyze and discuss such subjects as the welfare diversion policy, job creation and development, and sources of local revenue for the individual programs. The findings from these two types of analysis are, therefore, not extensively discussed in this document.

FINDINGS ON PROGRAM IMPACT AND COST

The supported-work program achieved a substantial measure of success in meeting its short-term objectives of increasing employment and earnings, reducing welfare dependency, producing useful goods and services, and reducing criminal activities. It provided ample evidence of a strong interest in work among the four target populations, particularly the recipients of AFDC. It also showed that temporary supported employment could lead to a substantial reduction in average welfare benefits and a decreased number of participants on the welfare rolls. Finally, for the ex-addicts, it demonstrated that providing a pay check can lead to a direct and dramatic reduction in criminal activities.

The findings on long-term impact are more mixed. For the AFDC participants, it appears that program effects endured after their experience in supported work and into the postprogram period, and that the level of impact did not decline over time. For ex-addicts, the program appears to have had a delayed effect, with no significant impacts observed during months sixteen to thirty, but substantial positive impacts during months thirty-one through thirty-six. Finally, for the ex-offenders and youth, the program does not appear to have had long-term impacts.

The analysis of program benefits and costs suggests that supported work has a substantial redistributive effect in accordance with its goal of reducing poverty through employment. It also indicates that, for the ex-addict and AFDC target groups, society as a whole receives benefits in the form of useful goods and services, reduced criminal activity, and increases in future employment that are considerably in excess of program cost.

Impacts on AFDC Women. Both in terms of operational measures and in comparison to the control group, supported work had its greatest success with the AFDC group. Statistics for all enrollees at the fifteen sites show that the AFDC women have the highest attendance rates at their work in the program (89 percent, compared to 84, 80, and 76 percent for the ex-addicts, ex-offenders, and youth, respectively), the longest average time spent in the program (9.5 months compared to 5 to 7 months for the other target groups), the highest rate of departures to a regular job (35 percent compared to 23 to 29 percent for the others), and the lowest rate of firings in the program (12 percent, compared to 37 to 42 percent for the other groups).

As Table 5-3 shows, supported work was extremely effective in increasing employment and reducing welfare dependency both when the participants were in the program and after they had left it. During the first nine months following random assignment, most experimentals were still in supported work and thus had a much higher employment rate than controls. As anticipated, this difference declined in the next nine months as participants left the program and as an increasing number of controls found jobs. The difference was cut still further during the postprogram period (somewhat arbitrarily defined as the months subsequent to month 18), when almost all experimentals had left supported work. However, statistically significant experimental/control differences—a factor most critical for the assessment of supported work's usefulness—continued into this postprogram period. On the average, during months nineteen to twenty-seven, experimentals worked 36 percent more hours and earned 46 percent more money per month than controls. Moreover, participation in supported work may have resulted in better quality jobs, since the experimentals working in nonprogram jobs earn an average of 46¢ an hour more than the working controls. Finally, an examination of the monthly data during this postprogram period indicates no further decay in program effect, suggesting that there may be some stability and durability to the program's impact on the work experience of these women.

As a result of higher earnings, employment in supported work contributed to a substantial reduction in welfare dependency by the AFDC women. Over the twenty-seven-month period, experimentals received $2,600 less in AFDC and food stamp benefits than members of the control group. By months nineteen through twenty-seven, about twice as many experimentals as controls had left the AFDC rolls (71 percent of the experimentals received welfare payments compared to 85 percent of the control group). The

TABLE 5-3

Experiment-Control Group Differences in Key Indicators During the 27 Months
Following Enrollment: AFDC Target Group

Outcome Measure	Experiment Participants	Control Participants	Difference
Percent employed during period			
Months 1 to 9	96.3	36.5	59.8
10 to 18	76.5	39.4	37.1
19 to 27	49.1	40.6	8.5
Average monthly hours worked			
Months 1 to 9	135.6	27.7	107.9
10 to 18	79.2	40.8	38.4
19 to 27	61.0	44.7	16.3
Average monthly earnings ($)			
Months 1 to 9	400.44	78.28	322.16
10 to 18	274.06	131.08	142.98
19 to 27	242.89	165.88	77.01
Percent receiving cash welfare payments[a]			
Months 1 to 9	93.8	97.7	−3.9
10 to 18	82.4	90.1	−7.7
19 to 27	71.4	85.1	−13.7
Average monthly amount ($)			
Months 1 to 9	169.82	277.90	−108.08
10 to 18	164.28	246.60	−82.32
19 to 27	172.06	224.00	−51.94
Food Stamps: average monthly bonus value ($)			
Months 1 to 9	44.83	63.46	−18.63
10 to 18	42.15	58.02	−15.87
19 to 27	47.14	60.25	−13.11
Average monthly total income[b] ($)			
Months 1 to 9	628.06	435.10	192.96
10 to 18	524.47	454.44	70.03
19 to 27	497.50	470.14	27.36

SOURCE: Stan Masters, *The Supported-Work Evaluation: Final Results for the AFDC Sample*, Manpower Demonstration Research Corporation, forthcoming.

NOTES: Data for the different time periods are from samples similar in size to those noted in Table 5-2. All data are regression-adjusted estimates that control for differences due to age, sex, race, education, prior work experience, marital status, cash welfare.

b. Total income includes earnings, unemployment compensation, welfare, food stamp bonus value, and other unearned income (Social Security, pensions, alimony, and child support).

increased earnings of the experimentals were also accompanied by reduced payments of Medicaid benefits and increased rental payments by families in public-housing projects.

Finally, when welfare and earned income are examined together, it becomes clear that increased earnings from supported-work employment are substantially offset by reductions in welfare benefits. (See Table 5–3.) Although the total income of the experimentals remains above that of the controls during the period the experimentals are in the program, by the postprogram period the difference is no longer statistically significant.

In another respect as well, the AFDC findings are both unanticipated and puzzling. Prior to the demonstration, the program operators had expected that competing child-care responsibilities, poor health, the lower monetary incentives provided to this group because of the welfare reductions that would accompany employment, and the stereotypically "male" job types at some of the supported-work programs might cut into program attendance or result in early terminations for the women. Quite to the contrary, however, their performance while in the program earned the AFDC employees the reputation of the most stable and reliable of the supported workers. In fact, their success raises the question of whether the AFDC participants needed "supported" work or just work. Unfortunately, there are no reliable findings on the success of a comparable group of women placed directly into private-sector or public-service employment jobs. There is, however, some evidence from the supported-work operational experience and research that the program environment was essential to the demonstrated success of the AFDC women.

As Table 5–1 indicates, the AFDC eligibility criteria targeted the program at a group of women who had been out of the labor force for a prolonged period of time. Throughout the demonstration, program operators commented on the needs of these employees for assistance in acclimating themselves to the world of work and on their anxiety about leaving supported work for a regular job. This impression is also reflected in the job placement data: fully 74 percent of the AFDC employees who left supported work found a job with the assistance of the program staff, in contrast to 42 to 50 percent using this method for the three other target groups.

A comparison of data for the four target groups also indicates that the primary explanation of the relatively strong AFDC findings was the poor performance of their comparison group, the AFDC controls. The members of the control group, despite their interest in working (as indicated by their volunteering for supported work) and their status as mandatory WIN registrants, had only limited success in getting jobs. And when the AFDC group is divided into subpopulations according to previous work experience, the program appears to have its largest impact on the individuals with the least prior employment experience. While not conclusive, all this information taken together suggests that the program served as a useful and necessary bridge between welfare and work, providing both an opportunity to get used to the world of work, and credentials and assistance in finding subsequent employment.

Impacts on Ex-Addicts. The comparison of the behavior of program participants and controls summarized in Table 5–4 suggests that supported work had a number of impacts on the ex-addict participants. During the early months after random assignment, participation in supported work resulted in a large and statistically significant increase in earnings and employment for this target group. This figure was substantially reduced, however, during the second nine-month period, when most of the experimentals had left the program; more detailed data show no significant differences for participants from months sixteen to thirty. Surprisingly, the data indicate a delayed program impact during the last follow-up period, when employment, earnings, and hours for experimentals were significantly higher than for controls. While extensive supplemental analysis confirms that this upturn does occur and is not the result of any special characteristics of the thirty-six-month follow-up sample, a full understanding of the belated program impact is not currently available.

Probably the single most important finding for the ex-addicts was that supported-work participation led to a dramatic reduction in criminal activities. During the first eighteen months after random assignment, there was a 24 percent reduction in the arrest rate for experimentals, 25.3 percent compared to 33.5 percent for the controls. In addition, the impact on criminal activities persisted into the postprogram period, with 38 percent of the experimentals arrested over the thirty-six months compared to 53 percent of the controls. Similar changes were observed in a large number of other measures of criminal activities, a few of which are included in Table 5–4. Particularly notable are the sharp reductions in the arrests of the experimental group for robbery and drug-related offenses. Finally, a comparison of the self-reported interview data, presented in Table 5–4, with arrest records from criminal justice agencies at two of the program sites, confirmed that the interview results reflected actual differences in experimental/control behavior.

Impacts for Youth and Ex-Offenders. A comparison of the activities of the youth target group in supported work and their control group counterparts indicates that the program does not have a lasting impact on employment and earnings or lead to significant changes in criminal activities or drug use. Supported work did result in temporary improvements in employment outcomes while the youth participated in the program, but the effects decayed rapidly in subsequent periods. The findings for the ex-offender

TABLE 5-4

Experimental-Control Group Differences in Key Indicators During the 36 Months Following Enrollment: Ex-Addict Target Group

Outcome Measure	Experiment Participants	Controls Participants	Difference
Percent employed during period			
Months 1 to 9	95.0	50.2	44.8†
10 to 18	63.9	53.1	10.8†
19 to 27	56.5	53.0	3.5
28 to 36	64.0	53.9	10.1*
Average monthly hours worked			
Months 1 to 9	119.7	41.5	78.2†
10 to 18	67.2	51.9	15.3†
19 to 27	60.4	59.0	1.4
28 to 36	70.0	52.9	17.1†
Average monthly earnings ($)			
Months 1 to 9	361.23	159.79	201.44†
10 to 18	259.62	220.42	39.20*
19 to 27	277.75	261.33	16.42
28 to 36	326.09	224.36	101.73†
Average monthly welfare[a] and food stamps benefits ($)			
Months 1 to 9	57.97	115.17	−57.20†
10 to 18	92.42	110.89	−18.47†
19 to 27	89.90	93.94	−4.04
28 to 36	94.34	103.79	−9.45
Percent using any drug (other than marijuana)			
Months 1 to 9	36.1	38.2	−2.1
10 to 18	34.1	32.7	1.4
19 to 27	28.0	27.5	0.5
28 to 36	23.4	20.7	2.7
Percent using heroin			
Months 1 to 9	20.7	22.0	−1.3
10 to 18	16.8	17.8	−1.0
19 to 27	13.4	11.7	1.7
28 to 36	10.1	8.8	1.3
Percent arrested			
Months 1 to 18	25.3	33.5	−8.2†
19 to 36	35.0	53.1	−18.1†
Percent arrested for robbery			
Months 1 to 18	2.3	7.5	−5.2†
19 to 36	0.2	13.4	−13.2†
Percent arrested on drug charges			
Months 1 to 18	4.1	7.9	−3.8†
19 to 36	6.8	14.0	−7.2
Percent convicted			
Months 1 to 18	13.5	17.8	−4.3*
10 to 36	19.3	32.9	−13.6*

SOURCE: Kathy Dickenson, *The Supported-Work Evaluation: Final Results for the Ex-Addict Sample*, Manpower Demonstration Research Corporation, forthcoming.

NOTES: See Table 5-3.

a. Welfare includes AFDC, GA, SSI, and other unspecified cash welfare.

* Statistically significant at the 10 percent level.

† Statistically significant at the 5 percent level.

group are less clear-cut. There is a similar pattern of strong in-program impacts and a rapid decay during months ten through twenty-seven. However, there is some evidence of a delayed program impact during months twenty-eight through thirty-six, although the upturn is small and less certain than for the ex-addicts. Additional follow-up and analysis will be required to clarify the pattern of program impacts over time. Finally, for the ex-offenders, there is some evidence that supported work affected the extent and nature of drug use.

Program Benefits and Costs. The preceding discussion suggests that supported work is a complex program that produces a large number of effects at substantial budgetary cost. It puts to work people who have previously been unemployed, who have been surviving sometimes on welfare, sometimes on criminal activities, and who frequently have a recent history of drug addiction and participation in costly treatment programs. As indicated in Tables 5–3 and 5–4, employment in the program often had measurable impacts on the participants themselves; for those benefiting from the program, it also most likely led to an increase in more intangible outcomes, such as their psychological well-being. The program also undoubtedly affected the lives of the people who were closest to the supported workers: the children of the AFDC participants and the families of all the supported workers. In addition, the public-at-large benefited from the goods and services produced in the program, the reduction in criminal activities for the ex-addicts, and the successful redistribution of income through employment. Finally, the nonparticipants, as taxpayers, achieved substantial savings from reduced welfare payments that also offset program costs.

Many of these program benefits are extremely difficult to quantify or measure. Thus, while the supported-work evaluation included a substantial effort to assess and measure the program's benefits and costs from the perspectives of society at large, the nonparticipants (as taxpayers), and the supported workers themselves, it includes only a subset of the measurable impacts and therefore provides at best only a partial estimate of the program's economic efficiency and redistributive impact. As a result, while a finding that social benefits exceed costs would be a strong indication of the program's social usefulness, a contrary finding need not mean it is socially inefficient. Rather, it would provide an estimate of the level of social subsidy required to gain the unquantified, intangible benefits.

From the social perspective, measured benefits include the output produced by participants while they were in the program, any increase in future earnings or reduction in criminal activities, and savings from reduced participation in alternative employment and training or drug-treatment programs; measured costs include the program operating cost (net cost of supported-worker wages) and the foregone earnings of the supported workers participating in the program. Findings on operating cost came from the demonstration's fiscal system; those on the behavioral changes and on supported-work opportunity cost were based on interviews with the experimentals and controls (valued where necessary using estimates from external sources); and conclusions on the value of output came from a study of a partly random sample of forty-four work projects conducted at eight of the ten survey sites. For the taxpayer and participant analyses, data were also collected on changes in tax payments and in the receipt of cash and in-kind transfers.

While this resulted in an unusually comprehensive and accurate set of data, considerable uncertainty still surrounds individual components of the analysis. As a result, the detailed reports on the findings present a range of estimates reflecting the sensitivity of the outcome to different assumptions about the component parts—for example, assumptions about the accuracy of the self-reported arrest data collected in the interviews or the extent to which the observed program impacts continue or decline after the twenty-seven- or thirty-six-month period covered by the interviews. In this paper, only the "benchmark" or best guess estimates are reported; however, with the exception of the ex-offenders, the overall results do not appear sensitive to reasonable variations in these underlying assumptions.

For the AFDC and ex-addict target groups, both from the overall perspective of society and from the more limited perspective of the taxpayer, the benefits of supported work appear to be substantially in excess of its costs. Per supported-work participant, net social benefits are estimated at $8,100 for the AFDC group and $4,300 for the ex-addicts, net taxpayer benefits at around $8,000 and $1,000 respectively. In both cases, substantial benefits result from the output produced during participation in supported work ($4,500 and $3,400 per participant respectively, reflecting their differing average lengths of stay in supported work) and from increases in their postprogram earnings; for the ex-addicts, large benefits also flow from the reduction in criminal activities (valued at $5,200) during and after the program.

For the youth group, the measured costs of supported work exceed the benefits, by a total of $1,500 per participant using the social cost-benefit perspective and by $2,400 per participant from the perspective of the nonparticipating taxpayers. In constrast to the other three target groups, the direction and magnitude of the ex-offender findings proved extremely sensitive to the specific assumptions adopted in the analysis. However, the range of estimates resulting from the sensitivity tests suggests that the costs probably exceed the benefits from both the social and taxpayer perspectives.

CONCLUSION

The supported-work demonstration was conducted to test whether the provision of a job in a special work environment could combat a number of societal problems: crime and drug abuse, long-term welfare dependency, and high youth unemployment rates. It applied, for the first time in the evaluaton of an employment program, the new techniques of social experimentation, in order to yield more reliable data than had previously been available on the effects of such an intervention and to determine the extent to which the high costs of providing the unemployed with a job would be offset by measurable benefits. The findings presented in this paper suggest that, for two of the target populations, the supported-work experiment vindicated its planners' conviction about the effectiveness of a job strategy. They also indicate that a large-scale demonstration can be structured as a social experiment.

The supported-work program had far-reaching impacts on the participants in the AFDC and ex-addict target groups. The program concept was most successful for the AFDC women, a substantial number of whom benefited from it, both as a sheltered introduction to work provided while they were in the program and as a bridge to unsubsidized employment. The cost-benefit calculation for this group reveals that from a number of perspectives society's investment in supported work was more than paid back in reduced welfare and other transfer payments, increased earnings and tax payments, and the goods and services produced while the women were in the program. Supported work also provided an important opportunity for the ex-addicts, who responded to the program's offer by earning income from legitimate sources, with a dramatic reduction in illegal activities. The magnitude of these changes was such that, even were there no postprogram employment effects, the program's benefits would exceed its costs.

For the ex-offenders and youth the overall conclusion is less clear. Supported work appeared unusually effective in getting particularly hard-to-employ individuals into a job. For the youth, there is no evidence of a more permanent effect on employment and earnings; for the ex-offenders there is some indication of a possible impact. For neither group is there a concomitant reduction in criminal activities. A judgment on whether or not the benefits for these groups, including the output produced by the supported workers while they were in the program, justify the cost ultimately depends on one's values. How much is it worth to put unemployed ex-offenders to work? To provide teenagers a job as an alternative to street life?

91

Employing the Unemployed

Those who place a high value on substituting work for welfare or unemployment might argue that even for these two groups the net costs seem small. Others could counter that similar redistributive effects could be obtained at less cost through additional welfare programs.

In assessing the supported-work findings, the reader should consider a number of additional caveats. First, the supported-work experiment was conducted in a period when a large number of alternative CETA and WIN services were available, particularly to the youth and AFDC target groups. As a result, the estimates of program impact may not show the full potential of the program, but only the marginal benefits that would follow its introduction in an environment of specific program alternatives.

Second, the impact findings were derived from ten programs operating under demonstration guidelines and may not be generalizable to a subsequent operating program. While there was an initial effort to choose sites reflecting a variety of administrative structures and local conditions and to operate the projects under procedures that could be replicated, the quality of the ten programs may in fact have been exceptional. In addition, the supported-work experience was by design quite different from the more familiar CETA programs, both in the structure of the work environment and in such diverse features as the variety and type of work projects and the emphasis on raising revenue from the sale of the products of the supported workers. Any expansion or institutionalization of the supported-work demonstration would have to consider how the key features of the program design could be preserved and implemented in a nondemonstration environment.

Third, a planned, more refined analysis of the interview data may suggest supported work is particularly effective for certain subgroups within the target populations and may point toward a refocusing of the eligibility criteria. For example, the program appears to be more successful in increasing the employment of AFDC women with extremely limited previous work experience and that of ex-addicts with a particularly extensive record of prior arrests.

Finally, any conclusions on the usefulness of supported work should follow from an assessment of the program's relative efficacy compared to alternative employment and training approaches. Given the differences in populations served—and therefore in the nature of program impacts and opportunity cost of labor—such comparisons should go beyond budget outlays to a detailed examination of social benefits and costs. Unfortunately, the paucity of reliable and consistent data on other programs and the differences in populations served makes such an effort extremely hazardous.

From another perspective, the supported-work demonstration provided some valuable lessons about the implementation of program evaluations. It demonstrated that social experimentation with randomly assigned participant and control groups is a feasible and extremely useful method to estimate the impacts of employment programs. It affirmed the importance of studying the effects of a program over an extended period of time, both by the indication that program impacts may be long-lasting and by the complicated patterns of decaying effects for the different target populations. In addition, the project confirmed that a multisite operational program can be implemented with sufficient discipline to satisfy the constraints of social experimentation. (However, as discussed in greater detail in other reports on the demonstration, this success was critically dependent on the existence of a central managing agency with sufficient influence and authority, probably through control of program funding, to establish and discipline compliance with essential operating guidelines and on the adoption of a sampling strategy that could be adjusted to meet program contingencies.) Finally, it suggests that, under certain circumstances, several separate federal agencies can combine resources to make possible a research project of interest to their distinct constituencies and which these constituencies most likely could not finance on their own.

In conclusion, the supported-work findings shed some light on the usefulness and nature of an employment strategy for individuals with substantial barriers to employment. Recent legislation has redirected the CETA program toward the more difficult-to-employ and imposed strict time limits on participation. The targeted jobs and WIN tax credits also seek to place some of the same groups directly into subsidized private-sector jobs. The supported work experience suggests that for many of these people direct placement in a public agency or private job will not succeed. A transitional, sheltered environment is an essential bridge between their prior prolonged unemployment and a regular job. Moreover, for some subgroups of this population, the supported-work research suggests that twelve to eighteen months of work, even in this specially tailored environment, will not be sufficient in obtaining a lasting change in work behavior.

LESTER C. THUROW

Manpower Programs as Income Redistribution

WHERE ARE WE?

All income-redistribution programs have to be seen in the context of the changes that are occurring in the market distribution of earnings (Table 6–1). In the economy, the fourth quintile of the work force has made large gains in its share of total income (up from 23.4 percent in 1948 to 26.4 percent in 1977) at the expense of everyone else. While everyone has lost ground relative to the fourth quintile, the losses are particularly sharp for those in the lowest quintile and diminish as you go up the income scale. The poorest quintile's share of earnings has been cut 35 percent from 2.6 percent to 1.7 percent of total earnings. In contrast the share of the richest quintile fell by only 2 percent.

The net result is a situation where the earnings gap has risen between each of the bottom three quintiles of the population and the top two quintiles of the population. Between the poorest quintile and the richest quintile of the population, the gap in average earnings has risen from nineteen to one in 1948 to twenty-eight to one in 1977. Between the poorest quintile and the fourth quintile, the difference in average earnings has risen from nine to one in 1948 to sixteen to one in 1977. Given an economy where earnings differences between the bottom 60 percent and the top 40 percent are expanding rapidly, income-redistribution programs have to expand very rapidly just to hold the distribution of income constant.

Manpower Programs as Income Redistribution

Part of this movement toward a more unequal distribution of earnings is caused by an increasing dispersion in annual hours of work and part is caused by widening gaps in earnings. Regardless of the source, however, it leads to an Alice in Wonderland world where manpower programs have to run very rapidly just to keep from falling behind. And as we can see, they have not succeeded in doing this in the thirty years since World War II.

This macrofailure is not surprising given the small size of most manpower programs relative to the size of the economy, but it is surprising given the change in the distribution of education (Table 6–2). Education is not a small

TABLE 6–1
Distribution of Earnings Among Workers

Quintile	1948	1977
1	2.6%	1.7%
2	8.1	7.7
3	16.6	16.1
4	23.4	26.4
5	49.3	48.1

program relative to the economy and has succeeded in substantially equalizing the distribution of educational attainment among the work force. From 1965 to 1976, the proportion of the work force with less than a high school education has fallen from 50 percent to 25 percent, while the proportion with more than a high school education has risen from 11 percent to 35 percent. Yet the distribution of earnings has become more unequal. Even among white males employed on a full-time full-year permanent basis, increasing educational equality has not led to increasing earnings equality.

For many years, each new cohort came into the labor force with a more equal distribution of education than the previous cohort. This process is now slowing down as the distribution of education stabilizes. Older, more poorly educated cohorts continue to retire, but new cohorts do not bring a much more equal distribution of education than their immediate predecessors. As a result, whatever countervailing power a more equal distribution of education has to mitigate rising dispersion in the distribution of market earnings, this power will be less than it has been.

If instead of looking at the earnings gap between rich and poor workers, you look at the gap between economic minorities and economic majorities, there is a mixed pattern of success and failure. The best way to look at this pattern is to use three measures of a group's earning performance. (1) What is happening to a group's relative unemployment rate? (2) What is happening to the relative earnings of those that escape unemployment? and (3) Is

TABLE 6–2

Distribution of Man-years of Education of the Work Force

Years	1965	1976
0 to 7	17.4%	5.3%
8	15.0	5.3
9 to 11	17.7	14.3
12	29.8	40.4
13 to 15	8.9	17.7
16	6.8	10.1
17 and up	4.2	7.0

the group making a breakthrough into the best jobs in the economy?

If you examine the employment position of blacks, there has been no improvement and perhaps a slight deterioration. Black unemployment has been exactly twice that of whites in each decade since World War II. And the 1970s are no exception to that rule. Whatever their successes and failures, manpower programs have not succeeded in opening the economy to greater employment for blacks. In the immediate post–World War II period, it was possible to argue that blacks were moving from farms (where underemployment does not show up in our statistical indicators) to cities and that constant unemployment rates masked a real improvement in employment prospects. This is undoubtedly true, but it does not explain the consistency of black unemployment rates in the last fifteen years. Given a lack of progress over a substantial period of time, there is nothing that would lead anyone to predict improvements in the near future. To change the pattern, there would need to be a major restructuring of existing labor markets.

Viewed in terms of participation rates, there has been a slight deterioration in black employment. In 1954, 59 percent of all whites and 67 percent of all blacks participated in the labor force. By 1978 white participation rates had risen to 64 percent and black participation rates had fallen to 63 percent.[2] This change came about through rapidly rising white female participation rates and falling participation rates for old and young blacks. In the sixteen- to twenty-one-year-old age category, black participation rates are now 15 percentage points below that for whites.

At the same time, there has been some improvement in the relative earnings for those who work on a full-time full-year basis. In 1955 both black males and females earned 56 percent of their white counterparts (Table 6–3). By 1977 this had risen to 69 percent for males and 93 percent for females. While black females made good progress in catching up with white females, this has to be viewed in a context where white females are slipping slightly relative to white males. If black males were to continue their relative progress at the pace of the last twenty years—5 percentage points every ten years—it would take black males another sixty years to catch up with white males.

While the greatest income gains have been made among young blacks and one can find particular subcategories that have reached parity (intact, college-educated, two-earner families living in the Northeast), there still is a large earnings gap among the young. Black males twenty-five to thirty-four years of age earned 71 percent of what their white counterparts earned in 1976. Among full-time full-year workers, the same percentage stood at 77 percent. Young black males are ahead of older black males, but they have not reached parity. As with black females in general, young black females do better than young black males. Females twenty-five to thirty-four years of eage earned 101 percent of their white counterparts and full-time full-year black females earned 93 percent of what white women earned.

Using the top 5 percent of all jobs (based on earnings) as the definition of a "good job," blacks hold 2 percent of these jobs while whites hold 98 percent. Since blacks constitute 12 percent of the labor force, they are obviously underrepresented in this category. Relative to their population, whites are almost seven times as likely to hold a job at the top of the economy as blacks. At the same time, this represents an improvement in the position of blacks relative to 1960. Probabilities of holding a top job have almost doubled, with most of the gains going to black males.

Separate data on Hispanics has been collected only since the end of the 1960s and is not as extensive as that available for blacks, but during the 1970s, Hispanics seemed to have faired slightly better than blacks in the labor market. From a position of relative inferiority, they have risen to a position of parity or better. With blacks this is probably due to the fact that Hispanics are much more heavily concentrated in the Sunbelt, with its rapidly expanding job opportunities.

Instead of having unemployment twice that of whites, Hispanic unem-

TABLE 6–3
Relative Earnings of Full-time Full-year Workers
Blacks/Whites

Year	Males	Females
1955	56%	56%
1960	59	68
1970	65	83
1977	69	93

ployment is only 45 percent higher. Labor force participation rates are rising even more rapidly than those for whites. In terms of relative earnings, full-time full-year males earn 71 percent of what whites earn and females have reached 86 percent of parity. While there are substantial differences in family income among different Hispanic groups, earnings are very similar among the major groups. In 1976, for all persons with income, Cuban-Americans, Mexican-Americans, and Puerto Ricans were all within $200 of each other.

In terms of the best jobs, Hispanics hold 1 percent of these jobs but constitute 4 percent of the labor force. Relative to their population, whites are only three times as likely to be in the top 5 percent of the job distribution as Hispanics. In terms of breaking into the good jobs of the economy, Hispanics are far ahead of blacks.

American Indians are the smallest and poorest of America's ethnic groups. They are poorly described and tracked by all U.S. statistical agencies. Despite the existence of the Bureau of Indian Affairs, only the roughest estimate for their economic status is available. In terms of family income, reservation Indians probably have an income about one-third that of whites. Where nonreservation Indians stand no one knows.

Female workers hold the dubious distinction of having made the least progress in the labor market. In 1939 full-time full-year women earned 61 percent of what men earned. In 1977 they earned 57 percent as much. Since black women have gained relative to black men, white women have actually fallen slightly relative to white men over this forty-year period. Adult female unemployment rose from 9 percent higher than men in 1960 to 43 percent higher in 1978. From 1939 to 1977 the percentage of the top jobs held by females has fallen from 5½ percent to 4 percent, although women's representation in the labor force rose from 25 percent to 41 percent. Relative to their population, a man was seventeen times as likely as a woman to hold a job at the top of the economy in 1977.

While one can certainly point to professions and businesses where women have broken into new job opportunities, these breakthroughs have not been large enough to keep up with a growing economy and a growing female labor force. Although it can only be speculation (there are no hard data), part of the problem may be traced to a declining proportion of working women who are full-time full-year lifetime workers. Leaving the labor force for any period of time can be a severe handicap in landing one of the economy's top jobs.

With the exception of breaking into the top jobs in the economy, much of this decline can be attributed to rapidly rising female participation rates. With more women in the labor force, there is simply more competition leading to lower wages and more unemployment. At the same time, the results indicate that the structure of the economy has not changed and women have not broken through into a world of equal opportunity. In such a world, they would compete with men and not just with each other.

At the bottom of the labor force stand the young—our modern lumpen proletariat. In 1978, 49 percent of all unemployment was concentrated among sixteen to twenty-four-year-olds. Unemployment rates for them were three times that of the rest of the population. Among male full-time full-year workers, earnings stood at 40 percent for fourteen to nineteen-year-olds and 65 percent for twenty to twenty-four-year-olds. Among females the same percentages were 64 and 104. In terms of holding the top jobs, sixteen to twenty-four-year-olds held 0.5 percent, although they constituted 24 percent of the labor force.

While low earnings can be dismissed on the grounds that the group is acquiring skills and will in the future earn higher incomes, the unemployment is not so easy to dismiss. Unemployed young people or young people who have dropped out of both school and the work force represent individuals who are not acquiring skills and good work habits. What this portends for the distribution of earnings in the future is hard to say since we have never before had a period where so much of the unemployment of our society is concentrated among the young, and especially among young minorities. Certainly, it is hard to think that it will do anything except make the distribution of earnings more unequal in the future. The cohort with the large population bulge will probably suffer higher unemployment all through its working life.

MANPOWER PROGRAMS AS DIRECT REDISTRIBUTION

Manpower programs impact the distribution of earnings through two avenues. First, they directly constitute a source of wage and salary income. Those in the programs earn wages that they otherwise would not be earning. Second, they have the potential to alter the distribution of market earnings by changing the distribution of skills in the labor force.

In fiscal 1978, $10.2 billion was spent on manpower-training programs in the Labor Department, $3.6 billion was spent on manpower-training programs in other departments (mostly HEW), and $0.6 billion was spent in the form of tax credits for training. These expenditures constituted 1.4 percent of the wage and salary income reported in 1977. Assuming that most of this money goes to workers who are in the bottom 40 percent of the work force in terms of earnings, manpower training directly resulted in an 18 percent increase in the share of total wages and salaries going to the bottom 40 percent of the work force. While adding 1.4 percentage points of income to the bottom 40 percent of the work force did not stop their relative position from deteriorating from 1948 to 1977 (Table 6–1), the bottom 40 percent of the work force would have gone from 10.7 percent of total earnings to 8.0 percent of total earnings without manpower-training programs. With these training programs, the share of the bottom 40 percent only fell to 9.4 percent. Viewed as a vehicle for raising the share of total earnings for low-wage workers, manpower programs have been successful as a direct redistribution program.

The second avenue of redistribution has to be viewed in the context of an underemployed economy with skill surpluses almost everywhere. Even those who argue that the economy is now at full employment do so in terms of a shortage of prime-age white males and not a shortage of this or that skill. Unemployment rates differ across occupation (Table 6–4) but in every occupation, unemployment rates are substantially higher than they were in the boom years of the late 1960s.

In a world of underemployment and skill surpluses, different manpower programs can be effective in a microsense (those trained have a higher income than they would have had without training) but there is no impact in the macroworld of the entire distribution of earnings. If a trainee gets a job, he or she gets a job that would have gone to someone else in the absence of a training program. This someone else now has lower earnings than he or she would have had if the training program had not existed. The net result is

TABLE 6–4

Percentage of Unemployment by Occupation

	1969	1978
Total	3.5	6.0
Professional	1.3	2.6
Managers	0.9	2.1
Sales	2.9	4.1
Clerical	3.0	4.9
Craft	2.2	4.6
Operatives except transport	}4.4	8.1
Transport Operatives		5.2
Nonfarm laborers	6.7	10.7
Service workers	4.2	7.4
Farm workers	1.9	3.8

no change in the distribution of earnings even when manpower programs are successful at the microlevel. Manpower programs can only alter the distribution of earnings in an economy of skill shortages where a job filled does not mean someone else unemployed. I have labeled this effect the "push-in, push-out" effect. Manpower programs push a new trainee into the economy and the economy pushes out someone who now needs training.

This reshuffling process is not without merit, however, if those pushed out of the economy were significantly different in their characteristics (race, sex, age, and so on) than those pushed in. If prime age white males were pushed out in this process, one could argue that despite the zero-sum earnings effects, programs were valuable since they did not have a zero-sum unemployment effect. Those driven into unemployment do not have the same characteristics as those driven into employment. Unfortunately, if you look at the structure of unemployment, if has, if anything, been becoming more unequal in the 1970s. Manpower programs are swimming against a strong current of rising proportions of economic minorities in the labor force and have not succeeded in making progress against these currents. Unemployment has not been reshuffled so as to narrow unemployment differentials.

Thus manpower programs must be viewed primarily as a direct form of earnings redistribution. Indirect earnings redistribution could occur in an economy with skill shortages, but in an underemployed economy, no change in the distribution of earnings is apt to occur even if the manpower programs are microsuccesses.

Both the size and the frustrations that would occur in a program large enough to affect the entire distribution of earnings can be seen in the one government manpower program large enough to affect the entire economy—education. Table 6–5 presents data on the relative earnings of two male cohorts (twenty-five to thirty-four-year-olds and fifty-five to sixty-four-year-olds) as the distribution of education changes. In each case very large changes in the distribution of education are needed to make relatively small changes in average earnings.

Among males twenty-four to thirty-four years of age who work full-time full-year, the percentage with less than a high school education (the reference point) has fallen from 26 to 12 percent, while the percentage with more than a high school education has risen from 34 to 52 percent from 1968 to 1976. With this enormous change in the distribution of education, the relative earnings of the bottom three educational classes rose 5 percent and the relative earnings of the top three educational classes fell 6 percent. To close the gap between top and bottom by 11 percent required 13 million man-years of education above that which would have been necessary to

TABLE 6-5

Distribution of Relative Earnings for Males by Educational Attainment for Those Who Work Full-time Full-year

Educational Attainment (in years)	Twenty-five to Thirty-four Years of Age				Fifty-five to Sixty-four Years of Age			
	Relative Earnings		Percent of Labor Force		Relative Earnings		Percent of Labor Force	
	1968	1976	1968	1976	1968	1976	1968	1976
0 to 7	63%	70%	5.2%	2.0%	63%	62%	21.5%	10.3%
8	78	85	5.3	1.6	75	75	20.3	11.2
9 to 11	85	86	15.5	8.8	86	87	17.6	14.8
12	100	100	39.8	35.7	100	100	22.8	35.5
13 to 15	111	109	14.8	21.4	114	122	7.9	12.7
16	138	122	10.6	18.0	199	157	5.3	7.7
17 and up	143	137	8.8	12.4	190	190	4.7	7.9

hold the distribution of education constant at 1968 levels. Using direct costs of $3,000 per man-year of education, $39 billion dollars were necessary to achieve this change. If we expand this to the entire labor force, an expenditure of $365 billion would be needed.

But as we can see, there is also reason to believe that the effects of a more equal distribution of education disappear with age. Among those fifty-five to sixty-four years of age, the changes in the distribution of education were if anything more dramatic. The percentage of the full-time full-year work force with less than a high school education fell from 59 percent to 27 percent and the percentage with more than a high school education rose from 18 to 28 percent. Yet in this age group, there was no rise in the earnings for those with less than a high school education. Those with more than a high school education saw their relative earnings fall by an average of 6 percent. Thus the equalization effect on the oldest group of workers was about one-half as large as that on the youngest group of workers.

While education did succeed in narrowing average earnings differentials across educational classes, it did not succeed in narrowing the distribution of earnings. This can be seen by looking at the distribution of earnings for white males who work full-time full-year (Table 6–6). Despite dramatic movements toward equality in educational attainments and despite significant narrowings in the average earnings differentials between educational classes, the entire distribution of earnings has not become more equal, even for the most preferred group in the labor force.

This has occurred because although the average wage gap between educational classes has narrowed, the variance of earnings within each educational class has widened substantially. There is after all no one wage for college-educated workers, only an average wage made up of various different actual wage rates. This increasing variance within educational classes has counterbalanced both a more equal distribution of educational attainment and a more equal distribution of average earnings. The net result

TABLE 6–6
Distribution of Earnings for White Males
Who Work Full-time Full-year

Quintile	1968	1976
1	7.7%	7.7%
2	14.3	13.9
3	18.2	18.2
4	23.5	23.5
5	36.3	36.7

is no progress in equalizing the distribution of earnings, even given very large manpower programs, which have succeeded in substantially changing the characteristics of the labor force.

In a strict neoclassical economy with its zero-unemployment rate, the previous result could not occur. In the process of eliminating unemployment, workers bid for jobs and lower wages until each wage has reached the market clearing price given the supplies and demands of that skill. A more equal distribution of skill inputs must lead to a more equal distribution of wages. This effect could be offset if changes in skill demands were raising the wage gap between skills at the same time, but as we have seen, this is not the case in the United States. Wage gaps between educational skills are falling, differences in educational attainment are falling, yet earnings are not becoming more equal.

Here again, we see the difference between what would happen in a full employment world (either due to macroeconomic full employment policies or due to the existence of a neoclassical full employment economy) and our actual world of underemployment. Pumping a more equal distribution of skills into an economy that has a surplus of those skills does little to equalize the distribution of earnings.

Both the existence of unemployment itself and the lack of success in narrowing the distribution of earnings with educational programs point to a labor market that clears based on factors other than wages. If workers are selected for jobs based on the background characteristics that they bring into the labor force (rather than on their willingness to work for lower wages) and if most workers acquire some substantial fraction of their skills informally, on the job (rather than in formal training programs), the heart of the earnings redistribution process centers on the allocation of jobs rather than on the allocation of formal training opportunities. Formal training programs have a role to play in reallocating job opportunities, but by themselves they will not alter the distribution of earnings in an underemployed economy.

ALTERING THE DISTRIBUTION OF EARNINGS WITH MANPOWER PROGRAMS

While one can argue as to whether we actually have a current shortage of prime-age twenty-five to fifty-five white males (their current unemployment rate is low but still twice that of the late 1960s), any successful effort to reduce earnings inequalities would have to focus on the problem of equalizing job opportunities and reshuffling unemployment. In 1978 age-sex-race unemployment differentials officially ranged from 3 percent for prime-age white males to 38 percent for black female teenagers. Since black teenage participation rates are now 15 percentage points below those of white teenagers, unofficial black teenage unemployment stands above 50 percent.

Since there are too few jobs to go around and since macroeconomic policies are not likely to produce enough jobs to go around in the forseeable future, any earnings redistribution must come through the reshuffling of unemployment. In addition to whatever merits it has as a program for altering the distribution of earnings, it also has to be an important part of the anti-inflationary program advocated by those who see a shortage of prime-age white males as the key bottleneck in our economy.

Prime-age white males are often seen as the key factor in wage inflation since they possess a large proportion of the economy's skills, are the preferred workers for many employers, and tend to dominate union politics. If shortages of prime-age white males develop, their wages rise. Rather than shift to young, female, or minority workers, employers simply pay higher wages to prime-age white males and pass the costs through in the prices of what they sell. As a result, many government policymakers see the unemployment rate of prime-age white males as the key ingredient in stopping wage inflation. White males are the wage setters for the economy and everyone else trails along. To keep the wages of white males in check, their unemployment rate must be high, but this requires much higher rates for everyone else, even though high unemployment among these other groups does not provide very much help in reducing wage inflation.

Since it is a paradigm example of a zero-sum economic policy where some American gains exactly what some other American loses, it is not surprising that programs to reshuffle but not lower unemployment have little political appeal. Whenever such a program is suggested, say lower minimum wages for young people than adults, it meets vigorous opposition. As the labor movement says, it does not weigh "sons and daughters taking jobs away from mothers and fathers." But taking jobs away from fathers (or at least prime-age white male fathers) and giving them to minorities, women, and the young is the only way to equalize the distribution of earnings in an underemployed world. It is also the only way to reduce inflationary pressures if you think that the current U.S. inflation is due to a shortage of prime-age white male workers.

The essence of the problem can be seen among young people. In 1978, 49 percent of all those unemployed in the United States were 16 to 24 years of age and their unemployment rate was more than three times as high as that of the rest of the labor force. Given this extraordinary level of surplus labor, one would expect to see strong downward pressures on wages. This is especially true in a period of inflation, since employers can lower real and relative wages without having to lower money wages. Yet this is not what has happened.

Among males with earnings, relative wages were unchanged between 1972 and 1977 at 11 percent for the fourteen to nineteen-year-olds and 62 percent for the twenty to twenty-four-year-olds. If one looks only at those who work full-time full-year, the fourteen to nineteen-year-olds held their own at 40 percent of the national average in both 1972 and 1977 and there is a statistically insignificant slip from 67 percent to 65 percent for the twenty to twenty-four-year-olds.

For fourteen to nineteen-year-old females, relative earnings rose from 21 to 24 percent and from 62 to 64 percent for full-time full-year permanently employed females. Among twenty to twenty-four-year-old females, there was a slight slippage in relative earnings from 111 to 104 percent for all females and from 89 to 85 percent for full-time full-year females. At the same time, participation rates are rising for both males and females so that the stable earnings cannot be explained on the grounds that more people have dropped out of the economy and simply aren't being counted. On a quality-adjusted basis (relative to educational attainment), one can argue that youth wages have fallen, but when one reaches the bottom line, high unemployment has not succeeded in lowering the wages of those who do find employment.

Given that the relative wages of young workers have not responded to their enormously high unemployment, it is not surprising that employers have not been changing their hiring patterns to hire more young workers and fewer older workers. They have no incentive to do so since young workers have not become cheaper.

If relative wages do not change in the market, the option is to use government policies to change relative wages. Any wage subsidy program can serve this role if it is targeted at those groups with high unemployment. It would also be possible to change relative wages by altering government rules on fringe benefits. Employers, for example, might be forgiven their share of social security taxes for young workers, for workers who are new entrants into the labor market, or for workers who come from groups with high unemployment. Many of our current manpower programs have a strong element of wage subsidy now and this could be expanded. Conversely, a wage tax could be placed on the employment of preferred groups.

At the same time, there are several characteristics of a wage subsidy effort

Manpower Programs as Income Redistribution

to alter relative wages and relative unemployment that are needed but do not now exist. The most important is that it would have to be open-ended and available for everyone in some particular category. The budget for the program could not be controlled by limiting the total number of slots.

The need for this requirement is easy to see. Suppose that you were to announce a 20 percent wage subsidy for sixteen to twenty-four-year-olds looking for full-time work but you limit the program to 1 million young people. While unemployment rates are high for economic minorities at any point in time, millions are employed. If you announce a limited program of youth wage subsidies, employers have an incentive to substitute eligible youths for ineligible ones, but they have no incentive to substitute youths for older workers. The latter incentive only exists if all young workers carry the subsidy with them.

What this means in budgetary terms is that subsidies have to be paid for the employment of millions of currently employed young people in order to provide a subsidy for currently unemployed young people and to encourage the hiring of more young workers. This obviously makes any wage subsidy program expensive. In 1977 a 20 percent wage subsidy for sixteen to twenty-four-year-olds would have cost $13 billion dollars for those who were already employed on a full-time full-year basis. When one adds in those who would like full-time full-year work and would find it if a wage subsidy existed, the total cost would be even higher.

While paying for employment that would have existed anyway can be viewed as inefficient, it is an inefficiency that is a necessary part of any effort to restructure hiring patterns. It is also an inefficiency which we tolerate when it comes to capital subsidies. The 10 percent tax credit is designed to subsidize and lower the cost of investment, but here we also pay billions of dollars in tax credits for investment that would have occurred anyway in order to get the marginal effect. A wage-tax credit would have to be operated in the same way. The program would have to be open-ended (available for everyone) and carry the same burden of "necessary inefficiency."

While wage subsidies (direct or indirect cuts in fringe benefit requirements, and so on) are not outside the bounds of current political discussion regarding young workers, poor workers, or potential workers on welfare, they do seem to be outside the bounds of discussion vis-à-vis minority and female workers. Although one can make the argument that minority workers are slowly gaining on majority workers in the course of economic growth, female workers do not seem to be gaining on any of the three dimensions— unemployment, earnings, or top jobs. Since educational and formal skill attainments of minority workers are still behind those for whites, further improvements in these input variables should bring some further future improvements in output—earnings. Females, on the other hand, do not lag behind males in terms of educational attainment and the other skills that can be acquired in formal training programs. The female work problem lies directly in the area of job allocation within the private firm or public agency.

Part of the problem springs from a clash between the way our economy allocates its good jobs and the physiological imperatives of child bearing. If you were to look at a group of twenty-five-year-old white males and attempt to predict who would be economically successful (earn the highest income), you would have great difficulty in predicting economic winners and losers. If you were to look at the same group of white males at age thirty-five, it would be relatively easy to predict who would be the most successful. Those who are going to make it are already well-established on the economy's fast track. If a white male doesn't show signs of economic success between twenty-five and thirty-five, he is very unlikely to show them later.

But it is exactly this decade where female participation rates have traditionally been the lowest. In the past most women either did not work at all or were out of the labor force for some substantial period of time. Recently, average participation rates for females twenty-five to thirty-four years of age have risen very rapidly so that the sharp drop of earlier years has vanished, but this is still a decade where many fewer women than men are in the labor force without interruption. Yet this is the decade that is most vital. Dropping out of the labor force before twenty-five does not seem to make much difference and after thirty-five individuals are well-enough established that they can take some time out and still return to a good career. One solution is to have children before twenty-five or after thirty-five; the other solution is to alter the timing of the make or break career period.

Discrimination against female workers is one of those areas where neither public policies to help them nor theories to explain what is occurring seems adequate. Since females are falling behind males, the programs obviously aren't working. When applied to females, none of the discrimination theories developed for minorities makes much sense. It makes no sense for men to maximize their income vis-à-vis women since they lower their own family income in the process. At the same time, the barriers to advancement are both real and formidable.

With similar personal input characteristics, female work advancement is clearly going to succeed or fail based on affirmative action pressures. The economy is making no progress in the normal course of events. Personal characteristics (other than sex) are not a source of disadvantage; wages at every skill level are well below those for men. Only forced changes in the allocation of job opportunities are going to narrow the gap.

CONCLUSIONS

To end is to begin. The starting point was a distribution of market earnings that had grown substantially more unequal since World War II. The ending point is a distribution of market earnings that is still moving rapidly in that direction. Given existing manpower programs, the distribution of earnings is more equal now than it would have been without these programs. As they have grown in size, they have become a significant source of direct redistribution. As a mechanism for indirectly altering market earnings by changing skills and relative wages, they fail. They are working in an underemployed economy where they cannot cause the desired changes.

In an economy of high unemployment a more equal distribution of earnings can only come about if we adopt policies to reshuffle employment opportunities and alter the structure of unemployment. Low unemployment rates are to be raised; high unemployment rates are to be lowered. Generally, across the board wage subsidies are probably the best vehicle for bringing this change about.

While low-wage workers are not catching up with high-wage workers, economic minorities do seem to be catching up with whites. Male wage gaps are closing slowly and female wage gaps are now small enough that all females share a common problem of catching up with white males rather than each other. How this is to be done in a world that vigorously resists affirmative action quotas is a mystery.

7

J O H N P A L M E R

Jobs versus
Income Transfers

CONCERNS over the work disincentive effects of income-transfer programs and the provision of "jobs not welfare" are themes that currently dominate discussions of social-welfare policy.[1] These are not new concerns, but they now have a strength that has not been in evidence since the depression. Employment and training programs have expanded considerably over the past several years and are being increasingly redirected toward income-maintenance objectives. After more than a decade of federal welfare policies that did little more than pay lip service to work rhetoric, Congress is debating an administration welfare-reform proposal that virtually guarantees a job or training slot to one adult in all low-income families with children. States and localities wish to experiment more with "work relief" programs for Aid to Families with Dependent Children (AFDC) recipients. And several proposals to reduce work disincentives in public retirement, unemployment insurance, and disability programs either already have passed Congress or are receiving serious consideration.

Contemporary American society clearly has both ambivalent and evolving views of the "jobs-versus-income-transfers" controversy. National polls repeatedly show that a large majority believes that government should guarantee every adult a job, while an equally large majority opposes a government-guaranteed income. Yet our social-welfare policies have brought us much closer to the latter than to the former. Why is this? In part the answer lies with the more general macroeconomic and structural barriers to achieving truly full employment. However, another major factor is that income-maintenance objectives often can be met more efficiently through direct income-transfer programs than through employment and training policies. But this is not always the case. Furthermore, much broader and often more intangible values relating to the role of work in our society must be considered in any debate over jobs-versus-income-transfers. This chapter explores several of the more important issues in the jobs-versus-transfers debate in order to illuminate some of the current policy choices and relevant considerations.

HISTORICAL PERSPECTIVE

Prior to the 1930s, America's policies for assisting its poor and unemployed were deeply grounded in the British Poor Laws. The British principle of "less eligibility"—the notion that those on welfare should always be less well off than the poorest worker—held forth in America as well. Local governments and their overseers of the poor were responsible for administering welfare policies, and the local tax base financed those operations. Private groups, church-related organizations, and the extended family shared in this responsibility of caring for the poor. The federal government played virtually no role in relief.

In the early 1900s several states began programs of categorical assistance for selected needy groups in the population who were deemed unable to work—widowed families, the blind, and the aged poor. Most states by 1929 had also instituted workman's compensation provisions. But on the brink of the depression, no state had passed an unemployment insurance law. A few employers and unions had established voluntary unemployment protection plans, but the percentage of workers covered in 1929 was less than one percent.

The Great Depression overwhelmed the existing systems for providing assistance. Localities could not meet rising relief costs, private groups were unable to fill the gap, and state emergency relief programs were stymied by dwindling revenue bases.

When Roosevelt took office, state emergency programs were providing over one million unskilled jobs to the recently unemployed. But with fifteen

Employing the Unemployed

million out of work, the need for a federal income-maintenance function was clear. Roosevelt's first relief effort was in the form of substantial grants-in-aid to states and localities, to provide whatever mix of direct and work relief was determined to be needed for families whose breadwinner was unemployed. Between 1933 and 1935 more than three-quarters of these funds were spent for direct relief, usually consisting of in-kind provisions of food, clothing, or housing. Compensation for work performed, on the other hand, was usually cash. The work provided was most often manual labor, the amount paid was on the basis of need, and eligibility was restricted to those receiving direct relief.

All told, at least $15 billion was spent on work-related programs during the depression, which employed as many as 3 million individuals at any one time. It is interesting to contrast this to the British experience, where the public-sector relief jobs available during the decade never exceeded 100,000. What accounts for such a dramatic difference?

Roosevelt's and Harry Hopkins's stubborn determination that jobs take precedence in America's relief effort was a factor. They considered "the dole" a narcotic. But more important was the built-in protection against unemployment afforded to workers in each country. At the beginning of the depression, the United States had no old-age insurance, no unemployment insurance, and a hodgepodge of state categorical-assistance programs. Britain, on the other hand, had established old age and unemployment insurance in 1911 in addition to centralizing its categorical cash assistance. After World War I the British had greatly expanded unemployment coverage so that virtually all workers were eligible for benefits. The United States, having no such systematic cushion, turned increasingly to work relief to soften the blow as the need for some form of income maintenance grew.

Passage of the Social Security Act in 1935 marked the American adoption of social insurance to replace a portion of earnings lost due to the death, retirement, or temporary unemployment of a worker and authorized federal financial help as well, to states that provided means-tested cash assistance to their dependent children, aged and blind.

The period from World War II until well into the 1960s was marked by a conspicuous lack of relationship between income maintenance and employment concerns. Social Security grew tremendously during this time, but little public concern was expressed over any work disincentive effects of the various income-transfer programs.

Certain themes emerged in the 1960s that bear directly on the environment in which the issues surrounding work and income transfers are debated today.

First, transformations in public assistance from the 1950s accelerated as AFDC rolls and expenditures exploded and urban black families with absent fathers became dominant. These and other factors led to increasing concern over the lack of work effort on the part of recipients and the perceived pattern of long-term dependence on welfare. As a result, steps were taken in a series of amendments in 1962, 1967, and 1971 which: (1) insured that AFDC recipients who worked would be better off than those who did not by allowing a substantial portion of their earnings to be disregarded in calculating their benefits; (2) provided a limited amount of training, job placement, day care, counseling and other services aimed at facilitating the transition from relief to work; and (3) first authorized and then required states to institute a work requirement and to reduce a family's benefit if able-bodied adults without custodial responsibilities refused to register for work or training and accept a suitable job if offered.

Second, the 1960s also saw the emergence and growth of contemporary manpower programs. While it was hoped these programs would help to reduce dependence on income-transfer programs, none of them were designed to serve income-maintenance objectives *per se*.

Toward the end of the 1960s both the attempts to increase the work effort of AFDC families and the broader manpower-training and services strategy were viewed, at best, as having met limited success. The belief began to grow that what was really needed were jobs.

A third theme, growing out of the War on Poverty, was the increased recognition of, and concern for, the plight of the "working poor"—basically, two-parent families in which the adults worked either sporadically or regularly at low-wage jobs and were unable to earn enough to avoid poverty. Two steps were taken to assist them: a large expansion of the food stamp program and a policy change enabling states to pay AFDC benefits to families where the father became unemployed.

The confluence of these three themes and their consequences became evident in the early welfare-reform planning of the first Nixon Administration. The Family Assistance Program (FAP) as it was first envisioned was a remarkably bold and imaginative blueprint, which not only instituted a uniform federal cash-assistance structure for all low-income families—single parent and two-parent, working and nonworking—but also contained a large public-sector jobs component to insure that employment would be available to all those who (it was believed) should work. But the final FAP proposal did not contain this ambitious jobs component, and it ultimately failed to win congressional approval partially because of the conviction that it would have too discouraging an effect on the work effort of family heads.

Employing the Unemployed

What concern over the plight of the disadvantaged and the poor could not accomplish in the 1960s, concern over wide spread middle-class unemployment did accomplish in the 1970s. For the first time since the depression, public-employment programs were instituted to meet the growing income-maintenance needs of the average worker, first on a modest scale in 1970 to 1972 and then on a large scale under the Comprehensive Employment and Training Act (CETA) in 1975 to 1977. Although there was considerable rhetoric during both periods about focusing the jobs on the economically disadvantaged, and welfare recipients in particular, these populations received low priority. More recently, however, this priority has become more of a reality, both within CETA public jobs components and under the private-sector-oriented employment tax-credit program.

Work and welfare became most closely linked by the Carter Administration in its 1977 welfare-reform proposal—the Better Jobs and Income Program. In addition to federalizing and expanding eligibility for income-tested cash assistance to the entire low-income population, this proposal included 1.4 million public jobs for primary earners of all families, to insure the availability of sufficient employment opportunities. Congress, however, balked at (among other things) the price tag ($15 to $20 billion) of this proposal. In 1978 the administration introduced a much scaled down and less controversial proposal along similar lines that is still being considered by Congress in 1980.

CURRENT CONCERNS

We have arrived at a point today in the United States where income transfers are broadly available to populations on the basis of widely varying criteria. Some groups are clearly treated better than others and the distinctions are generally related to societal views about who should work and who is deserving of assistance on the basis of prior work effort. Both social insurance and welfare programs have a strong categorical philosophy; the level and duration of benefits vary with the cause of income loss or deficiency. But even where a strong presumption exists that work is not expected of a particular population, there is growing concern about work disincentive effects of the income-transfer programs covering them. On the other hand, long-term unemployment, temporary and partial disability, and

114

low income due to intermittent and low-wage employment provide little basis for receiving income transfers. For people with these difficulties there is both considerable unease about coverage through income transfers and growing interest in the use of employment-related measures to meet their income maintenance needs.

The Aged

There is a clear consensus that the aged should not have to work and should be eligible for public-income transfers either on the basis of past work history (Social Security) or low current income (Supplemental Security Income, SSI). But there is also a belief that major reductions in the labor-force participation and work effort of the aged have been caused in part by the growing generosity of Social Security benefits. This is disturbing to many people who either believe the mental and physical well-being of the aged is enhanced by continued work activity or that, as the baby boom generation ages, a healthy economy will depend on greater participation of senior citizens. For these reasons there are growing pressures in Social Security policy both to increase the reward for later relative to earlier retirement and to eliminate the "earnings test" that now applies to those under age seventy.

The Severely Disabled

There is also a clear consensus that those who are totally and permanently disabled should not have to work and should be eligible for income transfers on the basis of either prior work history (Social Security disability) or low current income (SSI). However, those who are only temporarily or partially disabled are generally not eligible for public cash assistance unless they are fortunate enough to be covered under Workmen's Compensation or Veterans programs.

Despite this consensus, the design of income-transfer programs for the totally and permanently disabled is becoming increasingly controversial. There is a growing recognition, fueled in part by the rapid rise in the disability caseload over the past decade and its fluctuation in tune with the general availability of jobs, that the definitions of "permanent" and "total" are somewhat arbitrary and often apply to people capable of work. To be eligible a person must have no, or very low, current, earnings. And since the program payments are often quite generous relative to either past earnings or to present earnings capabilities, little incentive exists to earn more than is consistent with retention of eligibility. Also, since eligibility for Medicare and Medicaid is generally tied to receipt of disability cash assistance, far more than just the cash benefits may be at stake. Thus, these programs are coming under attack for fostering the continued dependence of many persons who might have the ability to support themselves through their own work.

The Unemployed

Our society clearly believes that those adults without custodial responsibilities (for young children or incapacitated relatives) or disabilities should have to work for their living if they do not have an independent income. Unemployment insurance provides protection for many people, but only on a time-limited basis and only for those with an appropriate prior work history who are involuntarily separated from their jobs. Recipients must be willing to continue their job search activities and accept a suitable job if offered.

As unemployment insurance benefits have become more broadly available and more adequate, concerns have grown both about their work disincentive effects and even their appropriateness in some instances. Some of the major focal points are:

- The work test as usually applied is lax in its requirements regarding active job search and acceptance of a suitable job offer. Eligible workers generally can be more or less assured of collecting benefits for the maximum number of weeks if they wish to do so.
- Benefits are generally 40 to 60 percent of prior earnings and occasionally range as high as 90 percent. Since they are generally not taxable, have no offsetting work expenses (such as commuting costs), and useful work around the home can be performed while benefits are being received, the financial sacrifice of remaining on unemployment insurance rather than returning to paid work may not be very substantial for some workers, especially for two-worker families. The duration as well as the level of benefits can constitute a strong work disincentive.Normally benefits are available for only twenty-six weeks, but states can extend this with federal assistance to thirty-nine weeks when national or state unemployment rates exceed trigger levels. And during the 1974–1975 recession, Congress acted to extend them, at full federal cost, to sixty-five weeks and it also provided payments to workers not covered in the permanent system.

The public and Congress are uneasy about all of these factors. There is considerable discussion about capping benefits as a percent of prior earnings. Questions are being raised about the wisdom of extending the duration of benefits for as long as has been done in recent recessions rather than relying more upon employment measures.

Low-Income, Single-Parent Family Heads

These, of course, are AFDC adults, overwhelmingly the "welfare mothers" about which there is so much controversy. About the only aspect of social agreement about them is that it would be desirable for far more of them to be working. The reduction in benefits (particularly when AFDC is considered in combination with other programs, such as food stamps and Medicaid) relative to the earnings capacity of recipients can represent a considerable disincentive to work. However, views differ considerably on the extent to which these work disincentive features, lack of motivation, or inadequate child care and employment opportunities are at the root of the problem.

Low-Income, Two-Parent Families

These are working poor families who, by virtue of some combination of large family size, low wages, and periods of joblessness not covered by unemployment insurance, have incomes near or below the poverty level. Their needs have been addressed gradually over the past two decades by income-transfer programs—the earned income tax credit, food stamps, the unemployed father's component of AFDC, continued liberalization of retirement, disability and unemployment-insurance programs, and the general assistance programs of state and local governments. However, while there is a growing consensus about the desirability of using direct public measures to raise all such families above the poverty level, there also is growing concern that it be done in a manner that rewards rather than discourages work effort.

Other Workers

Several other groups of workers, who do not fit neatly into the categories listed above, traditionally have not been aided as much as others by public income-transfer programs. However, much as with two-parent families, the assistance that they receive through income-transfer programs has been increasing gradually in recent years. Societal preferences for these workers clearly are for providing additional assistance through job-related means and not through direct income-transfers.

Two particularly noteworthy subgroups of this population are youth and the partially disabled. In recent years youth employment programs have been both considerably expanded and more targeted to those from low income families. However, the problem of youth unemployment has worsened and many youth programs have been criticized for not improving the employability of participants. The partially disabled are at a serious disad-

117

vantage in the job market, often the result of discrimination rather than truly lower productive capacity. They are somewhat aided by vocational rehabilitation programs and a network of privately and publicly subsidized sheltered workshops, but only very sparsely by income-transfer programs. On balance, they probably remain the most underserved population in our society in need of assistance.

PRO: EMPLOYMENT MEASURES

The most generally and oft heard argument for preferring employment approaches is that they attack the causes rather than the symptoms of inadequate earnings. In this view it is better to teach a man to fish than to provide him food.

There is, in fact, considerable uncertainty regarding both the nature of most individuals' employment problems and the efficacy of alternative methods of redressing them. For example, it is often difficult to assess the extent to which a particular worker's problems stem from a lack of available jobs, a lack of training or good work habits on the part of the individual, or barriers such as inadequate commuter transportation or poor information on the part of either the worker or potential employers that inhibit an appropriate worker-job match. Different explanations yield different policy approaches.

Employment programs add to socially useful output. The extent to which subsidized jobs programs add to socially useful output depends upon the value of the output actually provided by the program participants and the extent to which this output substitutes for, or displaces, nonprogram output that otherwise would have been produced. Both of these factors can be expected to vary considerably with particular circumstances (including the state of the macroeconomy) and their quantification has so far proven elusive to researchers.

Numerous studies have produced no consensus on the extent of displacement in subsidized-employment programs, with results ranging from as little as 10 to 20 percent up to 100 percent. The degree of displacement should be lower as the program wage gets less, and the more narrow targeting on the disadvantaged will result in fewer workers being attracted away from regular employment. In addition, the program output will be less similar to that already available in regular markets.

Employment programs improve the long-term earnings and employment of participants. Assessments of training programs are quite mixed. On balance, they appear to be mildly favorable, but they are dependent upon a myriad of program details and other circumstances in a way that is not well understood. Far less attention has been paid so far to the long run consequences of subsidized-employment programs; the results to date are less encouraging than for training programs. This may be largely due to the low overhead costs and accompanying lack of emphasis on support services, skill acquisition, and transition to regular employment, which have been characteristic of most of these programs until recently.

Employment measures can increase the overall level of employment with little inflationary pressure. There is a growing discussion of and body of support for this notion. Essential prerequisites are that employment programs target on workers least likely to have alternative means of employment and that they pay relatively low wage rates. Even if these conditions are met, the potential effectiveness of such programs in expanding employment with less inflationary pressure than, say, macroeconomic policies is uncertain.

Employment measures are a means of overcoming the work disincentives effect of direct-income transfers. The fact that income-transfer programs, particularly those that are income tested, reduce the work effort of recipients is well known. In addition, there is an impressive amount of evidence quantifying these effects with a fair degree of precision. In general they are small, though significant, for prime-age male heads of families and quite substantial for most other segments of the working population. Furthermore, the work requirements embodied in present transfer programs appear to have little effect on actual work effort. Thus, employment measures, used as either a total substitute for direct transfers or as a means of enforcing work requirements, have the advantage of providing assistance to target groups in a way that could increase, rather than decrease, their work effort.

An important question is whether either the individual or society as a whole is better off as a result. The answer to this question cannot be inferred directly from whether or not the immediate work effort of the recipient is increased. Rather, it depends upon a weighing of other considerations, such as time that might have been spent searching for a better job, caring for children, or furthering one's education.

Employment measures improve the social, psychological, and physical functioning of the worker and his or her family. The issue here is whether, putting aside short- or long-term direct economic benefits to the individual or society at large, there are less tangible benefits from receiving income through work rather than direct transfers. This is a commonplace belief that is deeply held in our society, a society that strongly values work for remuneration. The evidence on the subject is meager, but suggests such positive effects if certain conditions are met. Presumably the answer depends to a great extent upon the nature and quality of the work at issue, as well as the opportunity or ability of the individual to be otherwise engaged in activities that lend his or her life meaning and dignity.

PRO: DIRECT INCOME TRANSFERS

The most general argument for favoring direct income transfers to meet income-maintenance needs is that they clearly accomplish the immediately intended purpose. In this view the most pressing problem is lack of income, defined either relative to some minimal standards that vary with such factors as family size or relative to some prior achieved standard of earnings. Direct income transfers can be more efficiently and equitably designed and delivered to meet this need than can employment programs. However, the more adequate are the benefits, and the greater the extent to which they are limited to those with low earnings or income, the more they discourage work effort.

Income transfers are less costly than employment measures. Except in the case of workfare projects (requiring welfare recipients to work), training allowances and wage rates in employment programs are generally above the benefit levels of relevant transfer programs. Gross costs per worker are considerably higher, in turn, than wages or allowances since substantial overhead usually is required for support services, supervisory personnel, materials, and equipment. These overhead costs are likely to be on the order of 25 to 33 percent of wage levels in programs with any reasonable training

120

content, and they may easily approach or exceed 50 percent of wage costs for programs specializing in disadvantaged workers.

In addition, if the employment program does not entirely substitute for direct income transfers and participants are still eligible for the latter, then the total public costs may be considerably higher than the employment program costs alone. The substantial disregard for earnings and work-related expenses in many direct income-transfer programs can result in employment-program participants receiving sizable transfer benefits, even while earning more than the maximum benefit levels in the transfer program.

Income-transfer programs are more equitable than employment measures. The potential for an inequitable distribution of resources is much greater when employment programs attempt to serve income-maintenance objectives. Even though current earnings or family income might enter into the initial eligibility determination, the guiding criterion for wage payments is usually "equal pay for equal work." If the employment measures are not supplemented by direct income transfers, then the income assistance provided to participants will not vary with their need (as measured by income and family size). Also, whether or not wages or training allowances are supplemented by direct income transfers, those benefiting from employment measures generally will be better off financially than those receiving only income transfers; and the allocation of subsidized job and training slots is likely to be based at least partially on criteria that are somewhat subjective and unrelated to income needs.

Income transfers may cause less disruption of labor and product markets than employment measures. As we noted earlier, direct income-transfer programs can disrupt labor markets by creating disincentives for recipients to work. This discouragement factor is stronger, the weaker the attachment of the recipient to the labor force. But as we also noted earlier, employment programs may disrupt both labor and product markets through displacement effects. The former occurs by workers being drawn into or held in subsidized employment when they otherwise would have been employed in unsubsidized jobs. The latter results from the diversion of other resources from regular markets and the production of output that otherwise would have been produced with unsubsidized labor.

The extent of the disruption of labor and product markets by employment programs will depend upon many factors. In general, it will be more severe the higher the wage rate paid, the stronger the participants' attachment to the labor force, the lower the overall unemployment rate, and the more similar the program output to that provided in the regular economy.

Conclusion

These general arguments in favor of direct income transfers or employment measures do not, indeed cannot, lead to a preference of one over the other. Our ability to quantify many of them is rudimentary. Their applicability differs according to the state of the economy and the characteristics of workers in question. And, finally, they involve the consideration of many intangible values. However, they can be helpful in providing a backdrop for consideration of alternative policy directions that might be pursued. We now turn our attention to some alternative policy directions.

POLICY DIRECTIONS

Presumptive Groups for Income Transfers

This category includes the aged, the severely disabled, and most short-term unemployed who are not in low-income families and who have at least a modest prior employment history—all groups currently receiving the most adequate coverage under cash-assistance programs. There appears to be little or no societal interest in either requiring work as a condition of assistance to these populations or making substantial use of employment measures as an alternative to providing direct income transfers. But, as we noted earlier, there is a strong and growing interest in reducing the work disincentives inherent in the income-transfer programs for which these groups* are eligible.

Such steps might be desirable, but they are not without their problems. There are only two fundamental approaches for increasing work incentives in these programs and the pursuit of either immediately causes conflicts with other highly valued objectives. The first approach is to reduce the level or scope of income-transfer benefits so that the amount people receive without working is less than what they could earn. This, of course, reduces the adequacy of the income-transfer program and particularly penalizes those whose income derives largely or totally from the program. The second approach is to increase the disregard for earnings in calculating program benefits so that working adds relatively more to the total income of recipients. This has the disadvantage of adding to total program costs while

---

*As a modest contribution to policy, we will make distinctions among groups where preconceptions favor the use of income transfers or employment opportunities.

providing no additional assistance to the most needy (those with no other source of income).

The difficult trade-offs posed by this particular triangle of income adequacy, work incentives, and costs—whereby no gains can be made in any one of the three dimensions without sacrificing on one or both of the other two—severely limit the potential for improvements in work incentives in income-transfer programs.

The dilemma this poses for the aged and severely disabled is not too problematic since their work effort is low. Disregard for earnings can be expanded while maintaining the adequacy of benefit levels, with only a small percentage increase in program costs. However, expanding disregard for earnings of those on unemployment insurance would engender a much greater percentage increase in program costs because of the close attachment to the labor force of this population. Thus, selective restrictions in benefit levels (either directly, or indirectly through taxation of benefits) that compromise adequacy as little as possible may be a more promising route for reducing work disincentives for the short-term unemployed.

Presumptive Groups for Employment Measures

Three major groups can be identified: disadvantaged youth, adults with low income, two-parent families, and the long-term unemployed. There appears to be a strong societal interest in having the income-maintenance needs of these groups primarily met through work, with direct income transfers playing only a supplementary role under certain circumstances. If employment can be assured for these populations, then basic societal values will be upheld and the income adequacy/work disincentive/costs dilemma discussed above can be avoided. But as we have seen, there can be problems as well as benefits in placing a heavy emphasis upon employment measures to meet income-maintenance objectives. How do they apply to these populations and what are the important policy choices and considerations that must be faced?

Disadvantaged youth. Employment programs for disadvantaged youth that have been partially motivated by the desire to provide income maintenance to this population have largely failed to improve the employability of participants. A prime example of this was the SPEDY Program. Because the primary concerns were keeping youths off the streets and providing them with some legitimately acquired money, little attention was paid to the quality of the work experience. All too often there was little or no supervision and the jobs entailed trivial tasks at best. As a result, the experience was of little future benefit to the youths and even of negative value in many instances.

The lessons from this experience seem clear. The value of employment measures for disadvantaged youths is in their ability to enhance future employment opportunities by contributing to good work habits, a sense of self-worth, and marketable job skills. They should be utilized only to the extent that there is a strong potential for meeting these objectives. If income-maintenance needs still exist for these youth and their families after the use of effective employment measures is exhausted, these should be addressed through other, more appropriate, means.

Adults with low-income, two-parent families. The socially sought after objective appears to be to lift these families above the poverty level in a manner that maximizes reliance upon work effort, minimizes reliance upon welfare-type cash assistance, and does not add too much (however that is judged) to public costs. The Carter Administration's welfare-reform proposals were crafted to respond to these concerns through (1) the use of food stamps, (2) an expanded income tax credit to keep the working poor out of poverty, (3) enabling employers, through CETA and tax credits, to provide more job openings for welfare clients seeking employment, and (4) the extension of AFDC to all two-parent families.

The proposal of subsidized jobs and training slots rather than just cash transfers adds considerable costs to this expansion of income-assistance to two-parent families. But it also insures that the work effort of these families will increase, not decrease, as a result. Whether or not this approach will be judged successful will depend largely on the ability of the jobs programs, particularly public-service employment (PSE) under CETA, to realize the advantages of employment measures previously discussed. While the CETA-PSE jobs have by and large provided useful social output, they have been criticized for entailing considerable displacement and for not improving the future employability of the participants.

There are two other approaches that have been advocated for providing income assistance to these families. Both would eschew the use of direct income transfers, even for an initial temporary period, but would provide jobs immediately for all family heads—in one case through work-relief projects and in the other through the guarantee of a CETA-type PSE slot.

The major criticism of work relief is that the jobs are unlikely to provide any substantial advantages beyond insuring that the recipient is working. The whole "work gang" ethic surrounding the jobs—minimum wage, low overhead, lack of a training component, no job search assistance, part-time employment with hours of work varying across workers, and so on—does not promote most of the possible benefits of employment measures discussed in the previous section. Furthermore, there is concern that they might undermine the prevailing wage structure and substitute work relief for existing state and local public jobs.

The major criticism of the CETA-type PSE job guarantee approach is that such extensive use of PSE is likely to cause undesirable disruptions of labor and product markets and to exceed the bounds of our present ability to utilize this tool effectively as an employability device. Under normal circumstances many hundreds of thousands of workers would be drawn into PSE who would otherwise be in unsubsidized employment. Also, if the unemployment rate rose much, the program might be deluged with applicants, all of whom it would be forced to accommodate. It would not be possible to provide constructive employment experiences to all program participants or to provide socially useful output while avoiding large-scale displacement.

The long-term unemployed. In a high-employment economy, if workers experience extended unemployment, it is likely to be mostly structural in nature and not a result of a general lack of available employment opportunities or malingering. At some point the provision of remedial employment measures, rather than continuing direct income-transfer support to such persons, seems appropriate. In fact, this group has become a prime target group for programs under the structural titles of CETA in recent years.

More difficult issues arise, however, in the context of a low-employment economy. Extended unemployment is clearly often cyclical in nature and becomes the common experience of millions of workers who would have no difficulty finding unsubsidized jobs in a more favorable economy. Does it make more sense to extend the duration of unemployment benefits beyond the usual twenty-six to thirty-nine weeks to a year or longer as has been done during recent recessions, or to provide subsidized-employment opportunities as an alternative form of income maintenance? During recessions, many of the factors that favor the use of employment measures take on more force, that is, it is easier to implement expansions of output that are socially useful and to avoid disruption of regular labor and product markets.

If the societal preference for work over direct income transfers is sufficiently strong, then a work-relief-type approach, which would substitute at little additional expense for extended unemployment-insurance benefits for the more employable part of this population, might be considered. Increasing the employability of participants is not an issue; all that is being sought is some immediately useful output in return for public support until more normal economic conditions once again prevail. However, this approach would meet considerable opposition, both because of the concern about undermining public-employment wage structures and because it would be even more difficult politically to apply work relief to middle-class workers than to the working poor.

A second approach would be to eliminate extended unemployment insurance benefits but to greatly expand CETA-PSE jobs and employment tax credits to private employers so that virtually all workers who are unemployed beyond twenty-six to thirty-nine weeks are guaranteed a job. This could involve the creation of several million subsidized jobs between the public and private sectors that pay prevailing wage rates. Even though they would be implemented on this scale only during recessions, there would be grave concern about their effectiveness and potential for disrupting regular markets. In addition, these programs would provide a very considerable economic stimulus. Thus, they should be evaluated in a macroeconomic context and weighed against other policy measures designed to expand economic growth and jobs.

Some expansion of subsidized employment—in both the public and private sectors—during times of low or negative economic growth is undoubtedly desirable, and those workers who have experienced the longest spells of unemployment are a logical priority group. However, trying to serve all of long-term unemployed through this means would not be sound policy. The expansion should be constrained by relevant macroeconomic considerations on the one hand, and a sense of how large a jobs program can be effectively managed on the other hand. Furthermore, it is important to try to distinguish those whose unemployment is solely countercyclical in nature from those whose employability is low even in the high-employment economy and to provide more training, transitional assistance, and other appropriate forms of support to the latter group.

Groups about Which There Is Ambiguity

The primary group about which there is considerable ambiguity is single-parent heads of low-income families—typically AFDC recipients. Because of the society's ambiguity about whether work effort should be expected of single parents in return for public income support, there are strong policy pulls in different directions. Those who believe that they should not be expected to work emphasize the need for AFDC benefits to be as high as the poverty level. On the other hand, many of those same people would advocate generous disregard for earnings and child-care expenses and the provision of sufficient subsidized jobs so that those AFDC recipients who wished to work would be able to and would receive substantial financial benefit from doing so. The combination of these, of course, would yield a far more expensive set of programs for this population than we now have.

For those who believe these AFDC recipients should be expected to work, the policy concerns and choices are similar to those already discussed for the two-parent families, but there are two related exceptions. The first is the issue of whether it is socially desirable to force young children into day-care situations rather than allow mothers the freedom to care for them if they so choose. The second is the higher public costs attendant with insuring work effort on the part of AFDC mothers due to the greater need for child care and other support services among this population. These considerations are primarily responsible for the current policy that exempts adults with children age six or less from the AFDC work requirement, although the requirement has little meaning for those recipients without very young children, since training and support services for AFDC recipients has been inadequate relative to need.

Given the state of the economy, our limited ability to mount effective employment programs, and the conflicting societal values, there seems to be no entirely satisfactory approach to deal with the issues surrounding this population. Certainly it does not appear desirable to contemplate a complete substitution of employment measures for the AFDC program, even for those mothers with older children. However, greater employment provisions on a voluntary basis for AFDC mothers with children of all ages seem called for. The apparent success of the supported-work projects in increasing the employability of long-term AFDC mothers should encourage greater efforts in this direction.

CONCLUSION

Only occasionally in the jobs-versus-income-transfers debate is the appropriate issue the stark need to choose one assistance program over another. Far more often the relevant concerns revolve around how much emphasis should be put upon one approach vis-à-vis the other and how employment and income-transfer programs should be designed and integrated to promote societal objectives relating both to work and to income maintenance. Typically, there are no clearly correct or incorrect answers to these questions. Rather, there exists a range of alternatives whose assessment depends as much upon a weighing of competing social values as on technical merits.

Employing the Unemployed

Given the labor-market difficulties experienced by many of the primary target groups for income assistance whom society expects to work, it seems logical to make greater use of employment measures for those populations. However, as a general rule, the use of such measures should not be expanded beyond their ability to be effective on their own terms. They should have a purpose and value in their own right and not be simply an alternative form of income maintenance.

8

R O B E R T   M .   S O L O W

Employment Policy in Inflationary Times

FINE DISTINCTIONS make bad policy. They may, however, be necessary for clear thinking. So it is with selective-employment policies: there are practical limits to the refinement with which programs can be tailored to meet very particular circumstances. But if the task is to understand whether selective employment policies become especially advantageous, compared with more generalized macroeconomic policy tools, in a period of substantial inflation, then some precision about objectives may be called for.

THE CASE FOR SELECTIVE-EMPLOYMENT POLICY

There are three distinguishable, though connected, reasons why selective-employment policies might be preferred to other fiscal policy devices, such as tax reduction or general government expenditure, whether or not the background is inflationary.

1. Selective-employment policies may be more effective, in the sense that they generate a larger increase in aggregate employment per dollar of gross government expenditure, or per dollar of incremental net budgetary deficit. This criterion is commonly described by the slogan "more bang for a buck," though often without clear definition of the "bang"—employment, wage bill,

useful output—or the "buck"—gross or net outlay.

2. Even if not more efficient in that sense, selective policies might be preferred precisely because of their selectivity. That is, the same dollar outlay might generate the same increment in employment, only more concentrated on disadvantaged groups or depressed areas—blacks, the young, welfare recipients, large cities, the rural South. This is an argument about equity, not about effectiveness.

3. The third reason is closely related to the second, but not identical. Added employment of disadvantaged groups and in depressed areas might be desired not because it is fair, but because it is noninflationary, or at least less inflationary than the same increase in employment of adult white males. The idea here is that some sectors of the labor market, especially the big industries employing experienced, skilled workers, are always tighter than others and have lower unemployment rates. These are the sectors that tend to set the pace for wages, costs, and prices. On both accounts, an extra thousand jobs in these sectors will contribute more to inflation than an extra thousand jobs in sectors where unemployment is high and wage pressures are weak.

The main topic for discussion here is the validity of these reasons. Let me call them the efficiency, equity, and stability arguments respectively. Do they provide a defensible case for preferring selective-employment policies to generalized fiscal expansion under ordinary circumstances? In context, however, there is a preliminary question worth discussing: the connection with inflation. Suppose that background economic conditions are characterized by ongoing "inertial" inflation at an uncomfortably high rate and, simultaneously, by so much unemployment that one would urgently like to see less of it. (Inertial inflation means inflation that represents primarily the successive passing on—or passing back and forth—of cost increases. Such an inflation could have originated in a past burst of excess demand, as from the Vietnam war, or in a massive outside cost increase, as from OPEC, or from both. Not everyone would be willing to characterize the current inflation in that way. But those who would not would probably find the subject matter of this chapter uninteresting in any case.) Under those circumstances is there any special power or significance to be attached to the arguments favoring selective-employment policies?

In the case of the stability argument, the connection with inflation is self-evident. If it is indeed true that a given increment in aggregate employment brought about by selective policies is less inflationary than the same increment brought about by generalized expansion, and if selective-employment policies can in fact increase employment, then selective-employment policy is exactly what a country needs when it is suffering simultaneously from inflation and unemployment.

There are two "ifs" in that statement, and both need to be checked. Obviously the heart of the problem is to decide whether, or to what extent, selective policies can increase employment in a less inflationary way than general policies. The other condition can also be questioned: according to some views of the way labor markets work, any attempt to employ more disadvantaged workers must simply displace other disadvantaged workers or other mainstream workers. This is an extreme view, and has very little support from the facts. If employment of disadvantaged workers merely displaces other disadvantaged workers one-for-one, or nearly so, then there just is no such thing as selective-employment policy. If mainstream workers are displaced, then one might still opt for selective-employment policies on the basis of the stability and equity arguments: reduction of inflation combined with a "fairer" distribution of employment. But of course, if selective job creation merely displaces mainstream workers, only a naive observer could believe that selective job creation will be a politically viable policy option.

There seems to be no intrinsic connection between the equity argument and ongoing inflation. If it is fair to provide jobs for the disadvantaged when prices are rising, then it is fair when they are not rising. But one only needs to think about the fate of various proposals for a youth exemption from the minimum wage laws to realize that what sounds equitable in the abstract need not sound so equitable when it comes down to the concrete risk that disadvantaged workers will gain ground at the expense of mainstream workers. (Perhaps it is worth pointing out that the equity case for the young is not so strong as that for blacks or for the residents of depressed areas. Everyone runs the risks associated with being young at one stage of the life cycle, but not everyone spends a few years being black or from West Virginia. The case for singling out youth is that there are a lot of them; and bad labor-market experience at the beginning may have prolonged effects.)

The efficiency argument does have a connection with inflation, though a peculiar one. If "bang for a buck" is very important, it can only be because bucks are scarce. Suppose for the moment that the relevant "bang" is simply the number of direct jobs created. Then one might want to minimize, or at least hold down, the gross dollar cost per job slot simply in the interest of small government. There are those who, as a matter of principle, like to see the smallest possible flow of dollars through the treasury. For them, the efficiency argument certainly makes sense; but it would seem to make the same amount of sense in noninflationary times as it does in inflationary times. Alternatively, one could believe that it is really the net budgetary cost per job slot that matters, the ultimate deficit per job, but one could simultaneously despair of the capacity of the political process to generate tax revenues, even in inflationary circumstances. In that case, a concern for net cost would masquerade as a concern for gross cost. More often than not, therefore, the efficiency argument rests on a desire to minimize the resulting deficit per job slot created.

This is not the place for an attempt to separate myth from reality in the ideological debate that seems forever to dog the idea of (federal) deficit spending. In the immediate context, fortunately, we can get away with a relatively noncontroversial proposition. Nearly everyone would agree that *if* the aggregate volume of spending in real terms is close up against the economy's capacity to produce without demand-pull inflation, *whether or not* that is the main cause of the ongoing inflation, *then* actions that add to the budget deficit by adding to gross expenditure are likely to worsen the inflation. In more direct words, the efficiency argument makes more sense in a prosperous economy than in a depressed one. There is controversy over whether our economy was prosperous, in the appropriate sense, in 1977, but there is more general agreement that it was at least close in 1978–1979. So currently, at least, inflation lends importance to the efficiency argument. If the economy is really prosperous, however, there would seem to be less urgency about creating more employment in the first place, except for the equity and stability arguments again.

The rough conclusion of this survey seems to be that the peculiar benefits of selective-employment policy in an inflationary environment stem mostly from the stability argument, and perhaps also from the efficiency argument. The main relevance of the equity argument—not in general, remember, but with respect to inflation—may come from the fact that when there is relatively full employment in the mainstream labor force, there is likely to be less resistance to policies that seek to benefit disadvantaged workers differentially.

RESEARCH FINDINGS

What does economic research tell us about the validity of the efficiency, equity, and stability arguments? One realistic answer is not very much. There has been quite a lot of study of the operations of individual manpower programs in the small, with a growing fund of results summarized in other chapters of this book. Much less is known about the more global questions having to do with the interaction of manpower policies and the economy at large, and not all of that information is indisputable. There are several reasons why hard knowledge is so difficult to come by in this field. In the first place, there is not much experience to analyze. A small program, conducted on an experimental scale for a relatively short time, can tell you what you want to know about operational details like administration, cost, and concrete results; and even then the results from a pilot project may not generalize accurately to the full-scale real thing. But the same experimental program may be much too small and last too short a time to reveal anything about the possible effects of a permanent full-size program on the economy as a whole, and vice versa. Even the large Public Service Employment program launched in 1977 has only a very short history so far. The evidence for firm conclusions is simply not there, though it may come.

Secondly, there is always too much happening at once. When, as in 1977, a fairly substantial policy initiative occurs, its interaction with the economy gets entangled with those of other macroeconomic policies and those of other extraneous events. Careful experimental design can isolate some aspects of a particular selective-employment policy from contamination with "noise," but there is no way to isolate the results of the same policy, which are bound to be fairly small, from contamination by OPEC, the Siberian wheat crop, or the Federal Reserve System. This problem is endemic in macroeconomic research; the case is not impossible, but it is difficult.

The third difficulty is closely related. Because the facts are hard to interpret, there is no way to do without theory in interpreting them. Even if the facts tried to speak for themselves, they would be drowned out. But there are differences of opinion about the way modern labor markets operate. How segmented are they, that is, how easily are impulses transmitted from one region or skill level or demographic group to others? How responsive are wage rates to variations in the supply of and demand for different categories of labor? What are the short-run and long-run objectives of business firms (and trade unions, for that matter) in their labor-market dealings? None of these questions is settled, and proponents of opposed views will inevitably interpret the none-too-clear facts in different ways.

Despite the obstacles, there are some sensible things to be said about the macroeconomics of selective-employment policies. They will not tell us everything we would like to know about the significance of selective-employment policy in a period of inertial inflation, but they are enough to rule out some simplistic pseudo-answers.

The Efficiency Argument

With regard to the efficiency criterion, the consensus is that selective-employment policy does have an advantage over more general macroeconomic policy tools; but the margin is slight, smaller than superficial considerations might suggest.

Take incremental jobs per dollar of net cost as the criterion. There are two

133

important considerations favoring policies targeted toward disadvantaged workers with high unemployment rates. The more obvious is that a given sum of money will go further when it is used for the direct employment of low-wage workers than when it is spent in other ways. Public service employment is more labor-intensive (involves less expenditure on materials and equipment) than construction, say; and since the average wage is lower, any amount paid in wages will employ more people.

The second factor enhancing the efficiency of selective-employment policies is that the workers employed directly by such programs will almost certainly spend a very large fraction of their earnings. Only about half of the employment-creating effects of expansionary policies is represented by the direct employment generated by the program in question, whether in special public-employment projects or in commercial heavy-construction firms or airplane factories. A further effect, of the same order of magnitude, occurs when the recipients of the added wage income spend it on food, clothing, or for that matter, booze. Those additional expenditures create a market for goods and services and eventually lead to still further employment in private industry. This "secondary" increment in employment cannot be visibly connected with the initiating cause, but it is no less real. It will increase as there is an increase in the fraction of earnings that the primary beneficiaries spend. Since mainstream workers probably spend some 80 percent of incremental income, the difference is not overwhelming even if PSE workers spend 100 percent, but it counts.

These efficiency advantages of selective-employment policy are weakened by a few offsetting factors. The most important of them goes under the heading of "displacement." Suppose the employment of disadvantaged workers is subsidized, and suppose the eligibility requirements are adequately policed (though this has not always been the case). Potential employers or prime sponsors may find it profitable to hire eligible workers and to collect the subsidy; but in the absence of strong demand for their services, they may lay off mainstream workers who had earlier been performing the same or similar functions. The end result may be an improvement according to the equity criterion, but it surely weakens the efficiency advantage of targeted policies. If displacement were 100 percent, the policy would not work at all. The key question is: How much displacement is there likely to be in practice? It is hard to say. There have been some attempts to estimate the displacement rate statistically, in effect by observing what happens to the aggregate employment by prime sponsors after PSE programs are authorized or increased. The typical finding has been that the immediate displacement rate is quite low; at the very beginning, increases in PSE are almost entirely net increases in employment. As time goes on, however, non-PSE

134

workers diminish and after a year or so, the displacement rate is quite high, perhaps as high as 60 percent or even more. These estimates must be taken skeptically. They depend, obviously, on the ability of the method to predict what employment by prime sponsors would have been in the absence of the selective-employment program. The results themselves provide plenty of internal statistical warnings that they cannot do that very well. So this econometric evidence is not to be ignored, but it is not to be treated as reliable either. There have also been some recent attempts to make direct estimates of displacement by resident observers of individual prime sponsors. This technique has led to more optimistic, that is, lower, estimates of the displacement rate, perhaps only 20 percent. These "direct" observations contain no internal statistical check; since what is being "observed" is not something you can see, but a complicated inference, the results cannot be taken literally either. We have to live with uncertainty about displacement, and therefore about the efficiency of selective-employment policies.

A second offsetting factor has to do with the secondary employment effects, which come, it will be recalled, from the increased spending by primary beneficiaries. Primary beneficiaries can spend only from increased after-tax income. One might think this consideration would add to the effectiveness of selective-employment policies, because mainstream workers are subject to higher tax rates than disadvantaged workers. No doubt that "ought" to be so. But when the earnings of the primary beneficiary may be accompanied by losses of public assistance benefits, food stamp eligibility, public housing privileges, and Medicaid benefits, it can easily turn out that the implicit tax rate is higher than that faced by mainstream workers. In that case the efficiency advantage of selective-employment policies with respect to secondary employment could vanish.

The conclusion to be drawn is a modest one. Selective-employment policies probably do have a small efficiency advantage over generalized expansion. This advantage could be enlarged and made more certain if careful targeting, maintenance-of-effort requirements, and similar devices can keep the displacement rate small, and if the implicit tax rate on recipients of public assistance were reduced (which would be a good idea anyway). No miracles are to be expected; but a reasonable case can be made for favoring selective-employment policies in periods of inflation, when mainstream labor markets are not seriously depressed, so that net job creation per dollar of net budgetary cost is among the valid criteria of choice.

The Equity Argument

The point has already been made that the equity argument is in principle indifferent about inflation. Considerations of *Realpolitik* do suggest, however, that selective-employment policies are more likely to attract widespread support when the mainstream labor market is tight than when unemployment is general. From that point of view, a year such as 1977 is especially favorable for such programs, and a determinist would no doubt conclude that "it is no accident" that manpower programs bulked large in the stimulus package of 1977.

There is logically a prior question that needs at least to be raised. However legislation is written, it is not always the case that selective-employment policies are so very selective in practice. Normal creaming of applicants or simple political preferment can steer a program away from its intended beneficiaries. Some students of the manpower programs of the past decade have concluded that, on the average, they have tended to benefit the middle of the skill distribution. In that case the selectivity is simply lost, and the policies are not different from general expansion after all. This may help to explain why it is difficult to statistically detect the aggregative effects of past policies. The issue here is primarily administrative; only effort and experience will tell whether it is possible to operate selective-employment policies in such a way that the actuality corresponds with the explicit intent. Otherwise equity considerations hardly matter. A related point will come up later in connection with the comparison of direct employment and wage subsidies as techniques for selective policy.

The Stability Argument

The main reason for believing that selective-employment policies are especially preferred in inflationary periods is the stability argument. In detail, it goes like this. It is generally accepted that, other things being equal, wages will rise faster in a tighter labor market, that is, one with a lower unemployment rate. Rising wages will carry the price level with them. (Recent revisions of the ideas underlying this relation have turned mainly on the *durability* of the "Phillips curve" trade-off. Extreme views aside, I think there is still a consensus that the relation persists quite long enough in a short run to be of importance for economic policy. This is compatible with the trade-off being swallowed up by inflationary expectations in the long run.) If that were all, if the rate of inflation responded just to the aggregate unemployment rate, then a job would be a job and there would be no special advantage to selectivity on this score. There are, however, bits of evidence that suggest a more complicated response, perhaps providing an edge for selective policies. It is important to understand how this is supposed to work.

One line of thought starts from the premise that the general wage level is really determined in an industrial and occupational core of the economy. This core comprises large firms in major industries—one might once have thought exclusively of manufacturing and transportation, but the core is now broader than that—employing many highly skilled and moderately skilled workers in regular jobs, paying high wages, which have often been determined by collective bargaining. Once wage rates have been determined in this industrial-occupational core, wages in the periphery tend to fall into line according to traditional differentials. (This could be a valid description by and large even if sometimes, especially in very tight labor markets, peripheral wages took off on their own, partly because otherwise the fringe industries would lose workers to better jobs now available in the core, and partly because core wages would be slowed down by the existence of long-term contracts.) This picture of the labor market has straightforward implications. In an inflationary period with some remaining unemployment, general expansion of the economy would further tighten the core labor market and push wages up faster there. This acceleration would then spread to the periphery. The end result would certainly be faster inflation. Selective-employment policies might take the form of direct public service employment or subsidization of the private employment of the sort of unskilled and inexperienced workers not often found in the core industries. In either case, the incremental jobs could be confined to areas exercising little influence on the general wage level. The effect on inflation might thus be minimal.

This general argument can take another form, one that has some serious empirical support. It is easy to accept the statement that the movement of wages is governed by the balance of supply of and demand for labor. Suppose we mean by "labor" something more complicated than "number of workers or hours"; there is obviously a sense in which a skilled worker supplies more "labor" per hour than an unskilled worker, as evidenced by the fact that any employer will willingly pay more for it. Now start from the kind of situation we are concerned with: inflation with unemployment. General expansion will increase the demand for "labor" and thus generate a wage response. If selectivity can confine the expansion of opportunities to the disadvantaged or to depressed areas, the very same increase in the number of people employed will entail a smaller increase in the demand for "labor." If the initial hypothesis is correct—and there is some statistical evidence in its favor—the selective approach will disturb the supply-demand balance less and will generate less additional pressure on wages and prices.

There is a more complicated line of reasoning that leads eventually in the same direction. This argument emphasizes the fact that "the" wage level is really an average of wage rates in many different industries, occupations, and regions. Each sectoral wage rate will rise faster if unemployment in that sector of the labor market falls. But the appearance of an extra job slot in sector A may generate a large increase in the A wage rate than an extra slot in sector Z would generate in the Z wage rate. There are at least two different reasons why this might be so. It is often thought that the wage-inflation effect of an added thousand jobs is larger if it occurs in a sector in which the unemployment rate is already low and employers are scrambling for workers than if it occurs in a sector in which there is a lot of unemployment and workers are relieved to find employment. Then it is certainly better from the inflation-control viewpoint to target new job slots to sectors with relatively high unemployment rates. Those are typically depressed industries and areas offering unskilled occupations. Alternatively, there may be structural reasons why the A wage is more sensitive to changes in employment than the Z wage is. (The jargon is that sector A has a worse Phillips curve.) Degree of organization and union militancy is one possible explanation but so are the speed with which information travels, the degree of competition among employers, and no doubt still other characteristics. Whatever the reason, it is clear that selective placing of jobs can hope to reduce the net impact on the wage level and the price level.

There are almost too many arguments here: One clear and convincing argument would be enough. In this case, however, the more the merrier. The various reasons for believing selective-employment policy to be less inflationary than general expansion are not competitive with one another. They could all be true, and all add to the strength of the overall case. In fact, they are all plausible, and there is evidence to favor each of them. It is harder to get any reliable quantitative measure of the extent of the advantage that might be achieved by selectivity. Part of the difficulty is technical, but part of it probably reflects the fact that the advantage in question is small, and perhaps irregular.

DIRECT JOB CREATION AND WAGE SUBSIDIES

So far I have been using the neutral phrase "selective-employment policy" to cover any device that has the effect of differentially targeting job creation toward the disadvantaged. The ingenuity of specialists is great and the number of policy variations they can invent is correspondingly large. All or nearly all of the possibilities, however, fall into one of two broad categories. The first may be described as direct job creation: a public or semipublic body expends funds to employ eligible workers who perform services of one kind or another. Public service employment in any of its forms is the prototype.

Employment Policy in Inflationary Times

The second category of policy devices is wage subsidies: the government offers to pay a specified fraction of the wage of any eligible worker hired and employers may take advantage of the subsidy as they wish. The offer can be hedged about with restrictions and the class of eligible employers may be limited, but the intent is to create or widen a cost advantage in favor of hiring certain workers and, from that point, to let market incentives take their course. The New Jobs Tax Credit in 1977 is a prototype; it has since been revamped into the Targeted Jobs Tax Credit. It is no part of the task of this book to compare direct job creation and wage subsidies as general policy alternatives. It is possible, however, that the choice between them may have some bearing on the amount of inflationary pressure generated by a given policy-induced increase in employment. In that one respect, the comparison belongs here.

One would expect wage subsidies to be more efficient than direct job creation, provided they work at all. In most variations of public service employment, public budgets carry all or nearly all of the cost of hiring workers in the target group. Wage subsidies, by contrast, cover only half—or some other fraction—of the same costs, relying on market incentives to induce private employers to incur the rest. If relative wage rates have any flexibility at all, then they cannot be infinitely far from the point that would make employment of target-group workers profitable. After all, unemployment rates are not 100 percent in the usual categories of disadvantaged workers. A subsidy of 50 percent, say, ought to be enough to tip the balance. Then new jobs per dollar of gross or net budgetary cost ought to be higher for wage subsidies than for direct job creation. (Completeness requires me to mention that there is an extreme view, committed to the assumption that labor markets are always in equilibrium, according to which market wages are bound to move to neutralize the effect of a wage subsidy and thus restore the old unemployment rates. According to this doctrine, the very same mechanism would operate to nullify the effects of direct job creation: an initial reduction in the unemployment rate of the target group would stimulate broad wage increases until the old unemployment rates were restored. So the comparison would be a stand-off. But a believer in this view would also "know" trivially simple ways to end inflation. It must be a good feeling.)

There is an opposite point of view, more common among manpower specialists, according to which wage subsidies will not work at all because market incentives are ineffective. There cannot be much direct evidence on this because there is very little experience with wage subsidies. Recent studies of the New Jobs Tax Credit of 1977 contradict this skepticism. They found that after one year of operation not all firms knew about the existence of the NJTC, but those that did know about it had indeed taken advantage of it, that is, they had increased their employment levels significantly more rapidly than those that did not know about NJTC. This result certainly suggests that profit incentives operate more or less as they are supposed to. The fact that many firms were unaware of NJTC is sobering; but presumably a more extensive effort at notification and explanation could improve the situation. The conclusion about the effectiveness of profit incentives does have to be qualified, however. It is possible that the correlation between awareness and employment growth is not causal; perhaps the better-run firms knew about NJTC, and they outstripped the others in employment growth not because they were stimulated by NJTC, but because they were better run. Moreover, the eligibility criterion in NJTC was simply that employment rises by more than a specified percentage above its level in a base period. NJTC rewarded rapid growth of employment, not the employment of specified target groups. One is not entitled to assume with complete confidence that market incentives will work in one context because they work in another, but the case is certainly strengthened. NJTC has since been replaced by a Targeted Jobs Tax Credit, and so direct study will soon be possible. In any case, I would say that the burden of proof is on those who argue the ineffectiveness of market incentives.

The presumption is, therefore, that wage subsidies have some advantage over direct job creation according to the efficiency criterion. They are probably also to be preferred according to the equity criterion: they offer at least the possibility of a start in the mainstream labor market, whereas direct job creation at least runs the risk of creating a sort of caste. I do not see much difference between the two with respect to the stability criterion. Perhaps direct job creation might be favored slightly on the grounds that public service employment, precisely because it is somewhat insulated from the mainstream labor market, is likely to generate less inflationary pressure per additional thousand workers employed.

There is an additional, potentially important, factor that confers a definite advantage on wage subsidies in inflationary periods. One of the pervasive statistical findings of macroeconomic research is that the price level responds primarily to costs. (That is why many discussions of inflation start with the labor market—not out of prejudice, but because wage costs bulk so very large.) It follows that a policy measure that has a direct impact on unit costs is likely to have a direct impact on the general price level. This is especially so in a situation such as the one that has existed since 1973, when supply-side influences—food, raw materials, imports, oil—have been dominant and account quite logically for the uncomfortable combination of rising prices and a soft economy. The advantage of selective wage subsidies is that they provide an incentive for the employment of disadvantaged workers while *reducing* unit production costs. Whatever the indirect effects, the impact effect contains an anti-inflationary component. Thus wage subsidies are a preferred selective-employment policy tool in an inflation context for the same reason that excise-tax or payroll-tax reduction is a preferred fiscal policy tool if general expansion is called for.

CONCLUSIONS

This brief survey has not produced a lot of hard evidence. What there is consists mostly of educated guesses. That is perhaps distressing, but it is hardly surprising. We have very little experience with selective-employment policies on a scale likely to make any dent at all on macroeconomic facts; and only experience can provide hard evidence. Nevertheless, the general indications that emerge are not so terribly ambiguous.

The macroeconomic effects of selective-employment policy and generalized expansion are likely to differ, but only slightly. Selective-employment policy is probably not the answer to a maiden's prayer, if the maiden happens to be suffering from simultaneous unemployment and inflation. Only the equity argument—the least viable one politically—offers a really sharp difference.

But the slight differences are meaningful and usable. They make a modest but significant case that selective-employment policies *are* somewhat better adapted to a period of inflation with excessive unemployment but not mass unemployment. A desired increase in employment can be maneuvered probably with less, and surely without more, additional pressure on the price level if it can be successfully targeted on depressed areas and disadvantaged groups than if it results from wholesale expansionary fiscal and monetary policy. There is thus every reason to promote selective policies as especially adapted to the time, provided it can be done without overselling.

Within the general class of selective-employment policies, wage subsidies offer some particular advantages over direct job creation. The cost per hire is likely to be lower, and the supply-price effects can only be favorable.

I realize that if St. Bernard had preached in temperate terms like these, the Crusades might never have captured the imagination of Christendom. But then it is not clear that the Crusades ever accomplished very much good anyway. We could hope to do better.

9

ROBERT H. HAVEMAN

Direct Job Creation

IN THE AREA of labor-market policy, the 1970s have seen a major redirection of policy away from programs designed to change the productivity of individual workers and toward direct job-creation policies. By fiscal year 1980, nearly $4 billion was obligated for direct job-creation efforts, three-fourths of it for public-sector job creation. This outlay reflects a major change of emphasis from the earlier training-education placement efforts in the manpower field, and the expansion of income-support policy in the transfer program area. The effort to directly provide jobs to the unemployed would appear to reflect dissatisfaction, perhaps frustration, with policies to increase income and employment via increasing earnings capacity, and to maintain the income of those for whom work is unavailable. This increase in the direct provision of jobs can be viewed as the first serious step to implement the Full Employment Act of 1946 and to move the United States toward a full employment-guaranteed job economy. Support for direct job-creation measures is not unrelated to that motivation driving the Humphrey-Hawkins bill and the Full Employment and Balanced Growth Act of 1978, which emerged.

Direct public provision of jobs is a relatively unorthodox venture for the market-oriented U.S. economy. It represents an admission that the current structure of the market economy, despite aggregate monetary and fiscal measures, is unable to secure adequate economic performance. Support for direct public-job provision comes in part from a belief that this instrument can reduce some of the current constraints on labor-market performance. It is by improving this performance that direct job creation holds promise as an effective instrument for reducing the number of persons living in poverty, and for solving what has come to be known as the structural unemployment problem.

WHAT IS DIRECT JOB CREATION?

It is perhaps easier to indicate what direct job-creation policy is not than what it is. It does *not* refer to normal public employment—that employment which provides direct public-sector services—even though standard public employment can include a direct job-creation aspect. Here, direct job creation is defined by measures that are undertaken to accomplish two major objectives. They are, first, an increase in labor demand for specific groups in the economy, such as youths, minorities, the handicapped, or those with little education or skills. Because normal labor demand for these groups is often inadequate when other groups are fully employed, they are referred to as the structurally unemployed. Because these groups tend to be found at the bottom of the earnings distribution, the reduction of persons below the poverty level is a second objective of direct job-creation efforts. In short, then, any policy measure designed to increase the demand for the labor of specific groups experiencing high unemployment (or nonemployment) or income poverty will be considered direct job creation.[2] This includes direct public service employment programs and employment subsidy programs designed to create jobs in the private sector.

Most prominent among the recent policies fitting this definition is the Comprehensive Employment and Training Act—CETA. As originally developed in 1973, CETA was designed to enable local officials to coordinate manpower programs so as to meet their particular concerns and to provide jobs for unemployed and disadvantaged workers. Although the original act included a provision for public service employment for those with low skills, the major thrust of CETA came with a 1974 revision that established an untargeted, countercyclical public employment program. With federal support provided to areas experiencing high and sustained unemployment, transitional employment opportunities were provided by state and local government agencies at close to prevailing wage rates. Of the nearly 300,000 slots created in the first year of the program, less than one-half were filled by persons from low-income families, and nearly three-fourths were filled by high school graduates.

Employing the Unemployed

After 1976, the emphasis in CETA shifted toward disadvantaged and hard-to-employ workers. The 1976 amendments reserved 250,000 job slots for disadvantaged workers, and with the Carter Administration's sponsorship a target of 750,000 public service jobs was established with eligibility criteria targeted toward disadvantaged workers, welfare recipients, and the long-term unemployed. By 1979, 43 percent of the nearly 700,000 CETA jobs were being performed by the structurally unemployed, and by 1980 this proportion is expected to increase to 57 percent.

Although CETA is the most prominent direct job-creation program, it is not the first. One predecessor was Operation Mainstream, which, by the mid-1970s, was directly employing about 40,000 older, disadvantaged, and chronically unemployed workers in community service activities at wage rates slightly above the minimum wage. As in CETA, little training was provided. Moreover, relatively few workers were placed in regular public or private jobs.

An even larger predecessor was the Neighborhood Youth Corps, which was perhaps more a work experience than a public-employment program. As part of the War on Poverty in the 1960s, Neighborhood Youth Corps provided short-term summer and during-school employment at low wage rates to over 6 million poor youths during a ten-year period. Another predecessor (which has received publicity out of all proportion to its magnitude) was the Work Incentive (WIN) program. This publicity came from the 1971 legislative requirement that welfare recipients register for work. While over 2 million recipients were so registered by the mid-1970s, only a few thousand were placed in public jobs, and most of those were in work-experience or on-the-job training programs rather than regular public employment. Another direct job-creation program, but with a countercyclical emphasis, was the Public Employment Program (PEP) of the early 1970s. During its two-year life, PEP employed 340,000 workers in transitional public jobs and an additional 300,000 workers were hired in summer jobs. Targeting to specific groups in PEP was not extensive, and while nearly one-half of the workers had been unemployed for a long time, over three-fourths were high school graduates, and relatively few were from low-income families.

All of these direct job-creation programs involved the special provision of work in the public sector. Technically, workers in these programs were public employees. In the 1970s, however, direct job-creation efforts were also aimed toward the provision of jobs in the private sector, in part because the magnitude of the problem exceeded the potential of the public sector to provide jobs. The major private-sector program designed to increase the demand for labor, particularly for low-wage labor, was the New Jobs Tax

Credit (NJTC) enacted in 1977. The NJTC provided a tax credit equal to 50 percent of the first $6,000 of wages paid to the fifty workers who were hired above the 102 percent mark of the firm's previous year's employment level. While this two-year program (1977 to 1978) did not distinguish among workers by their unemployment or poverty status, the subsidy—and hence the incentive to hire low-wage workers—was a higher percentage of low-wage employees' earnings than it was for those of more skilled workers.

In 1979, the NJTC was replaced by a directly targeted employment subsidy program, the Targeted Jobs Tax Credit (TJTC). This tax credit equals 50 percent of the first $6,000 of wage cost for the first year of employment of any newly hired person from a designated set of categories—youths from low-income families, disabled workers, Vietnam era veterans, and Supplemental Social Security (SSI) and general-relief recipients. The subsidy falls to 25 percent for the second year of employment. By eliminating the 103-percent employment threshold and explicitly designating target groups, the substitution of TJTC for NJTC represents a shift in emphasis from cyclical unemployment toward structural, low-wage unemployment.

One final direct job-creation measure—proposed but not yet enacted—should be mentioned. In 1977, President Carter proposed direct job creation as an integral part of his welfare-reform plan—the Program for Better Jobs and Income (PBJI). Work, he stated, would be substituted for welfare as a primary source of income for many current welfare recipients. In his plan, 1.4 million new minimum-wage jobs would have been created by the government and would have been filled by able-bodied welfare recipients not encumbered with substantial child-care responsibilities. In order to continue receiving income-support payments, these recipients would have been required to find employment in regular public- or private-sector jobs or to participate in the PBJI program. While congressional concern with the budgetary cost of PBJI led to its demise, a new, scaled-down version has been proposed. Direct job creation is a central element in it as well. In this new 1979 proposal, 400,000 new positions for welfare recipients would be created within CETA.

In both labor-market and income-support policy, then, the direct creation of jobs through public-employment and employment-subsidy programs has begun to play a pivotal role. While training remains a component of some of these programs, work *qua* work is now seen as their primary purpose. For recipients, the work provided has value in itself as an alternative to unemployment, as human capital in providing experience in the world of work and some on-the-job training, and as earned income rather than income support from transfer programs For taxpayers, direct job creation is viewed as more desirable than cash grants with no *quid pro quo*

145

in providing income support to the disadvantaged and, in addition, outputs meeting some private or social need are produced.

These recipient and taxpayer gains are judged to be at least equal to the costs of creating work where no real—or at least well-articulated—demand for output exists. The costs of creating jobs are not trivial, and estimates range from an annual budget cost of about $3,500 per job in the Neighborhood Youth Corps program to over $10,000 per job in the WIN and CETA programs. These per job costs, however, are substantially below the government outlays required to create employment by means of tax cuts or general spending increases.

WHY DIRECT JOB CREATION?

High unemployment rates among certain groups, large and growing welfare rolls, and substantial and concentrated numbers living in poverty are not new phenomena. Why, then, did the government wait until the 1970s to turn to direct job creation to combat these problems? The answer, it seems, is not one which fosters confidence in either policymakers or economists.

Though rarely admitted, the political rationale for direct job creation rests on a pair of less than inspiring propositions. The first is frustration over the apparent failures of early labor-market programs. The decisions made in the 1960s to provide education, training, and skills to poor and unskilled workers were optimistic ones, based on the human-resource investment notions of economists and other social scientists. The poor, it was believed, could earn their way out of poverty if given additional education and skills. The problem was thought to arise on the supply side of the labor market, and tens of billions of dollars were spent during the decade after the War on Poverty was announced to correct supply-side deficiencies. To supplement this strategy, income transfers were expanded through increased coverage, additional programs, reduced eligibility requirements, and more generous benefits. From 1965 to 1974, income transfers targeted on poor and disadvantaged workers grew from about $30 billion to $170 billion.[3]

This period also saw the rising importance of evaluation research. Hundreds of evaluation studies were made of the numerous education, training, and income-support programs, and the results were not positive. Participants in the training programs generally recorded earnings increases, but they were often not large enough to cover the costs of providing training. Gains in educational attainments were also recorded, but these were largely short-lived and not substantial.[4] Welfare and transfer benefits expanded and incomes were supported, but serious work disincentives were created, horizontal inequities remained severe, and administrative complexities and claims of fraud supported the belief that there was a "welfare mess." Perhaps most serious, the national poverty count did not fall markedly, especially after 1969, and the unemployment rate of minorities, youths, women, and other groups remained many orders of magnitude larger than the average rate. The supply-side training, education, and income-support strategy apparently had not really worked. The failure of the supply-side approach increased the relative attraction of a demand-side strategy; this resulted in direct job creation, in part by default.

The other political rationale for direct job creation arises from dissatisfaction with the growth in the income-support system. The substantial increase in education, training, and other social-welfare expenditures brought with it the strong opposition of those nonpoor who were paying the bill. Failures were emphasized, work disincentives cited, and the absence of tangible reductions in poverty and unemployment were noted. Income transfer and social policy came to be viewed as encumbering the economy and restraining initiative, investment, and growth.[5] This opposition also argued against what to them was the senseless strategy of "give-aways." Little could be expected from a system of money or food or housing or medical care gifts in which no *quid pro quo* in the form of effort was required or expected, and in which the gift was withdrawn as effort increased. The remedy was clear: Provision of income support should be granted only in payment for work provided. Again, direct job creation—the new "putting out" system—met this requirement. Unfortunately, what was required to satisfy the political need for a *quid pro quo* was the presence of an individual in a job slot—an input—and not the value of the output which his or her services yielded.

This characterization of the political rationale for direct job creation may be too cynical, but perhaps not by a great deal. Arguments concerning the self-esteem associated with work as opposed to welfare were raised, as was the value of work experience and the outputs produced. Moreover, the provision of jobs would reduce a primary constraint on the success of training programs—the lack of jobs—and offset the work disincentives of standard transfer programs. It is, however, difficult not to believe that these arguments were little more than dressing for the real need for a policy alternative to the discredited supply-side strategy—an alternative which entailed some *quid pro quo* for income support. Direct job creation was such an alternative.

While the political rationale for direct job creation is a questionable one, the economic rationale failed to be clearly articulated in time to have substantial impact on legislation. With but few exceptions, economists had neither fully thought through nor convincingly argued this rationale until well after major public-service employment and wage subsidy programs were in place. And, as we will see, that rationale is not an unimpressive one. The Brookings economist Henry Aaron's characterization of policymaking guiding social science—rather than the reverse—is nowhere better illustrated.[6]

What then is the economic rationale for direct job creation? This rationale starts from a perception of the adverse economic effects of existing legal and institutional constraints on the operation of the labor market. Because of these constraints—minimum-wage laws, discriminatory behavior by the employer, union power and influence, supply disincentive caused by income transfer and income and payroll-tax programs, and the demand disincentives caused by unemployment insurance and payroll taxes—labor markets do not respond quickly to change in labor supply or demand, and a wedge is created between the gross wage paid by employers and the net wage received by workers. Employer-borne gross-wage costs are increased relative to the perceived marginal product of low-skill workers, and the net wage received by workers is reduced relative to the supply price of labor for these workers; the market-clearing effect of flexible wages is not permitted to operate. In this context, high unemployment among groups of low-skill workers—youths, minorities, women—is inevitable, as is the persistence of income poverty among these same groups.

Direct job creation measures—either public-service jobs or employment subsidies—directly reduce the cost of hiring additional labor as perceived by potential public or private employers. Indeed, in the case of public-service employment, a 100 percent subsidy of the wages of target-group workers is provided, driving the cost of hiring such additional workers to zero. This reduced cost will cause employers to substitute workers in the target group for both capital inputs and workers who are not members of the target groups. Thus, employers have an incentive to accelerate plant and equipment maintenance or inventory accumulation (especially if the program is not a permanent one), or, if confronting increased demand for output, to add a second shift of new workers rather than to increase overtime work. All of these reactions stimulate the demand for workers in the target group.

From an economy-wide perspective, a related effect will occur. If the direct job-creation program is targeted on workers who will increase their labor force participation in response to an increased labor demand, then potential output (Gross National Product [GNP]) will increase. Transfer-program recipients, handicapped workers, and low-income youth would

148

seem to be such groups, as large numbers of these workers are not employed—indeed, are out of the labor force—because of unemployment, minimum wages, and other labor market constraints.[7] In an inflationary situation, substantial increases in both the employment of these workers and GNP could occur without substantial upward wage pressure. Some economists have referred to this as "cheating the Phillips curve" by concentrating employment increases on sectors of the labor market experiencing excess supply.[8]

The benefits of expanding GNP in this noninflationary way are even larger if these target groups are unemployed or out of the labor force involuntarily. In such a situation the leisure foregone by the newly employed would be of small, zero, or even negative value. In economic welfare terms, the gain from employing such otherwise unemployed workers is the entire output which they produce, and not the output less the value of the inputs, as in the standard case.

Other gains also occur. Taxpayers will gain from the increased taxes paid by the newly hired workers, and the reduced welfare and other transfer payments. Thus, both the workers involved, and society as a whole, gain as recipients work their way out of welfare.

Two final effects should be noted: First, direct job-creation programs in the private sector may exercise downward pressure on prices by reducing total labor costs. This price-reducing effect complements that of the "cheating the Phillips curve" effect mentioned above. Second, selective job-creation measures will tend to shift the composition of employment and earnings toward low-skill, target-group workers. If less inequality in the distribution of income is desired, this is a major benefit.

This economic case for direct job creation can be thought of in yet another way. If the key causes of excessively high unemployment and poverty among some groups are the constraints on the operation of the labor market due to discriminatory employer behavior, the power of trade unions, and minimum-wage and welfare policies, two approaches seem feasible. The first would be the elimination of the constraints—revamping or abandoning minimum-wage and income-conditioned transfer programs and eliminating restrictive employer and union practices. The second would be to ameliorate or offset the adverse side effects of these policies and practices. These side effects were described earlier as wedges (1) between employer-borne gross wages and the perceived marginal product of low-wage workers and (2) between the net wage received by laborers and the supply price of their work. It is precisely the reduction of these wedges that is accomplished by direct job-creation programs. To employers, the program reduces the wage costs of hiring low-wage workers, while to low-wage workers, the program increases the possibility of finding a job and the rewards of holding one. In short, well-designed direct job-creation programs can serve to offset the adverse side effects of labor-market constraints, and in so doing can lead to increased employment and earnings of low-wage workers and to increased output and aggregate employment with little or no inflationary pressure.

Clearly, then, the economic rationale for direct job creation is a strong one, and surely more substantive than that which has motivated political support for such measures. Unfortunately, the pattern which Henry Aaron documented for other areas applies to this policy approach as well. Both theoretical and empirical work has followed rather than guided direct job-creation policy.

THE REALITIES OF DIRECT JOB CREATION

While the politics of direct job creation suggest a major and growing preference for public-service employment and wage subsidies, and while the economic rationale for such a demand-side strategy hypothesizes gains in both efficiency and equity, their effective design and implementation is not straightforward. Any ultimate appraisal of the role for a direct job-creation strategy must also confront several potential problems.[9]

The first problem associated with direct job-creation programs involves "displacement effects"—the reduction of employment somewhere as an offset effect of the job-creation impacts of the program. Because the primary objective for this strategy is employment creation, its evaluation must be in terms of its *net* job creation impact, defined as the difference between the employment level in the economy with the policy and the employment level without it. Clearly, because (1) the output produced by the subsidized workers competes with alternative outputs, (2) the financing of the program entails opportunity costs that represent displaced outputs, and (3) many of the subsidized workers would have been working even in the absence of the subsidy, the *net* job-creation impact will be smaller than the *gross* number of workers hired or subsidized. The ratio of net to gross job creation is an indicator of these displacement effects.

Although several studies have estimated this ratio or its equivalent for public-employment programs, estimates vary widely. For example, one evaluation of CETA, in which few constraints were imposed on the governmental units that administered the program, suggested that this net-to-gross jobs ratio approached zero in the long run. The implication is that fiscal authorities were able to divert nearly all of the CETA funds to expenditures that would have been financed alternatively in the absence of CETA. In general, the short-run net employment effects were found to be larger than the long-run effects.[10] Other studies evaluating public-employment programs—and critiquing the above study—were more optimistic. They placed the ratio of net-to-gross employment at between 40 to 60 percent after one year,[11] implying that about one-half of the funds was diverted from job creation through "fiscal substitution."

It seems likely that public-employment programs that constrain governmental units from diverting CETA funds to activities that would have been undertaken even without CETA would yield net-to-gross employment ratios higher than those estimated for CETA. Moreover, for public-service employment programs that are targeted on low-skill, high-unemployment groups, fiscal substitution is likely to be relatively difficult because the skill mix of target-group workers hired would not conform closely to that of regular public employees.

The only evaluations of direct job-creation programs aimed at the private sector are those of the New Jobs Tax Credit. These studies measured the net employment increases, taking into account displacement within industries, but failed to consider the possible displacements in other sectors of the economy. In one study, the employment increases in the construction and retailing industries attributable to the NJTC were estimated by means of a variety of time series regressions.[12] The estimated NJTC employment stimulus over the twelve-month period from mid-1977 to mid-1978 ranged from 150,000 to 670,000. For these industries, total employment growth over the period was 1.3 million. The preferred models attribute at least 20 to 30 percent of the observed employment increase in these industries to NJTC. This result is consistent with the observation that, during the period of estimation in both industries, rates of employment growth substantially exceeded the rates of output growth.

Other studies, based on different data and techniques, also suggest a substantial effect of the NJTC. While these studies focus on the net intrasector employment effects, and hence fail to consider some possible channels of displacement, the employment effects attributed to the job-creation measure appear to be substantial.[13]

A second problem involves the resource and budget costs of the net jobs created by this approach. As indicated earlier, the budget costs per *net* job created are quite high. The most recent "guesstimate" of budget costs is based on the assumption that displacement is 20 percent in public-employment programs and 80 percent in private-sector job-creation programs. It suggests a cost per job for private-sector programs of about $6,500 and a cost of public sector programs of over $9,000 per job.[14] Although these estimates do not consider the increased tax revenues generated by the extra employment, or the reduced transfer payments, they do suggest that the taxpayer cost per job created is close to if not in excess of the net earnings of the new employees.

This discussion of budget costs per job raises a third problem—the value of the output produced relative to the real costs of creating the jobs. The benefits attributable to such jobs involve not only the productivity of the worker while employed on the job, but also the contribution of the work experience or on-the-job training to his or her earnings in the future. The real costs of employing a worker in such a special public or private program include both the value of the equipment and materials with which he or she works and the value of what he or she would have been doing if the program had not existed. This foregone productivity might involve the worker's alternative market activities, or the home production (such as child care) in which he or she would have been engaging, or simply the value of the foregone leisure.

As with other effects, public direct job-creation programs are likely to differ from wage subsidies to private firms in their efficiency impacts. Economic theory suggests that the private sector approach will be the more effective in meeting an efficiency, or cost-benefit criterion. First, private employers already have a known production process and a set marketing channel for the products produced, whereas public-employment programs are often undertaken with no clear definition of the expected output and no easy measure of productivity. Partially offsetting this is the fact that, through competition, privately marketed outposts are more likely to displace other production than public outputs designed to fill an unoccupied economic niche. Moreover, if private employers use the subsidy to retain workers whom they would otherwise lay off, the opportunity cost of the workers retained will be low. At least in principle, direct public-employment programs would appear better equipped to hire very low-skill, low-wage workers with correspondingly low opportunity costs. In practice, however, the managers of public-service employment programs have found the hiring of such workers weakened their efforts to develop productive and smoothly functioning work arrangements, and have not, in fact, targeted job slots on these workers.[15] Finally, to achieve economic efficiency, actual wage rates should equal the marginal opportunity cost of labor. Direct public-employment programs, in effect, subsidize labor costs by at least 100 percent of true marginal productivity. Wage subsidies toward the private sector are likely to come closer to subsidizing the difference between observed wage rates and real opportunity costs.

In any case, it should be emphasized that this economic efficiency criterion is a difficult one to meet for either private- or public-sector direct job-creation efforts targeted on low-productivity workers. While diverting such workers into a direct job-creation program is likely to entail relatively small losses from alternative activities (especially if the alternative to participation is involuntary unemployment), these workers do require associated inputs in the form of materials, equipment, and supervisory personnel, all of which comes at full cost. The key issue, then, is the value of the output produced. Because the output of public job-creation programs is not marketed, its value is hard to measure. This is especially true if the basic motivation for the program is to "keep occupied" members of the target groups or to provide them with work experience or training, rather than to use the public sector to achieve some defined objective or to produce identifiable goods or services.

The difficulties of meeting the efficiency objective have been illustrated in a recent study of a large, well-organized program of special workshops for handicapped and other less productive workers in the Netherlands. Little fault could be found with the internal organization of the factories in this job-creation program, and its clients are clearly less productive workers. Production from the workshops competed in the private market at market prices, and workshop managers were able to pursue any contracts for which they could assure delivery. The subsidy provisions, however, did little to encourage effective cost control in the program. An analysis of the benefits and costs of this program turned up a balance sheet that was not particularly favorable. The *net* economic costs of employment in the program are on the order of $4,000 to $5,000 per year per worker (in 1979 dollars), similar to taxpayer costs of U.S. direct job-creation programs. Only if the sociopsychological benefits to the workers are judged to exceed this value can the program be considered a socially efficient one.[16]

Additional evidence on the economic efficiency effects of direct job creation is found in preliminary reports of the Supported-Work Experiment.[17] Only program sites employing Aid to Families with Dependent Children (AFDC) recipients showed clear-cut potential net economic benefits. This analysis, like the Dutch study, does not account for a number of potential intangible benefits from the program, in particular the willingness of nonparticipants to pay for income redistribution through work rather than welfare and, especially, the future employment and earnings of the participants attributable to the program.

Employing the Unemployed

A fourth problem of direct job creation concerns the effects on the macroeconomic relationships in the economy if the programs are successful. Consider, for example, direct job-creation programs for the private sector. It was argued above that such programs, if effective, would increase employment at a substantially greater rate than output, and the NJTC results have suggested that this has occurred. A direct result of this is a fall in productivity—output per unit of labor input—as we measure it in the U.S., as inputs grow faster than output. Similarly, if employment of target-group workers results in an increase in labor force participation by those who are discouraged workers, employment may increase but measured unemployment may remain relatively unchanged, or it may even increase.

One of the most widely accepted macroeconomic relationships is known as Okun's Law, which states that a 1 percentage point reduction in the unemployment rate will be associated with a 3.2 percent increase in GNP. This relationship depends on several other macroeconomic responses in the economy as aggregate output changes—for example, the skill composition of employment, average hours worked per employee, and the utilization of capital. If the change in unemployment is induced by a wage subsidy targeted on low-skill workers, all of these standard macroeconomic responses will be altered, and Okun's Law will be repealed. Indeed, during recent years it appears that just that sort of effect has been taking place; some recent estimates have placed the current Okun multiplier at about 2.0, down from the 3.2 figure in the "Law."[18]

Surely it is an open question as to whether or not such changes in macroeconomic relationships are desirable. Declining productivity, for example, does have implications for economic growth and the maintenance of international competitiveness. On the other hand, the reduction in productivity may be evidence that low-skill workers are being removed from unemployment and idleness and are being transferred into the productive sector. In this case, these adverse side effects on macroeconomic relationships indicate that direct job-creation efforts are, indeed, producing the intended effects.

The final problem concerns the administrative and design problems associated with direct job-creation programs. Such programs are exceedingly difficult to design and administer, surely more costly than a general expansion of aggregate demand. The administrative difficulties of public-service employment have already been referred to. As one critique of the Carter PBJI jobs program stated:

The mass creation of public service jobs for low wage-low skill workers is something with which this country has no previous experience. The effort is analogous to a private firm's promise to introduce a new product, the manufacture of which requires a technology which has not yet been developed. [T]he effort is fraught with uncertainty, and the possibility of an ineffective and unproductive program must not be neglected. [Consider these] potential problem areas. (1) Regarding the prime job sponsors, how would their competence and honesty be judged; . . . how would the limited number of jobs be allocated among them and would that allocation create inequalities and discrimination against the least skilled and least productive workers? (2) Can jobs be created which participants will not find demeaning and dead end; will they have a training component facilitating transition to regular employment; . . .what precautions would be taken to avoid competition with existing private and regular employment, competition which can lead to labor union objections and to displacement with little net job creations; . . . [Would the wage paid in public service employment programs be sufficiently below the private sector net wage to encourage transition out of the program?] (3) How would the transition from special public sector jobs to private sector jobs be facilitated; if the available supply of public service jobs should prove greater than the demand would there be incentives for contractors to terminate existing holders of public service jobs or to encourage their transition to regular employment? (4) What problems would . . . [high expected job] turnover create for the administration and, especially, the productivity of the public jobs program?[19]

The problems associated with employment-subsidy programs are equally difficult but of a quite different sort. For example, a marginal wage subsidy such as the NJTC will minimize displacement (and windfalls to employers), but it will be relatively ineffective in targeting the additional jobs created. On the other hand, a program that is effectively targeted on low-skill workers may find recruitment costs high, employment goals unattainable, and output objectives difficult to achieve. Such programs may also result in the displacement of a more skilled worker who is a family's primary earner (such as a father) with a target-group individual (such as a youth) whose earnings position in the family is more peripheral. Moreover, programs with the highest potential for stimulating target-group employment may increase labor turnover, cause procyclical inventory-accumulation policies, or stimulate additional growth in regions that are already the fastest growing.[20]

The realities of direct job creation must serve to temper the optimistic economic rationale for this strategy and to dampen the apparent political enthusiasm for jobs programs designed to reduce unemployment and poverty. Yet such tempering and dampening are not disastrous. One must, after all, consider the alternatives. And, as has been suggested, the overall marks awarded supply-side education and training programs have not been high. And, while income transfers have doubtless reduced income poverty, the administrative difficulties and the disincentives to work and advancement have discouraged even the most ardent supporters of the income-support antipoverty strategy.[21] Further, few would now argue that affirmative action, regional development, public works, or even a national service draft are likely to make great inroads into the unemployment problems of youths, minorities, or low-growth regions.

A balanced appraisal, it seems, would award a substantial role to direct job-creation efforts. The administrative problems are difficult, but no more so than those of training and transfer programs. And while displacement is a serious concern, even the most cautious appraisals suggest that the $6,000 to $10,000 budget costs of creating jobs in direct job-creation programs are but one-third to one-half the costs of creating jobs via general tax cuts or public-expenditure increases. Moreover, the targeting of effects on groups of greatest policy concern would appear to be more feasible under a direct job program, either public or private, than under alternative approaches. Perhaps the most telling consideration in support of a prominent role for direct job creation is its macroeconomic effect. In a period in which inflation is a serious concern, any strategy that holds out hope of increasing the employment of low-productivity workers and, thereby, decreasing their income poverty with little or no upward wage and price effects has to be awarded a relatively high grade. When the enthusiasm of policymakers and the optimism of the economic rationale are tempered by the hard realities of direct job creation, a nontrivial optimism regarding the potential role of this policy strategy still remains.

SOME SUBSEQUENT STEPS IN DIRECT JOB-CREATION POLICY

Accepting this cautiously optimistic conclusion regarding the potential role of direct job-creation policy, the question is: Can we build on past experience and research to develop improved efforts in this area? What are some potential directions for policy and what must be known in order to proceed efficiently?

One possibility concerns an *employee*-based employment subsidy arrangement. Until now, both of the major private-sector job-creation efforts (the NJTC and the TJTC) have been employer based. The employer verifies if a particular worker hired qualifies under the terms of the legislation for a subsidy, and if he or she does, a claim for payment is filed. The worker need not know if he or she is generating a subsidy, nor will coworkers know. Moreover, in such an employer-based plan, the individual worker has little ability to influence his or her hiring, even if he or she has knowledge of being in the target population. Response to the incentive lies only with the employer, and, as a result, any activities induced by the subsidy to match the job to the worker will be only on the demand side of the market. The labor supplier is a passive participant.

This incentive pattern would be altered if the subsidy were employee based.[22] For example, assume that each worker certified as a member of the target group were given a card indicating that any employer hiring the worker would be entitled to a subsidy of a designated form. Indeed, the subsidy terms could be identical to those in any employer-based, targeted program. Possessing the card would provide the worker with a labor-market advantage, and hence an incentive to search for a job. Knowing the rules of the program, the employer would have no less incentive to match job to worker than with an employer-based scheme. The advantage of such an employee-based plan, then, stems from the increased incentives on the labor suppliers to search for work, increasing the probability that they will be hired.

In evaluating such an arrangement, several questions immediately arise: (1) Would workers feel stigmatized if they were specially certified as card or voucher holders? (2) Would coworker resentment be generated if noncertified workers sensed special conditions or retention probabilities were associated with holding a certification card? (3) Would employers confront added (or reduced) administrative burdens if employee certification were handled in this way? (4) Are there possibilities for varying the terms of the subsidy depending on the circumstances (for example, income level or age or region) of the worker? (5) Would target-group members already employed be eligible for a certification card, and would their employers be eligible for the subsidy? (6) If the subsidy were paid only for hiring a new certified worker, wouldn't artificially induced job turnover be created? Given the benefits from the increased job-seeking activities that an employee-based plan would induce, the answers to the above questions would have to be rather strongly adverse to warrant abandonment of this idea without further consideration.

A second possibility relates to a concern already expressed about public-service employment: the apparently unproductive aspect of offering employment without a clear conception of the output or service to be provided. In the past, direct employment programs have had to look for general output rather than a clearly defined and accepted output that matches the skills of target-group workers. Indeed, this is one of the criticisms of the public-service employment component of PBJI, a criticism that carried weight. The suggestion here is that design of a new direct job-creation program be preceded by the clear specification of a public (or merit) good, the production of which would have gained public support, and be clearly visible and measurable. With such a clear delineation of output, the productive process could then be specified to maximize the employment of low productivity, target-group workers.

The strategy being suggested, then, is the reverse of the procedure heretofore adopted in the United States. One example of this approach would be that of the Netherlands, where a clear national commitment to a neat, clean, well-trimmed landscape has now been established as a public (merit) good. To obtain this "output" has required municipalities, with national government support to increase labor demands for sport field and playground improvement, roadway trimming and beautification, vacant field maintenance, and minor road repairs and clean-up. The provision of this output has entailed the employment of numerous low-productivity workers, including disabled and handicapped people. By focusing on attainment of this specific and visible output, public support is obtained. This support has the side effect of increasing the demand for low-productivity workers.

A third suggestion relates to the potential benefits of a combined training-job creation effort. Existing private-sector job-creation programs have neglected training in favor of direct employment. Evidence suggests that private-sector employment with on-the-job training over a continued period can have substantial long-run effects. If this is so, an explicit effort to link training and direct job creation may have merit.

Clearly, training provided by private-sector employers will only be commensurate with the net benefits that they expect to gain from such efforts. Hence, if a training component (or requirement) were to be coupled with employment subsidies, the subsidy provision would have to be appropriately enlarged.

Such an employment-training program is not without precedent. In 1978, Sweden introduced a temporary marginal employment subsidy designed to stimulate a general increase in employment. The program originated in response to an expected decrease in industrial employment during the latter part of 1978 and was designed to expire on July 1, 1979. Any establishment which experienced a net increase in employment by July 1, 1979 beyond its May 1, 1978 level was eligible for the subsidy. Employers are required to satisfy the union involved that the relevant employees receive a minimum of training (about two-months' worth), with the amount of the subsidy being set to cover the additional costs incurred. There is little doubt that a subsidy arrangement which both paid training costs and subsidized employment could be made attractive to private business. Again, numerous questions of design and implementation can be raised, not the least of which concerns the verification of training quality, effectiveness, and costs. However, the potential of such an approach would appear to warrant additional study and experimentation.

In conclusion, then, as we enter the 1980s, policies designed to directly create jobs would appear to be a permanent part of the economic landscape. As it now looks, the major problems of the 1980s will be continued inflation, structural unemployment of youths, women, and minorities, and other economic dislocations due to energy prices and changing retirement patterns. Public-service employment and employment subsidies have an important role to play in such an environment. The potential of these policies for "cheating the Phillips curve," targeting employment on less productive, hard-to-employ groups, and affording transitional employment opportunities during periods of dislocation, directly addresses these problems. Moreover, through the Full Employment and Balanced Growth Act of 1978, a legislative mandate to directly use federal policies to meet these problems is now on the books.

What is now necessary is that more be learned about the benefits and problems of alternative direct job-creation measures. Unless these measures can be designed so as to maximize their output and targeting potential while avoiding displacement and other adverse side effects, evaluation of them may ultimately be no more favorable than that of the education, training, and income-support strategies of the 1960s and 1970s. Such a result would represent an apparent missed opportunity. Experimentation with both employee-based subsidy arrangements and subsidized employment-training arrangements contracted for directly with private-sector businesses should be high on the policy agenda for the early 1980s. The results from such activities could serve as the basis for expanded job-creation policies that meet both efficiency and equity goals.

10

ISABEL V. SAWHILL
LAURI J. BASSI

The Challenge of
Full Employment

INTRODUCTION

THROUGHOUT history elections have been won and lost based on the state of the economy, and opinion polls regularly suggest a high level of public interest in the nation's economic affairs. Currently, anxiety about inflation tops the list of citizens' concerns, but any serious decline in output and employment could put unemployment back in first place.

This anxiety stems not only from the real hardship that inflation and unemployment produce, but also from the insecurity they breed and from doubts about our ability to cope with them. These doubts are especially pervasive among professional economists, including those who advise our national leaders.

In spite of such uncertainties, we now have legislation that commits us to act. The Full Employment and Balanced Growth Act of 1978 (more commonly known as "Humphrey-Hawkins" and hereafter referred to as the Full Employment Act) establishes specific goals for unemployment and inflation, complete with deadlines for achieving them.

In this chapter, we address some of the issues raised by this legislation and by the broader challenge it symbolizes, giving particular attention to the

160

possible role of labor-market policies in achieving the macroeconomic objectives stated in the act.

The chapter begins with a review of the Full Employment Act. We next attempt to probe its intellectual foundations, first exploring the various theoretical assumptions about the causes of unemployment and inflation, then reviewing evidence on the limits of macroeconomic policy, and finally, examining the potential of microeconomic interventions to fill the under-utilization gap. In a concluding section, we draw on the preceding review to assess the goals and policies proposed in the legislation.

THE LEGISLATIVE FRAMEWORK: THE FULL EMPLOYMENT AND BALANCED GROWTH ACT OF 1978

The responsibility of the federal government to promote "maximum employment, production, and purchasing power" was first established with the enactment of the Employment Act of 1946. No attempt was made to define "maximum" employment or purchasing power and the word "full" was deliberately avoided in the title of the act. This legislation also set up a Council of Economic Advisers, required the president to submit an annual economic report to the Congress, and provided for a Joint Economic Committee to review the economic report. While the experience of the Great Depression and fears of a serious post-World War II recession provided the original impetus for this legislation, it has subsequently come to symbolize the nation's commitment to a permanent role for the federal government in maintaining high levels of employment and has provided a cornerstone for economic policymaking in the United States for over three decades.

In 1978, this legislation was amended by the passage of the Full Employment and Balanced Growth Act. Relative to its predecessor, the 1978 legislation places greater emphasis on the problem of structual unemployment and the need for microeconomic as well as macroeconomic policies to deal with the problem. The profound effects of monetary policy on the economy are recognized, and much greater attention is given to the problem of inflation than was true in the original act. These shifts in emphasis are not surprising when read in the light of the past three decades of experience—a period that has seen the birth of structual explanations of unemployment, the discrediting of "fine tuning," the resurgence of monetarism, and, most recently, a marked acceleration of inflation.

Employing the Unemployed

The bill was finally passed after a four-year congressional struggle, which involved much redrafting of the legislation. Earlier versions had proposed more ambitious goals, including the first version, which would have guaranteed a job for any adult American who wanted to work. The basic provisions of the act, as finally passed on October 27, 1978, are here described.

Economic Goals

The act includes a long list of economic objectives. With some pruning and reorganization, this list boils down to the following more basic goals:

- A reduction of unemployment to 3 percent for adults and 4 percent overall by 1983.
- A reduction of inflation to 3 percent by 1983 and to zero by 1988, "*provided*, that policies and programs for reducing the rate of the inflation shall be designed so as not to impede achievement of the goals and timetables specified [for reducing unemployment]."
- The achievement of "balanced growth" and of gains in productivity and real income.
- Improvements in the balance of trade.
- The achievement of a balanced federal budget and the reduction of the ratio of federal outlays to GNP in an expanding economy, all in the context of meeting "national priorities."

In short, there appear to be five major goals clustering around unemployment, inflation, economic growth, the balance of payments, and the federal budget. With the exception of the federal budget objectives, these goals have been standard fare in the history of macroeconomic policy. The conflicts between them and the need for an equally large number of policy instruments if they are to be simultaneously achieved have also been much discussed in the literature. By contrast, the emphasis on a balanced federal budget as an *independent* objective appears to be a throwback to an earlier era when the analogy between private and public debt held moral sway; when it was believed to be as hazardous for a nation as for an individual to live beyond its means. Certainly, there are few modern economists who believe that federal deficits have any normative significance *beyond* their impact on inflation, unemployment, and growth. To pursue a balanced budget as an independent objective would be to leave an important policy instrument powerless to achieve more fundamental objectives.

The expressed interest in moving toward a reduced ratio of federal outlays to GNP is another noteworthy objective. This appears to be a rejection of an earlier faith in the benefits of larger social programs. Of course, by adding

162

language about the urgency of meeting "national priorities," liberals and conservatives alike can live with this provision, since "priorities" are never defined.

Proposed Means of Achieving Goals

Robert Solow has referred to the original Employment Act of 1946 as "piety without policy." Its more modern version might equally well be characterized as "policy without program." Unlike its predecessor, the Full Employment Act of 1978 attempts to establish a framework for policy and recognizes the need to coordinate different strategies. But no new programs are authorized and the specific means for achieving objectives are left to the president and the Congress to determine.

The authors of the bill do outline a wide range of strategies that *might* be adopted, although it is difficult to discern the specific role envisaged for each, what each is expected to accomplish, at what cost, and how each relates to the myriad of other policies directed toward similar objectives. Specifically mentioned are:

- Countercyclical employment policies including accelerated public works and public-service employment.
- Regional and structural employment policies, including efforts to reduce and then remove the gap between the national unemployment rate and the unemployment rates of minorities, women, and youth.
- Youth employment policies.
- Job training, counseling, and special employment projects under CETA or non-CETA auspices. With respect to the latter, the president is authorized to create reservoirs of public and private nonprofit employment projects to employ individuals aged sixteen and over who cannot be provided with other job opportunities, although this provision is not to be put into operation until two years after the passage of the act.

The legislative guidance is most precise in the area of job-creation programs. Creation of conventional jobs in the private sector via general economic stimulus is given first priority; federal assistance to generate private-sector employment (in connection with meeting national needs) is given second priority. Third priority goes to an expansion of regular public-sector employment. Finally, special "reservoir" jobs in the public sector are to be created only when all other efforts have proved insufficient. These jobs are to be structured in such a way as to avoid drawing workers away from the private sector. They are to be useful and productive, pay relatively low wages, and be targeted on areas of high unemployment and on the structurally unemployed.

Throughout the act there is an explicit recognition that general economic

163

policies alone will be unable to achieve the goals that have been set forth. The presumption is that various structural interventions will be needed and that employment and training programs will play a major role.

Administrative Provisions

The legislation repeatedly recognizes the need for coordination between different levels of government, between the public and private sectors, between the president and the Congress, and between monetary and fiscal policy. The recommendations for achieving this coordination are, however, very general in nature. The more specific provisions require:

- The president and Congress to set annual quantitative goals for the reduction of unemployment.
- The president and Congress to develop a comprehensive and consistent national economic policy annually to achieve the goals of the act.
- The appropriate committees of Congress and the Congress itself to work to implement the proposals set forth by the president to achieve the goals of the act.
- The Board of Governors of the Federal Reserve System to submit biannual reports to the appropriate congressional committees. These reports are to include (1) the objectives and plans of the Board of Governors and the Federal Open Market Committee and (2) the relationship of these objectives and plans to the short-term goals set forth in the most recent *Economic Report of the President*. Each committee receiving this report is then to submit a report to the House or the Senate containing its views and recommendations with respect to the Federal Reserve's intended policies.

These procedures, while in keeping with an accepted bureaucratic tendency to require additional reports in order to solve problems, are unlikely to achieve much in the absence of new or more effective programs. In its first report under the act, the Council of Economic Advisers stated:

> By any criterion these are very ambitious goals. The most difficult obstacle to achieving the 1983 goals arises from the potential inconsistency between the objectives for growth and unemployment and the need to reduce inflation. Economic plans for the next two years are designed to avoid any acceleration of inflation from the demand side, and to use macroeconomic instruments together with the pay and price standards to unwind the inflation from the past. It is clear, however, that the task of reducing inflation to an acceptable pace will not be completed by 1980. . . .
>
> Our prospects for achieving the 1983 goals depend upon finding ways to reduce the divergence of unemployment rates among various demographic groups. Much work needs to be done to improve existing employment programs and discover new approaches to structural problems if the goals of the act are to be realized.

. The Board of Governors of the Federal Reserve System appeared to be even more pessimistic in its economic outlook. In its second report, submitted in compliance with the Full Employment Act, the board projected inflation rates of 9.5 to 11 percent and 8.5 to 10.5 percent for 1979 and 1980 respectively and unemployment rates of 6.25 to 7 percent and 6.75 to 8.25 percent for those same years.

The reasons for the divergence between these pessimistic forecasts, which are representative of the current thinking of economists, and the optimism expressed in the Full Employment Act are examined in the next section.

INTELLECTUAL FOUNDATIONS[a]

Sound public policy requires an intellectual base: a set of assumptions about how the world works and how it can be reshaped in accord with the policymaker's preferences. The constant parade of academics before congressional committees is probably best understood in this light. While their views are not always sound, and certainly not always acceptable to individual members of Congress, many of their ideas eventually enter the mainstream and have a profound, if delayed and diffuse, impact on legislation. It is in this spirit that we now briefly explore the recent thinking of economists about the nature of inflation and unemployment. This review focuses first on theoretical developments and then on the empirical evidence relevant to assessing the goals and policies proposed by the legislation.

Theoretical Foundations

It is difficult, if not impossible, to arrive at a conceptual model of inflation and unemployment for which there would be broad agreement among economists. In fact, theoretical developments over the past decade have left the profession in some disarray; whatever agreement now exists is tentative at best and policy tends to be grounded in an admixture of old and new theories.

The older thinking can be traced back to A. W. Phillips's observations two decades ago of a strikingly consistent and negative relationship between wage increases and unemployment rates. This finding sparked a flurry of new research among economists, both to discover whether or not Phillips's results could be generalized, and if they could, to construct a theory that explained them.

165

Employing the Unemployed

This negative relationship between wage (or price) increases and unemployment rates, now referred to as the Phillips curve, has been found to hold in many economies. The theoretical underpinnings of the Phillips curve are less well developed, but the observed relationships are consistent with a disequilibrium view of labor markets. That is, given constant flux in the economy, at any point in time, there are some labor markets that are tight (have more vacancies than job seekers) and others that are loose (have more job seekers than vacancies). If wage adjustments are asymmetrical, rising in tight labor markets but failing to fall in loose ones, then the economy will have an inflationary bias even when there is no excessive demand overall. As James Tobin puts it, "full employment in the sense of equality of vacancies and unemployment is not compatible with price stability. Zero inflation requires unemployment in excess of vacancies." Thus, according to the Phillips curve doctrine, an agonizing decision must be made between how much unemployment to trade off for how much inflation. Moreover, if the economy is subjected to external shocks that raise prices in some sectors (energy or food, for example) with no concomitant declines in other sectors, the inflationary bias and the painful need to choose between inflation and unemployment are further exacerbated.

More recent developments in economic theory may relieve policymakers of this difficult decision. Most economists now believe the trade-off between inflation and unemployment is, at best, a short-run phenomenon. They argue that, in the long run, there is a single level of unemployment toward which the economy will always move. This "natural rate" of unemployment depends only on the efficiency with which individual product and labor markets operate; that is, on frictional or structural imperfections. Attempts to reduce the unemployment rate below the natural rate through expansionary policies will only be successful if *unanticipated* inflation fools workers into believing that *real* wages have risen when in fact only *money* wages are increasing. The unemployed respond to nominally "good" wage offers by accepting jobs more quickly while those already employed are less likely to quit as their paychecks fatten along with the Consumer Price Index. Once workers realize that they are no better off than before, that inflation has misled them into accepting employment that is not well paid in real terms, both search time and quit rates rise again, causing the economy to return once more to the "natural rate" of unemployment but now with a new, higher rate of inflation. The only way to *maintain* unemployment below the natural rate is to keep increasing the rate of inflation, thereby injecting a new dose of money illusion into the system. For this reason, the natural rate is the only unemployment rate consistent with a *stable* rate of inflation and is sometimes referred to as the nonaccelerating inflation rate of unemployment (or NAIRU). The NAIRU is viewed as the lowest unemployment rate achievable through aggregate demand management alone.

Finally, the most recent school of thought believes that people are not so easily fooled, and that the effects of any shift in policy are quite predictable. This leaves little room for any "money illusion" and makes the return to the "natural rate" almost instantaneous; in the face of such "rational expectations," even the short-run trade-off is nonexistent. However, most mainline economists would reject this view, since even those who accept the natural rate hypothesis believe that the near-term benefits of reducing unemployment (even if short-lived) may sometimes be worth the longer-term costs of a permanently higher rate of inflation. Politically, of course, one cannot ignore the fact that elections are relatively frequent events, and that this influences the time horizons of most presidents and their advisors.

The microeconomic foundations of the natural rate hypothesis have not held up very well under close scrutiny. Contrary to a fundamental assumption of the theory, much job search takes place on the job and does not require an intervening spell of unemployment. Moreover, quit rates rise rather than fall during expansions, involuntary unemployment (for example, layoffs) continues to be significant even when the economy reaches the NAIRU, and prices decelerate very little during recessions. Nevertheless, the fact that the rate of inflation has accelerated in the decade of the seventies whenever the unemployment rate has fallen below 5 or 6 percent, while it has tended to decelerate at higher rates, has gained converts to the natural rate view. Certainly, this is the ascendant orthodoxy within the economics profession, although it is still viewed with some skepticism, especially by those with front-line responsibilities.

If there is any eclectic synthesis of these theoretical developments that might attract reasonably broad support, our guess is that it would include the following elements:

1. We live in a world in which wage and price adjustments are sluggish and asymmetrical, in which formal or informal indexing is prevalent, and in which price increases tend to be validated by the central bank in order to maintain output and employment. In such a world, any disequilibrium that requires a price rise in one sector of the economy will not be offset by declines elsewhere. These price rises tend to feed the wage-price spiral leading to accelerating inflation as the initial effects are diffused throughout the economy. Inflationary expectations intensify efforts to make individual wages and prices inflation-proof and in the process make the economy as a whole more inflation-prone.

2. One way to slow the pace of inflation is to deliberately maintain economic

slack and relatively high rates of unemployment. However, there is nothing optimal about the unemployment rate consistent with nonacceleration inflation. In particular, it is *not* the equivalent of a full employment/unemployment rate or the rate at which all of the unemployed are engaged in voluntary job search.

3. Two additional ways of responding to accelerating inflation are available. The first is deliberate intervention in the wage- and price-setting process (for example, an incomes policy). The second is to prevent the disequilibria that give rise to price or wage increases in the first place. These preventive measures could include (a) monitoring government regulatory and tax policies for their inflationary effects, (b) long-term domestic energy production and conservation programs to protect the economy from foreign oil price shocks or price stabilization programs for other basic commodities, (c) encouraging competition through a reduction of trade barriers or increased antitrust activity, and (d) employment and training programs. In a market economy with freely adjusting prices and wages, these kinds of policies would not be required. They represent an attempt to compensate for various market imperfections, some of them introduced by the government itself.

With this proposed synthesis in hand, we turn to a review of the empirical research on (1) how far the unemployment rate can be reduced through macroeconomic policy before inflation begins to accelerate and (2) the ability of various microeconomic interventions, especially employment and training programs, to reduce the NAIRU still further. This review will be helpful in assessing the feasibility of achieving the goals of the Full Employment Act.

Empirical Foundations

The Limits of Macroeconomic Policy: If one accepts that there is a point, or zone, beyond which any attempt to stimulate the economy through monetary and fiscal policies alone will simply lead to an acceleration in the rate of inflation, then it is important to know, roughly, where the danger point is. While in practice we have tended to find this out through trial and error, economists have also been busy generating estimates of the danger point, or NAIRU, as it is called.

Techniques for estimating NAIRU and its changes over time have generally been based on the changing demographic composition of the labor force and the costs of being unemployed. It is assumed that as increasing numbers of youth and women enter the labor force the NAIRU rises, since these groups traditionally have higher unemployment rates than prime-age male workers. These changes in the composition of the labor force are thought to have increased the NAIRU by .6 to 1.0 percentage points over the last twenty years.

168

The Challenge of Full Employment

In addition to these demographic changes, increased coverage and extensions of unemployment insurance, increases and extensions in coverage of the minimum wage, and job-seeking requirements associated with welfare programs are all believed to have produced an increase in the NAIRU. As a result of all of these factors, there seems to be general agreement that the 1956 NAIRU of about 4 percent has now increased to somewhere in the range of 5.5 to 6.5 percent.

There is widespread agreement that the NAIRU will decline over the next decade as the baby-boom cohort ages, resulting in a labor force that has a demographic composition that is consistent with lower unemployment. The extent to which NAIRU will decline is, unfortunately, very difficult to predict. The only available estimates indicate that the decline over the next decade will be around .4 to .5 percentage points, with most of this reduction taking place by 1985. A rough guess is that demographic shifts will reduce the NAIRU by .25 percentage points by 1983, leaving it in the neighborhood of 5.0 to 6.5 percent by then, in the absence of other changes in the structure of the labor market.

The significance of these numbers should not, however, be overestimated. The estimates are all derived by more or less the same technique of adjusting for demographic and programmatic changes, and there is no rigorous analysis that indicates the nature of any causal relationship between these factors and changes in the NAIRU.

Some authors (Levitan and Taggart, Thurow, and Solow) have pointed out that there are many other factors, in addition to age and sex, that may have altered the NAIRU over time. They point out that better-educated workers generally have lower job turnover and, therefore lower unemployment rates. It might be reasonable to expect, then, that the better-educated labor force of the 1970s would have a lower propensity to be unemployed than the labor force of the 1950s. These same authors point out that while more women, who generally have higher unemployment rates than men, have entered the labor force, these women are less likely to be part-time workers than they were in the past, and that full-time workers have lower unemployment rates than part-time workers. Thus, after controlling for cyclical and other factors, we should expect the unemployment rate for women to have dropped over the last twenty years, while in fact it has risen. The important point that emerges is that the standard age/sex computations used in estimating the NAIRU are somewhat arbitrary and that different adjustment techniques can produce very different sets of numbers. This leaves us in the uncomfortable position of agreeing with the idea that there is a constraint on the use of macroeconomic policy, but it does not enable us to define or estimate the levels of unemployment at which this constraint begins to operate.

Fortunately, there is additional empirical evidence that sheds some light on the NAIRU. In a simple regression of the unemployment rate on the acceleration of inflation, Ashenfelter found that for the period 1950 to 1969, the NAIRU was 4.7 percent. The same regression over the years 1970 to 1977 yielded a NAIRU of 6.3 percent. These estimates are consistent with the estimates derived by the age/sex calculations. This by no means "proves" that these calculations are "right"; it only gives us two independent pieces of information that point in the same direction.

In short, the evidence indicates that it has become increasingly difficult to maintain low levels of unemployment without accelerating the rate of inflation. We can conclude, therefore, that increased efficiency in the use of microeconomic as well a macroeconomic policy will be needed if the goals of the Full Employment Act are to be met. The legislation clearly recognizes the need for such measures, stating that "general economic policies alone have been unable to achieve the goals set forth in this Act."

The Job Left for Microeconomic Policies. Assuming that the 1983 NAIRU is in the range of 5.0 to 6.5 percent, labor-market policies must reduce the NAIRU by between 1.0 and 2.5 percentage points. Remembering that these policies will, at best, simply prevent any further acceleration of inflation and will not actually reduce it, additional measures will be needed to *decelerate* the underlying inflation rate from its current high levels to the 3 percent target for 1983. The likely inflation rate in 1983 in the absence of these special measures is difficult to predict, since it will depend on the effects of any intervening recession, the rate of productivity growth, and other factors. A guess that inflation will continue to hover in the neighborhood of 8 to 10 percent in the early 1980s seems reasonable, leaving it up to additional microeconomic interventions (for example, an incomes policy, regulatory or tax policies) to shave 5 to 7 percentage points off the inflation rate.

Thus, the challenge for microeconomic policy is great. Although we know very little about the ability of such policies either to reduce the NAIRU or decelerate the rate of inflation, the evidence reviewed below suggests the Full Employment Act may be expecting more of these policies than they can deliver.

Using Labor-Market Policies to Reduce the NAIRU. In textbook models of the economy, labor is treated much like any other commodity. Any shift in demand or supply leads to an adjustment in wages with the result that unemployment, beyond some frictional minimum, will not exist. Observations of the real world, however, do not conform very well to these models.

170

The Challenge of Full Employment

Wages appear to perform their equilibrating role very crudely, adjusting mostly upward in response to excess demand in a particular market and hardly ever downward in response to excess supply. Any adjustments that do take place occur only very slowly, with all kinds of institutional constraints influencing the outcomes. The existence of unions, discrimination, personnel practices geared to long-term employer-employee relationships, the high costs of hiring and training new workers, minimum wages, a lack of complete information on the part of both employer and job seekers, family or community ties that reduce mobility, and high reservation wages set by income transfers and other sources of nonearned income all play a role. These and other institutional complexities create substantial barriers in the wage adjustment process and are capable of explaining a good deal of "structural unemployment." Thus, we are left with a situation in which wages may not always perform their market-clearing function, in which there is no single auction market for all types of labor but rather a multitude of partially segmented markets, and consequently a wide dispersion of unemployment rates around the national average. Labor-market policies are designed to deal with this kind of market failure.

Given the uneven incidence of unemployment, a nondiscriminating dose of macroeconomic policy wil be inflationary unless the economy is operating so far below its potential that virtually every labor market has excess capacity. As full employment is approached, an increasing proportion of these markets become tight, with the result that wages and prices are bid up long before the high rates of unemployment in other markets have fallen very far. Thus, the economy tends to exhaust its supply of prime-age white males long before it has made much of a dent in the unemployment rate of minority teenagers.

Labor-market policies can respond to this situation in three ways. First, special job-creation programs can be aimed at loose labor markets. The objective is to translate as much of an increase in labor demand as possible into rising employment rather than into rising wages. The fiscal stimulus is focused on those groups and areas with high rates of unemployment, on the assumption that wages are less responsive to increases in demand in these markets. There are a number of current programs that operate, more or less, on this set of principles. Public-service employment under CETA offers federally subsidized jobs in local government and nonprofit agencies to the low-income, long-term unemployed. The Targeted Jobs Tax Credit (TJTC), enacted in 1978, effectively increases the demand for low-income youth and some other disadvantaged groups by subsidizing their wages. Finally, the allocation of funds under a number of different programs (CETA, public works, revenue sharing) depends on local area unemployment rates.

Employing the Unemployed

A second role for labor-market policies is to influence the supply side of the labor market through education and training programs. There are several distinct contributions that these supply-side policies can make to the inflation problem. One is to ease the skill bottlenecks that push up wages in tight labor markets over the short run. Another is to improve the long-term rate of increase in productivity so that the impact of rising money wages on labor costs and prices will be minimized. Still another is to raise the productivity of the most disadvantaged groups to a level that is commensurate with the wage floor set by social or legal minimums or by income-transfer programs, thus reducing the amount of structural unemployment attributable to these factors. Although they have never been large, federally funded training programs have been operating for over fifteen years with these objectives in mind.

The third way in which labor-market policies can improve the trade-off between inflation and unemployment is by reducing frictional or "search" unemployment. A considerable proportion of measured unemployment represents the voluntary movement of workers in and out of the labor force and between jobs. Although some search may contribute to a better match between worker and job, much of this search is inefficient and does not require that an individual become unemployed in order to find a new position. Thus, better labor-market information and placement assistance, such as that provided by the federal-state Employment Service, are generally believed to be one way of improving the inflation-unemployment trade-off.

It is impossible to estimate with any confidence the potential for these labor-market policies to reduce unemployment in noninflationary ways. Thus far, there is only a trickle of empirical research bearing on these issues. The fact that there is so little information on such an important national issue appears to be related to several factors.

First of all, there is little agreement about the *direct* effects of employment and training programs on the participants. Jobs programs may fail to have their intended effects because they employ people who would have been employed anyway. Similarly, the observed outcomes for participants in training and placement assistance programs may not differ from the outcomes that would have occurred in the absence of the program. Without controlled experiments, or properly designed statistical models of program effectiveness, no one can say why a particular individual's employment experiences may have changed, although it is always tempting to attribute any observed improvement (or lack of it) to existing programs. Yet, because of delays in collecting and analyzing longitudinal data on CETA participants, we are relatively ignorant about these effects and may, in fact, be proceeding more on the basis of faith than of reason.

Second, even if the programs do improve the labor-market prospects of those who participate, they may not produce the desired macroeconomic outcomes. The programs may simply reshuffle existing employment and wages among groups or areas with no net effect on overall employment or price levels. (This may be desirable on equity grounds alone, but it should not then be viewed as a solution to unemployment and inflation.) In theory, by shifting demand toward target groups whose wages are relatively unresponsive to an increase in their employment opportunities, greater economic stimulus can be applied with little or no acceleration of inflation. Here, the empirical evidence is somewhat more convincing. Wages do appear to be less responsive to increased employment in low-wage, low-skill labor markets characterized by high unemployment.

To summarize, in order to reduce the NAIRU, employment and training programs must meet at least two conditions: first, they must change the distribution of employment or unemployment relative to what would prevail if there were a general fiscal or monetary expansion. Second, these distributional shifts must translate into a more favorable ratio of employment to price increases, thereby permitting a greater expansion of overall demand as well as a potentially more equitable distribution of existing opportunities. The evidence that these two conditions are being met under current labor-market programs is thin, but it suggests that there is room for cautious optimism.

Policies to Decelerate Inflation. It would be beyond the scope of this volume, as well as this chapter, to do anything more than mention the importance of microeconomic policies outside of the employment and training area for both unwinding the current inflation and for preventing any further acceleration. But a few critical points are worth emphasizing.

First, it would be a mistake to leave the impression that labor markets are the source—as opposed to the transmission belt—for most of our current inflation. Although the distinction may be no more valid than that between chicken and egg, it does suggest that if one can keep the rooster out of the barnyard or limit the number of eggs laid per day, one can interdict the process. Roosters come in the form of OPEC price increases, cost-increasing social regulation, payroll-tax increases, and other "exogenous" shocks. Once the rooster has been let loose in the barnyard, emphasis must shift to reducing the number of eggs laid per day by some type of incomes policy.

Second, while these measures have their own set of economic and political costs, the only alternative is to maintain a slack economy with high unemployment for a period of years, and this may be even *more* unacceptable. It is often argued that a credible policy of macroeconomic restraint will

173

eventually bring both lower inflation and less unemployment, but the short-term costs come very high.

If research on the ability of labor-market policies to reduce the NAIRU is still in its infancy, research on microinflation policies is newer still. One researcher's suggested menu of deflationary actions is listed in Table 10–1, along with some rough estimates of the likely short-run effects of such actions on the inflation rate. The longer-run effects depend on the extent to which a one-time reduction in prices contributes to a further unwinding of the wage-price spiral.

Having now reviewed the potential of both macroeconomic and micro-economic policies to combat inflation and unemployment, we are in a better position to assess the Full Employment Act of 1978.

ASSESSMENT OF THE FULL EMPLOYMENT ACT OF 1978

The Full Employment Act of 1978 is predicated on the assumption that we can mandate a solution to our economic woes, that the problem is a lack of commitment and coordination, not a lack of knowledge about how to simultaneously reduce inflation and unemployment within the framework of a democratic, free enterprise society. When every group attempts to maintain or improve its share of the national income but the latter is subject to real resource constraints, inflation is the ultimate reconciler. In fact, the commitment to full employment—by removing a major source of economic insecurity—may fuel the competition for higher incomes and, paradoxically, make the objective itself more difficult to achieve. What is needed is a new set of institutional arrangements to discipline this competition. Nothing so radical is envisaged in the Full Employment Act. Even voluntary incomes policies, a mild restraint at best, are nowhere mentioned in the legislation. In short, while we may be able to guarantee a job to everyone able and willing to work, if the wages offered on all existing jobs more than exhaust the social product, inflation, perhaps even accelerating inflation, is the inevitable outcome.

The result of this process is both inefficient and inequitable, especially when it generates political pressures for slow growth or deflationary policies to cope with a seemingly intractable inflation. Insult is added to injury when the levels of unemployment that this produces are labeled "full employment."

174

TABLE 10-1
Summary of Policy Proposals to Reduce the Price Level

Proposal	Annual amount (billions of 1977 dollars)	In gross private domestic deflator (percent)
Social Security		
Replace employer and employee payroll taxes with general revenue financing for disability and health insurance (fiscal 1979)	14.6	0.7[a]
Sales taxes		
Reduce state sales taxes up to 2 percentage points of personal income	27.4	1.6
Replace federal excise taxes with direct taxes	17.4	1.0
Agriculture		
Substitute deficiency payments for 1977–1978 wheat, feed grain, soybean, milk initiatives	3.6	0.2
Substitute deficiency payments for set-aside proposals designed to raise farm income by $4.4 billion[b]	4.4	0.3
Government regulation		
Pursue deregulation of airline, trucking, and the coastal maritime trade	5.3 to 10.4	0.3 to 0.6
Impose a shadow budget on social regulatory agencies	Unmeasurable with present data	—
Increase federal timber cut	0.3	0.02
Require fully incremental costing of all imported liquid and synthetic natural gas	Unknown, but up to 36.0	Up to 2.2
Reassess best-available-control-technology amendment to Clean Air Act	1.0 to 2.0	0.06 to 0.12
Foreign trade		
Substitute direct subsidies for meat, steel, and sugar import restraints	2.3 to 2.7	0.1 to 0.2
Minimum wage		
Replace 1978 minimum-wage increase with employment incentives	3.1	0.2
Hospital cost control		
Impose limited cost controls (fiscal 1978)	1.5	0.09

SOURCE: Robert W. Crandall, Table 12 in "Federal Government Initiatives to Reduce the Price Level," *Brookings Papers on Economic Activity*, 2: 1978, p. 438, compiled from information in the text.

a. Based on projection of fiscal 1979 gross domestic private product.

b. This is approximately the effect of some agricultural legislation being considered in Congress as of this writing.

Employing the Unemployed

It is the inequity and inefficiency of this process that the Full Employment Act refuses to accept. It incorporates a belief that unemployment is not an acceptable cure for inflation and makes clear that reducing unemployment is to have priority over reducing inflation. Given substantial evidence that (1) the costs of unemployment (in the form of lost production and income) exceed the costs of inflation, (2) inflation tends to redistribute income less inequitably than unemployment, and (3) unemployment is a relatively ineffective means of reducing inflation, these priorities seem to us to be the appropriate ones.

While the goals and priorities of the act are commendable, they are also unrealistic. To begin with, there are too many conflicting objectives, making the simultaneous achievement of all of them impossible. The most glaring example of this superfluity—the call for a balanced federal budget—has already been mentioned. Although most of the objectives are stated in such general terms that one need not attach much more than rhetorical significance to them, in the case of unemployment and inflation the establishment of specific numerical goals and timetables sharpens the mandate and compels a more searching assessment. Based on our earlier review of the state of the art in economic policymaking, we conclude that, even with the best of intentions, these goals are not achievable. To summarize our earlier review, this conclusion is based on the following arguments and evidence.

1. For whatever reason, inflation begins to accelerate when unemployment moves into the neighborhood of 5 or 6 percent. While demographic shifts in the early 1980s could lower the danger zone slightly and permit somewhat greater scope for macroeconomic policy, such shifts are not expected to have a major impact.

2. Labor-market policies are not a *proven* vehicle for reducing the unemployment rate consistent with nonaccelerating inflation. Cautious optimism appears to be warranted, but at the present time we can make only educated guesses about the likely effectiveness of these approaches. Further experimentation and research are badly needed.

3. Assuming that labor-market policies *could* reduce the NAIRU to 4 percent by 1983, we would nevertheless be far from having achieved the goals of the Full Employment Act since inflation might still be running in the neighborhood of 8 to 10 percent. Labor-market policies can potentially reduce unemployment in noninflationary ways, but they cannot eliminate or decelerate an existing inflation.

4. The major *known* mechanism for decelerating inflation is maintaining deliberate economic slack. By giving priority to the reduction of unemployment over inflation, the Full Employment Act rejects this option. As already indicated, the evidence suggests that this is not an effective remedy for reducing inflation. Moreover, it entails large social and economic costs.

5. While the Full Employment Act is long on labor-market policies, it is short on

what we have called microinflation policies. There is no mention of incomes policies, for example. Some interventions that would have a deflationary impact (such as rescinding increases in the minimum wage, agricultural price supports, and the Davis-Bacon Act) are explicitly prohibited. Some attention is given, however, to the need to stimulate productivity and economic growth. Over the longer run, this may be the best insurance against inflation, but it is not likely to have much impact by 1983.

6. The act, therefore, leaves us with virtually no means of reducing current levels of inflation, making the targets of 3 percent for 1983 and zero percent for 1988 completely unrealistic, short of some fortuitous deflationary event.

There appear to be only three options for economic policy at this juncture. The first is to rely on the old-fashioned remedy of macroeconomic constraint to decelerate inflation, accepting the natural-rate school's contention that the long-run impact on unemployment will also be favorable, if we are only willing to accept the short-run costs. The second is to adopt a much more aggressive set of microeconomic measures, some of which (such as wage-price controls or reducing government regulation) conflict with other social values. If combined with measures to improve productivity, such interventions might enable us to achieve the objectives of the Full Employment Act, if not by 1983, then a few years later.

The third alternative is to redefine our objectives. This might include some reassessment of the official data on unemployment and inflation. For example, some adjustment might be made for the upward bias in the CPI caused by the failure to measure the value of higher quality products, cleaner environments, safer work places, and other possible additions to real output. Given the widespread indexing of wages and other payments to the official data, if these biases exist, they contribute to the inflationary momentum.

Perhaps the greatest contribution of the Full Employment Act is to highlight how far our aspirations are from our capacity to achieve them. We have little or no knowlege about the macroeconomic impacts of specific sectoral interventions and no institutionalized means for acquiring it. Economic research is still essentially an activity carried out by academic entrepreneurs with minimal federal support.

Finally, we may need to open up a more serious debate about the fundamental compatibility of full employment and price stability in a society where every group expects its real income to be protected from the vicissitudes of a market economy. Inflation may be the cost of economic security, or to put it more accurately, of an economic system that has fewer and fewer downside risks to match its relatively abundant opportunities.

11

ELI GINZBERG

Potential and Limits

EACH of the contributors to this book has looked carefully at one or another aspect of the nation's manpower policy and programs during the past two decades and has reached some broad judgments about their value to the individuals involved and to the nation at large. They have identified both positive and negative conclusions about the different training programs.

Those who looked at the distributional effects on personal income of these manpower efforts concluded that long-term effects were usually nonexistent or trivial. However, they concluded that those who participated in these programs were better off than they would otherwise have been.

The three analysts who addressed the interface between manpower and macroeconomic policy concluded that there is a role for selective-employment programs that can expand the number of jobs for the hard-to-employ. Such jobs generally pay low wages and therefore have less inflationary potential than jobs stimulated through the use of macro measures. But these analysts see little or no possibility of reaching the goal of full employment in the near future.

Most contributors noted that weaknesses in the data base interfered with reaching clear-cut judgments. We know too little about every aspect of these programs—who entered; how long they stayed; what auxiliary services, such as occupational counseling, they received while they were in the program; whether they were assisted after they completed their programs; when they obtained jobs; how long those who obtained jobs held them; and how much they were paid.

But if better data had been available, that alone could not have assured that the assessments would be valid. Consider the following difficulties

178

reaching valid judgments: the programs were in constant flux, partly as a result of changes introduced because of experience (Job Corps); shifts in eligibility requirements modified, often radically, the kinds of persons accepted for training or employment; variations in the management, content, operations, and linkages to employers in the same program at different locations made each program more or less unique.

A second source of complexity reflects differences in the external environment. In a tight labor market, such as existed in the late 1960s, it may be possible to persuade employers to provide large-scale on-the-job training programs, but this kind of cooperation cannot be elicited in a loose labor market. A large public-service employment program will have better prospects of succeeding in a city that is under severe fiscal pressure and where its civil service workers have a relatively weak organization than in a city in which one or both of these conditions are absent.

Finally the political ambience and the public's mood are important factors in determining outcomes. It is easier to launch a new program or expand an existing one when legislators are enthusiastic and the public is supportive, as in early 1977 when Congress more than doubled the scale of the PSE program and passed the new Youth Act, than when enthusiasm has been dampened, as happened two years later.

These realities that constrain social intervention in a democracy are the justification for the broad assessment that is ventured below. That assessment is informed by the judgments of my collaborators but it is not bounded by them. I have relied in large measure on my ongoing research in the manpower arena, reinforced by the unique opportunity I have had since the onset of the federal programs to serve as the chairman of successive advisory bodies to the president, the Congress, and the secretary of labor.

CRITERIA FOR EVALUATING PROGRAMS

Since we have considered the difficulties of assessing federal manpower programs, it may be helpful to also consider how criteria, parameters, and target groups are likely to affect the outcomes. With respect to the criteria for evaluation, we can differentiate the effects on the individuals who participate, on others affected by the program, on the economy, and on broader considerations of social welfare. A few words about each. If we focus on the individual participant, we will want to consider whether the person in training or in a public-service job is better off in terms of income and other benefits than he or she would be otherwise. Since most manpower programs have been voluntary—the principal exception being WIN—there is a presumption that enrollees see advantages in participating. The allowances or wages paid them while in a program usually add an increment, sometimes a relatively large increment, to family income.

However the answer to whether the individual gains from participating in a program is elsewhere: the key question is whether, as a result of participating, the individual will have more employment and more income in the future. The answer, then, is in the postprogram effects and here a related question is whether the gains will be for a relatively short period, a year or two, or for a longer period.

Although the immediate and later impacts on the participant are important, they are only the beginning of a comprehensive effort at assessment. If one assumes, as most economists do, that the demand for labor at any point in time is determined by macroeconomic policy, then governmental efforts to improve the competitive position of one group of workers is likely to be at the expense of another group that will be pushed further back in the hiring queue. A concrete illustration of such "substitution" can be seen in municipalities discharging civil service workers for budgetary reasons at the same time that they are adding PSE workers who will perform some, if not all, of the tasks of those who were let go.

It is even more difficult to assess the impact on the economy of manpower programs. For instance, some economists believe that the demand for labor is not independent of the quality of the available supply. Consequently, they argue, building skills and competences in persons on the periphery of the labor force can make a difference in the total numbers who obtain employment. But even these economists find it difficult to determine when the balance tips from positive to negative outcomes in undertaking additional public investments to raise the skill level with an eye to expanding employment.

The current view, as indicated above, is that selective-employment programs aimed at expanding employment opportunities for the hard-to-employ are less inflationary than is macroeconomic policy. But even if we accept this conclusion, it does not provide much policy guidance as to the scale and design of these programs.

Much the same uncertainty exists in the case of policies aimed at reversing the decline of urban neighborhoods, cities, and regions by encouraging the employment of underused manpower resources. Unemployment and underemployment are serious wastes. The potential contribution of unemployed workers is permanently lost. But since large public resources are required to turn a declining area around, and since, even with such investments, the reversal may not occur, the outcome will be negative. The jobs that could have been created in other areas with these resources exceed the numbers that were in fact added.

To complicate the question we should consider further the difficulties of assessing, prospectively or even retrospectively, the trade-offs in a period of high inflation, such as at present, between short-term stimulation of the economy through a large effort at job creation and the impact of such a policy on the inflationary environment and on long-range employment.

Finally, we shall briefly consider the difficulties of assessing the social-welfare costs and benefits arising from different manpower programs. Some analysts believe that any public program that transfers income from the affluent to the poor justifies itself, and most evaluations suggest that the short-run distribution effects of manpower programs meet this test.

These illustrations are a reminder of the limitations of the available data as well as of accepted theory to definitively assess the impact of alternative manpower policies on the performance of the economy.

Opinion-survey data point up that the American people continue to place a high value on work. Hence they prefer that the unemployed work rather than live off governmental income transfers. But the critical issue is how fast can useful jobs be created and for what proportion of all potential job seekers? If job increases, private or public, call forth additional numbers of job seekers so that new entrants or reentrants obtain most of the newly created jobs, it may prove difficult, and in the short run impossible, to drive the unemployment rate down to a socially aceptable level without precipitating runaway inflation.

The American people have been energetically tackling the reduction and removal of discrimination against racial minorities and females in the labor market. To the extent that manpower programs are targeted on these groups, they should be assessed for their contribution to realizing this important societal objective.

Adults who do not have jobs use their time to seek some income, to keep busy, to find a role. We know that many young people who are out of school and without jobs engage in different kinds of antisocial and illegal activities from muggings to selling dope. We have no way of knowing what proportion of such youngsters, as well as older adults who follow a life of delinquency and crime, would prefer the alternative of a regular job if one were available. In any case, a democratic society will want to include the possible benefits of reduced antisocial behavior when it assesses the balance sheets of training and manpower programs.

These considerations of the criteria for assessing manpower programs—

the participants, other individuals, the economy, and the society—underscore the limitations of evaluations, even with improved data. The extant theories are inadequate to encompass and analyze the interacting variables in a changing world.

ADDITIONAL PROBLEMS

If the problem presented by these criteria could be effectively handled, two additional sets of difficulties would remain. They relate respectively to the types of assistance required by different groups and to the responsiveness in programmatic design elicited by changing conditions in the economy and society.

Different Client Groups

First, as we focus on groups with high claims for assistance, we can distinguish the following four categories of clients—young people, regularly attached members of the work force, the structurally employed (including in particular minority groups), and adult female entrants or reentrants into the labor market. One need do no more than list these four categories to appreciate that they have specific needs that cannot be met by one specific type of training or employment program.

The following observations are directed to distinguishing the needs of these several groups and the preferred responses to them.

If we postulate that most young people, as a result of their developmental experiences and with the help of their family, can make the transition from school to work without difficulty, we should focus on the cumulative deficits of those young people who cannot obtain steady work because they lack socialization and competence. Years of being buffeted in the labor market may reduce some of these handicaps but failure on their part to find and hold regular jobs will add new and telling deficits that future employers will weigh heavily in their hiring decisions.

To reduce significantly the number of disadvantaged youth entering the labor market would require improved developmental experiences through remedial education and skill acquisition and, above all, assistance in finding regular jobs.

With regard to the regularly attached members of the labor force, we can note the following conditions that warrant interventions: lack of opportunities for unskilled and semiskilled workers to obtain additional knowledge, training, and know-how in order to improve their job prospects. While many large employers provide such opportunities, many others do not, and this is the rationale for federally supported upgrading opportunities.

The U.S. economy continues to be buffeted by recessions that lead to large-scale layoffs and discharging of individuals who in better times would be firmly attached to their jobs and progressing in their careers. Since most of these individuals will be called back to work by their employers before their unemployment compensation runs out, a reasonable response to their plight is to insure that the unemployment-insurance system operates at effective benefit levels and duration, and to insure that some combination of income transfer and manpower assistance is available for those who exhaust their benefits or who have no prospect of being recalled to their jobs. Whether and to what extent public-service employment should be used to moderate cyclical unemployment is considered later.

Structurally unemployed adults are those who have never made a firm attachment to the labor force because of their developmental deficits, including inadequate educational preparation and lack of skills training, or whose attachment has been broken because of plant closure, area decline, or personal disabilities, including aging. The younger among the structurally unemployed are likely to need both training and job placement, including in many instances help in relocation from areas in decline. For older unemployed persons, especially those in declining areas, long-term public-service employment may be the preferred solution until they reach retirement age. Here is one arena where the prospects of selective-employment policies should be explored.

During the post–World War II decades, there has been a large and sustained influx of adult women into the labor force, an influx that continues. The overwhelming majority of these women has been able to find a job in the burgeoning service economy, primarily in clerical or sales positions. Their general education, maturity, and discipline are traits that employers seek. In recent years, the attention of students of this phenomenon has begun to focus on one group of mature women who find it difficult to enter or reenter the labor market—those who have been homemakers for a decade or two and who suddenly must find jobs to support themselves and often their dependents. There are no reliable data about how many "displaced homemakers" are seeking jobs, how many need help, or the types of help that would be most useful to them. The numbers are sufficiently large, however, to warrant governmental intervention.

The categories of present and potential claimants for manpower services have been kept deliberately short here to illustrate the range of problems they confront and the different types of assistance they require. If we were to add native Americans, migrant workers, veterans, the physically and emotionally handicapped, ex-offenders and ex-addicts, as well as the other groups that have been identified in the current legislation as worthy of special consideration, the complexities of meeting the discrete needs of so many different categories of claimants would appear horrendous.

Designing Manpower Programs for Changing Conditions

The other complication in assessing manpower programs flows directly from the changes characteristic of our dynamic economy and society, which can weaken or undermine sound efforts at intervention to enhance the employability and employment of persons who need assistance.

We called attention earlier to the differing responses of employers to on-the-job training in periods of tight and loose labor markets. However, the cyclical and structural changes in the economy impact every facet of manpower policy and programming, from expanding or contracting the numbers in search of assistance to the resources available and their effective deployment. Since the 1980s may differ from the growth trends of the two earlier decades, manpower policymakers may be faced with the new challenge of an environment of slow growth.

While opinions differ about how effectively the nation is dealing with its double-digit inflation, there is a consensus that until the present rate is cut substantially, the public agenda must continue to give priority to the issue. This preoccupation cannot fail to affect all economic and social policies and will certainly leave its mark on manpower programming in the years ahead.

National policy reflects responses to challenges on the international and domestic fronts as well as to changing national expectations. Although the Full Employment and Balanced Growth Act, which was passed in 1978, consisted of little more than a listing of objectives, the act included for the first time a national commitment to full employment, and it defined the commitment in terms of an acceptable unemployment level of 3 percent for adults and further stipulated that a level of 4 percent total, including youth, be achieved for 1983. The goal will not be achievable by 1983, but it will influence economic and employment policy as long as it remains on the statute books. There are many different interest groups that will remind Congress and the administration of this commitment and press them to take whatever steps appear possible to turn promise into reality.

The implementation of manpower programs has not been static in the past and the full-employment goal speaks to more changes in the future. In their first decade, federal manpower programs were federal in the sense that the federal government was responsible for the entire effort and the nongovernmental sector had a minor role. Since 1974, the principal actors have been state and local governments, with the federal role restricted largely to that of financier. However, the federal government continues to be responsible for a few specialized programs such as the Job Corps.

Recently there has been a new turn of the wheel and the administration, the Congress, and many other leaders of opinion are now looking forward to an enlarged role for the private sector. If the private sector becomes actively involved in the design and operation of manpower programs at the local level, the modest results achieved in the past may not be predictive of future outcomes.

There are two further references to possible changes. First, the administration has proposed that 400,000 PSE positions be reserved for the principal wage earner in families on welfare as the fulcrum for the reform of the welfare system. At this point we do not know whether the bill will be passed, but if it is, it will almost certainly leave its mark on the manpower system.

Second, there is a steadily increasing concern, in and out of Congress, with the large flow of undocumented workers into the United States whose presence, it is now realized, has a significant effect on the supply of unskilled workers, wages, and working conditions in selected labor markets. This presence must affect the opportunities open to the many hard-to-employ young people and adults who are the primary targets for manpower assistance. Any radical change in immigration policy would also influence future manpower programs.

Further complications that must be borne in mind stem from the weaknesses of the management-information system, the absence of control groups in most evaluations, and the wide differences in need, as earlier suggested, between different client groups, all of which impact the ability of Congress and the administration to design and improve manpower programs. It is further important to recall that good evaluations that point up the limited success of various programs do not solve the problem but only point to the need for improved programming.

JUDGMENTS ABOUT MANPOWER POLICY AND PROGRAMS

The thrust of these diverse considerations affecting the assessment of manpower policy and programs has been to underscore its continuing evolution. Even carefully developed analyses, based on firm data, will not permit more than a balanced judgment of past efforts in projecting policy into the future. We know that considerations germane to the environment within which the program initially operated and was evaluated cannot be uncritically projected.

The fact that objective inquiry is limited in all matters affecting public policy carries two implications: the necessity for the public to make judgments even when the facts are few and the theory weak and the correlative necessity of placing considerable weight on the judgments of informed persons. The need for judgment grows out of the imperative of a democratic society to weigh its options and to take action whenever it appears likely that a specific intervention will contribute to increasing equity and/or efficiency. If the public is unwilling to approve action until the case for intervention has been proved, action will be indefinitely delayed. Translated, this means that the status quo, with all of its shortcomings, remains entrenched.

Guided by these considerations, I consider it necessary to set forth as tersely as I can my judgments about the potential of manpower policy and programming based on the last eighteen years of American experience. I will follow this with a series of problematic formulations, which will remain unanswered until we move from conception to pilot model to full implementation.

With respect to the potential of manpower policy and programming, my views, as of the fall of 1979, are as follows:

- An advanced economy such as that of the United States must continue to experiment with manpower policies and programs for the reason that it cannot rely solely on the self-corrective forces of the market to assure optimal employment opportunities. Neither can it make use of fiscal and monetary policy alone to reduce the unemployment rates for specific groups to an acceptable level without generating unacceptable levels of inflation. Reworded, this means that there is latitude—how extensive remains to be discovered—for manpower policy and programs to play a constructive role in contributing to the employability and employment of selected groups in the population.
- The destructive effects of gross inequalities in opportunities and rewards reach across generational lines. The children of the poor, the unskilled, and the undereducated are likely to enter adulthood ill prepared to cope with the responsibilities of work and citizenship. While our society spends sizable sums on education and a variety of other measures contributing to the development of poor children, these efforts still leave many offspring of poor families so badly positioned that without special assistance they will remain on the periphery of society and the economy. It is not easy for manpower programs that deal with eighteen-year-olds to compensate for the cumulative deficits that a young person has sustained up to that age. But as the Job Corps experience underscores, a multifaceted effort directed at remedial education, skill acquisition, and job placement can make a real difference. Many young

people need a "second chance" not only on grounds of equity but also for the benefits that will accrue to society.

- The most favorable method for assisting low-skilled persons to improve their long-term occupational status and income is to provide them with training that leads to a desirable job, such as a year's course in practical nursing or in auto mechanics, where the demand for specific skills remains relatively high. Once they have acquired these new skills, they are likely to enjoy more or less permanent employment at wages double, or more than double, their previous earnings.
- Short training courses of approximately four to six months' duration have much to commend them when they are undertaken after the person has been hired or when arrangements have been worked out ahead of time with employers to hire all those who satisfactorily complete the course. In a tight labor market, such as existed in the late 1960s, the prospective placements may be sufficiently certain not to require such pretraining agreements. There is a disturbingly large body of evidence, however, that points to the failure of job placement following training, which serves to estrange still further the frustrated trainee who, having made a special effort at self-improvement, discovers that employers are still not interested in hiring him.
- A society with a large number of adults in need of jobs and income that the regular economy fails to provide, even under conditions of rapidly expanding employment such as existed during most of the 1970s, has every reason to experiment with public-service employment. It is clearly preferable for unemployed persons to be engaged in useful work than to deteriorate through idleness. Although as yet we lack effective mechanisms for preventing such workers from occasionally jeopardizing the jobs of regularly employed civil service workers, from restraining an upward pull on the wages of unskilled workers in the private economy, or for facilitating movement into regular employment after the PSE job has come to an end, these problems do not diminish the importance of public-service employment in an economy characterized by job shortfalls. Further efforts must be concerned with relating PSE wages to conditions in the marketplace rather than to the income needs of the assignees, with building in a training component to enhance the eventual transition to a regular job, and with linking the entire PSE effort more closely to the hiring practices of private- and public-sector employers.
- A beginning has been made in connection with the Youth Act to raise the contribution of the educational system to the occupational skills and goals of the student body and, more broadly, to improve linkage among the schools, employers, labor, and the manpower authorities. One must ascribe to manpower policy much of the credit for strengthening the educational system so that it is capable of making a larger contribution to the millions of high school students who each year complete their studies with or without acquisition of a diploma. Since the cumulative expenditures of the educational system for twelve years of instructional costs are three to four times as large as a year's remedial course in a Job Corps center, the importance of improving the productivity of the regular educational system is underscored. Given the fact that there is little prospect for young people to make a satisfactory transition from school to work unless they have acquired the basic competence that an educational system should provide them, one can assume that the manpower-

187

stimulated reform of the school system will continue even if progress will be slow and halting. Similar system-wide impacts can be seen in prospective role of job creation in welfare reform; in the reassessment of the limits of extended unemployment compensation benefits, with congressionally expressed preferences for recourse to manpower services after thirty-nine weeks in place of continued income transfers; and in prospective experimentation to use the unemployment-insurance system to compensate for short-time in order to reduce layoffs and discharges in periods of recession. It is fair to say that the potential effect of manpower policy on these related human-resources systems has only recently been recognized and judgment must be suspended until more evidence has been accumulated.

- Once a democratic society becomes cognizant of gross inequities and inefficiencies, as it did in the 1960s, with respect to the long-term neglect of minorities and the poor, it does not have the luxury of turning its back on its newly acquired knowledge and insight. Response is imperative. Had manpower programs been judged to have been less effective than the evaluations have found, the national effort to provide the disadvantaged with second-chance opportunities, and such other benefits as sizable income transfers, would nevertheless have to be seen as positive. This is not to say that a large proportion of the poor and minorities who participated in manpower programs (and one must remember that most did not have an opportunity to participate) succeeded in gaining a regular attachment to the labor force. But political tensions and social unrest would have been much greater had the federal government not demonstrated a concern and had it failed to act. Manpower programs may have fallen far short of what was needed, but they surely were preferable to a policy of indifference and neglect.

- The evolution of the manpower infrastructure has facilitated the launching of a variety of demonstrations focused on a number of groups on the periphery of society whose income and employment needs were overlooked in earlier years. Prominent among these are ex-offenders who in the past have been released from prison with little more than pocket money, a practice that virtually assured a high frequency of recidivism. Former drug addicts and released mental patients are two other large groups for whom manpower services have been designed in the hope that with training and a job many might eventually become regularly employed and lead normal lives.

PROGRAM ACCOMPLISHMENTS AND POTENTIAL

One can contend that the opportunities for experimentation with these hard-to-place groups have not been pursued with vigor and imagination; nevertheless, without a federal manpower effort in place and slow but steady gains in its capabilities to respond to a diversity of challenges, even such experimentation as occurred would not have been undertaken. The full exploitation of structured demonstrations and experiments to contribute to knowledge and policy lies in the future, but the potential exists.

The foregoing delineations of the potential of manpower policy and programs have been formulated conservatively in order not to exaggerate what has been accomplished and to avoid excessive expectations for the future. But by using a wide lens, the potential was found to be substantial. The interventions that were undertaken have enabled some hard-to-employ persons to become regularly attached to the world of work with significant gains in income; have provided jobs and income for large numbers of poor, near-poor, and unemployed persons through public-service employment; have taken early steps to improve the transition of young people from school to work, and in the process have challenged the schools to reappraise their orientation and performance in order to contribute more effectively to the employability of disadvantaged young people; and have initiated demonstrations and experiments aimed at (1) modifying important income-transfer systems such as welfare and unemployment compensation and (2) addressing the employment problems of the most disadvantaged groups in our society, whose lack of opportunities to work had not previously engaged the public's attention.

These significant potentials exist. But the critical questions that remain are how fast and how far they can be more fully realized. The following brief consideration of the problematic elements in the future use of manpower policy speaks to these questions.

- Although there is a renewed attempt to involve the private sector in various aspects of manpower policy and programming aimed at accelerating the training and employment of the structurally unemployed, it is premature to assess the success of this effort. The record leaves much to be desired: Only once in the past—and then reinforced by strong presidential leadership and a conducive labor market—did the private sector respond enthusiastically, and that was a decade ago. It is questionable whether even the sizable tax benefits provided by the Targeted Jobs Tax Credit Program (TJTC) and federal funding for the new Private Industry Councils (PICs) will entice more than limited employer response. If the president should lean heavily on the business leadership to play a leading role, stronger response can be anticipated. But effective business participation will require organization at the local level involving small- and medium-scale enterprises that do most of the hiring. This will surely prove difficult, perhaps impossible. However, unless the private sector participates, enabling enrollees in government-sponsored training programs and in PSE jobs to make the transition into regular jobs, the federal manpower programs will remain little more than stopgaps in the search of the hard-to-employ for work and income.
- There is an emerging consensus, even among left-of-center economists, that

so long as the nation is suffering from double-digit inflation, it would be unwise or downright foolhardy (a judgment depending on one's theoretical predilections) to drive the economy close to full utilization for fear of adding to the inflationary pressures. Given this major barrier to early or rapid movement toward the statutory goal of full employment, the question remains as to how venturesome the administration and the Congress will be in experimenting with selective-employment policies that hold promise of adding the unskilled to the nation's payroll without significant adverse effects on wage rates and inflation. At this moment such efforts are supported largely by theory; guidance is needed from experience as well. If Congress experiments along this axis, what will the experience reveal? If selective-employment policies can fulfill their promise, then manpower policy may, in the 1980s, really come into its own. We must recognize that unless we experiment with selective manpower policies on a controlled but expanding scale, millions of poor people will be doomed to a life of intermittent employment.

- One of the most difficult and perplexing aspects of structural unemployment has been the concentration of large pockets of peripheral workers in the cores of our major cities, in smaller communities that have suffered an erosion of their economic base, and in declining rural areas. Among low-income minorities, youth and adults alike, mobility is not likely to provide an escape mechanism from unemployment and poverty. There is no reason for a black youngster in Philadelphia to assume that he will be better off if he relocates in Houston or for a New York City youth of Puerto Rican extraction to be attracted to Denver. Accordingly, efforts to moderate the excessively high level of unemployment must focus largely on the areas where the structurally unemployed now reside. Although it is not practical in terms of public policy for the federal government to attempt to reverse the economic decline of every city, it may be able, with the assistance of state and local governments and the private sector, to contribute to the economic revival of many to the extent that their excessive unemployment is absorbed. We are in an early stage of improving the coordination of funding for federal manpower programs, with the funding for housing and economic infrastructure made available by the Housing and Urban Development Administration (HUD) and Economic Development Administration (EDA). To the degree that they succeed, these federal efforts will stimulate additional funding by other levels of government and the private sector. But the open issues are: How extensively will these different funding sources be coordinated? How well will the funds be invested in viable economic development projects? How much will they stimulate employment, particularly for the structurally unemployed? To list these questions is to underscore the complexity of what lies ahead.

- It is often overlooked that the U.S. economy has performed well in new job creation; the problem is that most of the new jobs are filled by persons other than the structurally unemployed. Recently, Congress has moved to target the federal manpower programs on the most needy. With total funding always insufficient for the numbers who can profit from manpower services, the logic of targeting on the most needy is appealing on grounds of equity and social welfare, if not always on economic efficiency. In addition, the reluctance of employers to hire the hard-to-employ must be anticipated. They may calculate

190

that the tax incentives, subsidies, or grants made available by the federal government will not overcome the additional costs of hiring only members of targeted groups. If this occurs, it may prove necessary for the federal government to increase the incentives, loosen the targeting criteria, and establish qualifying standards for eligible individuals, which might reassure skeptical employers of the unemployed to perform a day's work. A more radical proposal would be to make the financing of government contracts conditional upon the willingness of successful bidders to hire a given proportion of their workforce, say one out of three, from the rolls of eligibles certified by the employment service. More time must pass before a judgment can be reached about the present targeting regulations, and an even longer time will be needed to experiment with one or more of the above alternatives. But no manpower effort can fail to address and attempt to solve the issue of how to improve the outcomes for members of groups most in need of assistance.

- Ours is a society that looks to earnings from regular employment to provide most adults with the income required to support themselves and their dependents. During the last decades, however, our society has recognized the desirability of government's providing income to selected groups who are unable to work because of serious disabilities or competing responsibilities. Recently the availability of large income-transfer funds has been found to have an adverse effect on the work potential of many individuals who may gain little if any advantage, and on occasion may actually suffer losses, by accepting a job. While such dysfunctional effects of income-transfer systems can be reduced, they cannot be eliminated once one recognizes that the level of subsistence allowances from the welfare system may equal and even exceed earnings from low-paying jobs. A related problem in the work-income arena is posed by the increasing amount of income that people earn from off-the-books, illicit and illegal sources. The total of these streams may approximate $200 million annually, a sum that would translate into the equivalent of earnings for one out of every six jobs. Faced with these alternative ways of earning money, many young people, as well as adults, opt for a life of risk, excitement, and more dollars per hour of work, in preference to regular employment at an unskilled job with low wages and poor working conditions. The presence of these options—income transfer and illegal earnings—sets limits to the interim, and even long-term, goals that manpower programs can hope to achieve. There are a considerable number of individuals—the question is how many—who in the face of these irregular opportunities will probably eschew the assistance that manpower programs provide. They will play it their way, not society's way.

Even this abbreviated consideration of the limits that lie in the path of manpower policy and programs should suffice to dampen excessive optimism. It is unquestionably true that manpower policy has considerable potential to contribute to expanding the opportunities for many persons to improve their employability and obtain regular employment. But it is also true that the road ahead is uncertain. The constraints growing out of the continuing inflation, the wariness of the private sector, the difficulties of coordinating economic development with manpower policy, employer concerns about tight targeting, and the limits to a job policy introduced into the system by alternative sources of income are individually powerful, collectively that much more so. But even in total they do not cancel out the potential; rather they point to the difficulties that must be overcome in order to realize it.

POLITICS AND MANPOWER POLICY

While the interaction between potential and problematics will influence the future evolution of manpower policy and programs, the determining factor will be politics. Without undertaking an extended consideration of the political parameters and how they are likely to impact manpower policy in the years ahead, considerable illumination can be gained from a cursory review of the stances of the principal constituencies.

Most low-income persons belonging to minority groups have not benefited nearly so much as they need to from manpower programs. However, many CBOs have been established and expanded with the support of manpower funding and many among their leadership have made occupational and career advances as a result of manpower programs. Accordingly, one can assume that the spokesmen for minority groups will continue to be strong advocates of larger manpower programs, particularly if they are focused on the structurally unemployed.

While the trade unions have been supportive of manpower programs since their inception, their interest increased substantially once public-service employment was added to the range of available services. In a loose labor market that is likely to persist for some years to come, one can postulate that labor will remain a strong supporter of manpower programs and manpower policy since they offer assistance in moving toward the goal of full employment.

The third major constituency consists of the chief elected officials of medium-sized and large cities and counties, especially those that continue to operate close to their allowed taxable ceilings. The funding of manpower programs, particularly PSE, has been of major assistance to hard-pressed urban centers struggling to continue to provide basic and desirable services to their electorates. It is reasonable to expect that most mayors and county executives will remain strong supporters of manpower in the years ahead.

When it comes to the business community, both the leadership of the large corporations and representatives of small- and medium-sized enterprises, the outlook is uncertain. If the targeted tax credits and the work of the PICs find favor among large numbers of businessmen, one can look forward to support from a substantial segment of the private sector. However, if the present and prospective manpower programs impress only a small minority, the best that can be anticipated is neutrality, the worst, outright opposition.

This suggests that the future of manpower policy and programming will depend in considerable measure on how the average working-class and middle-class white voter reads the record and assesses the future. With the programs heavily targeted on low-income minority groups, the white voter may decide that there is nothing in them for him except higher taxes and may signal his legislative representatives to vote against such programs. In that event, the future of manpower programs is not encouraging. On the other hand, the political leadership may conclude, as did Vice-President Lyndon Johnson in 1962, that many, particularly blacks and other minority groups on the periphery of American life, will never be able to support themselves and their dependents unless assisted in obtaining training and employment.

The real choice that the American people face is not greater or lesser support for manpower programs in the future, but rather the basic decision as to whether or not they desire to affirm the nation's long-term commitment to a society built on work. In the event that they affirm this commitment, they have no option but to support the further elaboration of manpower policy and programming, which is a necessary if not sufficient condition for achieving this primary national goal.

NOTES

Chapter 1

1. I am indebted to Mr. William Hewitt, U.S. Department of Labor, for the $64 billion estimate. The best single source of data for manpower programs is the *Employment and Training Report of the President* (Washington, D.C.: U.S. Government Printing Office, 1979).

Chapter 2

1. Orley Ashenfelter, "Estimating the Effect of Training Programs on Earnings with Longitudinal Data," a paper presented at the Conference on Evaluating Manpower Training Programs (Princeton, N.J.: May 6–7, 1976), processed.

2. Orley Ashenfelter, "Estimating the Effect of Training Programs on Earnings," *The Review of Economics and Statistics*, Vol. LX, No. 1, (1978), pp. 47–57.

3. Steve L. Barsby, *Cost-Benefit Analysis and Manpower Programs* (Lexington, Mass.: Lexington Books, 1972).

4. Michael E. Borus, "A Benefit-Cost Analysis of the Economic Effectiveness of Retraining the Unemployed," *Yale Economic Essays*, Vol. 4, No. 2, (1964), pp.371–429.

5. Michael E. Borus, "Time Trends in the Benefits from Retraining in Connecticut," *Proceedings of the Twentieth Annual Winter Meeting* (Madison, Wis.: Industrial Relations Research Association, 1968), pp. 36–46.

6. Michael E. Borus, John P. Brennan, and Sidney Rosen. "A Benefit-Cost Analysis of the Neighborhood Youth Corps: The Out-of-School Program in Indiana," *Journal of Human Resources*, Vol. 5, No. 2, (1970), pp. 139–159.

7. Michael E. Borus, *Measuring the Impact of Employment-Related Social Programs: A Primer on the Evaluation of Employment and Training, Vocational Education, Vocational Rehabilitation, and Other Job-Oriented Programs.* (Kalamazoo, Michigan: W.E. Upjohn Institute, 1979).

Notes

8. Michael E. Borus and Edward C. Prescott, "The Effectiveness of MDTA Institutional Training over Time and in Periods of High Unemployment," *American Statistical Association 1973 Proceedings of the Business and Economic Statistics Section* (Washington, D.C.: American Statistical Association, 1974), pp. 278–284.

9. William F. Brazziel, "Effects of General Education in Manpower Programs," *Journal of Human Resources*, Vol. 1, No. 1, 1966, pp. 39–44.

10. Glen G. Cain and Ernst W. Stromsdorfer, "An Economic Evaluation of Government Retraining Programs in West Virginia," in *Retraining the Unemployed*, ed. Gerald G. Somers (Madison: University of Wisconsin Press, 1968), pp. 299–335.

11. Thomas F. Cooley, Timothy W. McGuire, and Edward C. Prescott, *The Impact of Manpower Training on Earnings: An Econometric Analysis*, Final Report MEL 76-01 to Office of Program Evaluation, Employment and Training Administration, U.S. Department of Labor (Pittsburgh: 1975), processed.

12. Steven M. Director, "Underadjustment Bias in the Evaluation of Manpower Training," *Evaluation Quarterly*, Vol. 3, No. 2, (1979), pp. 190–218.

13. Jon H. Goldstein, "The Effectiveness of Manpower Training Programs: A Review of Research on the Impact on the Poor" in *Studies in Public Welfare*, Paper No. 3, A Staff Study Prepared for the Use of the Subcommittee on Fiscal Policy of the Joint Economic Committee, 92d Cong., 2d sess. (Washington, D.C.: U.S. Government Printing Office, 1972).

14. E. C. Gooding, *The Massachusetts Retraining Program, Statistical Supplement* (Boston: Federal Reserve Bank of Boston, 1962).

15. Einar Hardin, "Benefit-Cost Analysis of Occupational Training Programs: A Comparison of Recent Studies" in *Cost-Benefit Analysis of Manpower Policies.* ed. G. G. Somers and W. D. Wood (Kingston, Ontario: Industrial Relations Centre, Queen's University, 1969), pp. 97–118.

16. Einar Hardin and Michael E. Borus, *The Economic Benefits and Costs of Retraining.* (Lexington, Mass.: D.C. Heath and Co., 1971).

17. Ketron, Inc., *The Long-Term Impact of WIN II: A Longitudinal Evaluation of the Employment Experiences of Participants in the Work Incentive Program*, Draft report prepared for the Employment and Training Administration, U.S. Department of Labor (Wayne, Pennsylvania: 1979), processed.

18. Nicholas M. Kiefer, *The Economic Benefits from Manpower Training Programs*. Final report prepared for ASPER, U.S. Department of Labor (Princeton, N.J.: 1976), processed.

19. Nicholas M. Kiefer, "Federally Subsidized Occupational Training and the Employment and Earnings of Male Trainees," *Journal of Econometrics*, Vol. 8, No. 1, (1978) pp. 111–125.

20. Sar Levitan and Robert Taggart, *Jobs for the Disabled*. (Baltimore: Johns Hopkins University Press, 1977).

21. Earl D. Main, "A Nationwide Evaluation of MDTA Institutional Job Training," *Journal of Human Resources.* Vol. III, No. 2, (1968) pp. 159–170.

22. Charles Mallar, *Evaluation of the Economic Impact of the Job Corps Program; First Follow-up Report.* Report MEL 79-04 prepared for the Office of Program Evaluation, Employment and Training Administration, U.S. Department of Labor (Princeton, N.J.: Mathematical Policy Research, Inc., 1978), processed.

23. Alfred Marshall, *Principles of Economics*, eighth ed. (New York: Macmillan, 1980).

24. National Council on Employment Policy, *The Imapct of Employment and Training Programs* (Washington, D.C.: National Council on Employment Policy, 1976).

25. Joe N. Nay, John W. Scanlon, and Joseph S. Wholey, "Benefits and Costs of Manpower Training Programs: A Synthesis of Previous Studies with Reservations and Recommendations," in *Benefit-Cost Analyses of Federal Programs*, a compendium of Papers Submitted to the Subcommittee on Priorities and Economy in Government of the Joint Economic Committee, 92d Cong., 2d sess. (Washington, D.C.: U.S. Government Printing Office, 1973), pp. 249–274.

26. John H. Noble, Jr., "The Limits of Cost-Benefit Analysis as a Guide to Priority Setting in Rehabilitation," *Evaluation Quarterly*, Vol. 1, No. 3, (1977), pp. 347–380.

27. Dave O'Neill, *The Federal Government and Manpower.* (Washington, D.C.: American Enterprise Institute for Public Policy Research, 1973).

28. David A. Page, "Retraining under the Manpower Development Act: A Cost-Benefit Analysis," in *Public Policy*, vol. 13, ed. John D. Montgomery and Arthur Smithies (Cambridge, Mass.: Harvard University, 1964) pp. 257–276.

29. Charles R. Perry, et al. *The Impact of Government Manpower Programs* (Philadelphia: Industrial Research Unit, The Wharton School, University of Pennsylvania, 1975).

30. Edward C. Prescott and Thomas F. Cooley. *Evaluating the Impact of MDTA Programs on Earnings under Varying Labor Market Conditions*, Final Report MEL 73-08 for the Office of Policy, Evaluation and Research, Manpower Administration, U.S. Department of Labor (Philadelphia: 1972), processed.

31. Myron Roomkin, "The Benefits and Costs of Basic Education for Adults: A Case Study" in *Benefit-Cost Analysis of Federal Programs*, a Compendium of papers submitted to the Subcommittee on Priorities and Economy in Government of the Joint Economic Committee, 92d Cong., 2d sess. (Washington, D.C.: U.S. Government Printing Office, 1973) pp. 211–223.

32. David O. Sewell, *Training the Poor* (Kingston, Ontario: Industrial Relations Centre, Queen's University, 1971).

33. Adam Smith, *The Wealth of Nations.* (New York: Modern Library, 1976).

34. Gerald G. Somers and Graeme H. McKechnie, "Vocational Retraining Programs for the Unemployed," *Proceedings of the Twentieth Annual Winter Meeting Meeting* (Madison, Wis.: Industrial Relations Research Association 1968), pp.25–35.

35. Gerald G. Somers and Ernst W. Stromsdorfer "A Cost-Effectiveness Analysis of In-School and Summer Neighborhood Youth Corps: A Nationwide Evaluation," *Journal of Human Resources.* Vol. VII, No. 4, (1972), pp. 446–459.

36. Ernst W. Stromsdorfer, "Determinants of Economic Success in Retraining the Unemployed: The West Virginia Experience," *Journal of Human Resources*, Vol. III, No. 2, (1968), pp. 139–158.

37. Ernst W. Stromsdorfer, *Review and Synthesis of Cost-Effectiveness Studies of Vocational and Technical Education* (Columbus, Ohio: ERIC Clearinghouse on Vocational and Technical Education, The Ohio State University, 1972).

Chapter 3

1. Bernard E. Anderson and Isabelle V. Sawhill, eds., *Youth Employment and Public Policy* (New York: Prentice Hall, forthcoming).

2. Bernard E. Anderson, "Community Based Organizations in Labor Market Intermediaries," *Report of a Conference on Labor Market Intermediaries* (Washington, D.C.: National Commission for Manpower Policy, 1978).

3. John F. Baum, *An Evaluation of a NAB/JOBS Training Program for Disadvantaged Workers* (Madison, Wis.: Industrial Relations Research Institute, 1973).

4. Andrew F. Brimmer, *The Status of Blacks in the American Economy* (Washington, D.C.: National Commission on Employment Policy, 1976).

5. Harrington Bryce, ed., *Revitalizing Cities* (Lexington, Mass.: D. C. Heath, 1979).

6. Richard D. Leone et al., *Employability Development Teams and Federal Manpower Programs: A Critical Assessment of CEP* (Philadelphia: Temple University Press, 1972).

7. F. Ray Marshall and Vernon M. Briggs, *The Negro and Apprenticeship* (Baltimore: Johns Hopkins University Press, 1967).

8. Charles R. Perry et al., *The Impact of Government Manpower Programs* (Philadelphia: Industrial Research Unit, The Wharton School, University of Pennsylvania, 1975).

9. Perry et al., *Impact of Government Manpower Programs.*

10. Robert Taggart, director, Office of Youth Programs, U.S. Department of Labor, in remarks before the National Council on Employment Policy, December 1978.

11. National Commission for Employment Policy, *Fourth Annual Report: An Enlarged Role for the Private Sector in Federal Employment and Training Programs* (Washington, D.C.: NCEP, 1978).

12. National Commission for Employment Policy, *Monitoring the Public Service Employment Program: The Second Round* (Washington, D.C.: NCEP, 1979).

13. Report of the American Assembly on Youth Employment (New York: American Assembly, 1979).

Notes

14. Ernst W. Stromsdorfer, "The Effectiveness of Youth Programs: An Analysis of the Historical Antecedents of Current Youth Initiatives," in B. E. Anderson and I. V. Sawhill, *Youth Employment and Public Policy* (New York: Prentice-Hall, forthcoming).

Chapter 4

1. Acknowledgment is made to colleagues who have worked with me on the monitoring study of the CETA-PSE program, Robert F. Cook, V. Lane Rawlins, Michael Wiseman, Janet Galchick, and the all-important group of field research associates responsible for the findings on which much of the material in this chapter is based.

2. *Monitoring the Public Service Employment Program*, March 1978 and *Monitoring the Public Service Employment Program: The Second Round*, March 1979. Both reports published by the National Commission for Manpower Policy.

Chapter 5

1. In preparing this chapter, the author drew heavily on published and forthcoming reports on the supported-work demonstration prepared by the research and operations staff of the Manpower Demonstration Research Corporation (MDRC) and by researchers at Mathematica Policy Research and the Institute for Research and Poverty, University of Wisconsin. The principal sources include the first and second *Annual Report on the National Supported Work Demonstration* (New York: MDRC, 1976 and 1978), the *Final Report on the National Supported Work Demonstration* (New York:MDRC, forthcoming), and a series of reports summarizing the findings from the impact analysis and the results and methodology of the benefit-cost analysis prepared by Robinson Hollister (principal investigator), Valerie Leach (project director), Peter Kemper, Rebecca Maynard, and Craig Thornton at Mathematica Policy Research, and Irwin Garfinkel, Stan Masters, Irving Piliavin, and Kathy Dickinson at the Institute for Research on Poverty (New York: MDRC, forthcoming).

Chapter 6

1. Unless otherwise specified, all data in this chapter was obtained from the U.S. Census Bureau, *Current Population Reports, Consumer Income*, Series P-60 (Washington, D.C.: U.S. Government Printing Office).

2. All employment and unemployment data was obtained from U.S. Department of Labor, *Employment and Earnings*, (Washington, D.C.: U.S. Government Printing Office).

3. Office of Management and Budget, *U.S. Government Budget Fiscal 1980* (Washington, D.C.: U.S. Government Printing Office).

Chapter 7

1. This chapter was begun while I was on the staff of The Brookings Institution and completed while I was employed at HEW. I am indebted to Arthur Hauptman for his considerable advice and assistance in the preparation of this paper and to Clive Smee for sharing his views with me.

Notes

Chapter 9

John Bishop, Robert Lampman, and especially Sheldon Danziger provided useful comments.

1. U.S., Congress, Joint Economic Committee, *The Effects of Structural Employment and Training Programs on Inflation and Unemployment*, 1979, p.27
2. Testimony of Isabel V. Sawhill before the Joint Economic Committee, U.S. Congress, *Hearings*, 21 February 1979, pp. 74–84.
3. Robert D. Plotnick and Felicity Skidmore, *Progress Against Poverty: A Review of the 1964–74 Decade* (New York: Academic Press, 1975).
4. Henry Levin, "A Decade of Policy Developments in Improving Education and Training for Low-Income Populations," in *A Decade of Federal Antipoverty Programs: Achievements, Failures, Lessons*, ed. Robert H. Haveman (New York: Academic Press, 1977).
5. Martin Feldstein, "Social Security, Induced Retirement, and Aggregate Capital Accumulation, *Journal of Political Economy* (October 1974), pp. 905–926, and Martin Feldstein, "Unemployment Compensation: Adverse Incentives and Distributional Anomalies," *National Tax Journal* (June 1974), pp. 231–244.
6. Henry J. Aaron, *Politics and the Professors: The Great Society in Perspective* (Washington, D.C.: The Brookings Institutions, 1978).
7. U. S., Congress, Joint Economic Committee, *The Effects of Structural Employment and Training Programs on Inflation and Unemployment*, *Hearings*, 1979, pp. 7–14.
8. M. Baily and J. Tobin, "Macro-Economic Effects of Selective Public Employment and Wage Subsidies," *Brookings Papers on Economic Activity*, Vol. 2 (1977), pp. 511–544. Also G. Johnson and A. Blakemore, "The Potential Impact of Employment Policy on the Unemployment Rate Consistent With Non-accelerating Inflation," *American Economic Review* (May 1979), pp. 119–123
9. R. H. Haveman and G. B. Christainsen, "Public Employment and Wage Subsidies in Western Europe and the U.S.: What We're Doing and What We Know," in a forthcoming report of the National Commission for Employment Policy.
10. G. Johnson and J. Tomola, "The Fiscal Substitution Effect of Alternative Approaches to Public Service Employment Policy," *Journal of Human Resources*, Vol. 12, (1977), pp.3–26.
11. M. Borus and D. Hamermesh, "Study of the Net Employment Effects of Public Service Employment-Econometric Analyses," *Job Creation Through Public Service Employment*, Vol. III (Washington, D.C.: National Commission for Manpower Policy, 1978), pp. 89–150.
12. John Bishop and Robert Haveman, "Selective Employment Subsidies: Can Okun's Law Be Repealed?" *American Economic Review*, Vol. 69, No. 2 (May 1979), pp. 124–130.
13. Jeffrey M. Perloff and Michael L. Wachter, "The New Jobs Tax Credit: An Evaluation of the 1977–78 Wage Subsidy Program," *American Economic Review*, Vol. 69, No. 2 (May 1979), pp. 173–179.
14. Testimony of Isabel V. Sawhill, *Hearings*, 21 February 1979.
15. Richard Nathan et al., "Monitoring the Public Service Employment Program," in *Job Creation Through Public Service Employment*, National Commission for Manpower Policy, (Washington, D.C.,: National Commission for Manpower Policy, 1978).
16. R. Haveman, "The Dutch Social Employment Program," *Creating Jobs: Public Employment Programs and Wage Subsidies*, ed. J. Palmer (Washington D. C.: The Brookings Institution, 1978).
17. Peter Kemper, David Long, and Craig Thornton, "The Supported Work Evaluation: Preliminary Benefit-Cost Analysis for the First 18 Months After Enrollment," prepared by Mathematica Policy Research for Manpower Demonstration Research Corporation, December 21, 1978.
18. Bishop and Haveman, "Selective Employment Subsidies."
19. Sheldon Danziger, Robert Haveman, and Eugene Smolensky, "The Program for Better Jobs and Income: A Guide and Critique," U. S., Congress, Joint Economic Committee, 1978, pp. 25–26.
20. John Bishop and Robert Haveman, "Categorical Employment Incentive Programs: Issues of Structure and Design," in a forthcoming report to be published by the National Commission for Employment Policy.
21. Sheldon Danziger, Robert Haveman, and Robert Plotnick, "Income Transfer Programs

Notes

in the United States: An Analysis of Their Structure and Impacts," U. S., Congress, Joint Economic Committee, forthcoming.

22. J. Bishop, "Vouchers for Creating Jobs, Education, and Training: VOCJET, an Employment-Oriented Strategy for Reducing Poverty," Institute for Research on Poverty Special Report (Madison: University of Wisconsin Press, 17 July 1977).

Chapter 10

We appreciate the comments received from Eli Ginzberg, Martin Baily, Robert Flanagan, George Johnson, Sar Levitan, and Ralph Smith.

ª This section draws heavily on one of the author's previous papers. See Isabel V. Sawhill, "Labor Market Policies and Inflation," in *New Approaches to Fighting Inflation*, ed. Richard Cornwall and Michael Claudon (New York: Academic Press, forthcoming).

1. Bernard E. Anderson, and Isabel V. Sawhill, ed., *Youth Employment and Public Policy*, (New York: Prentice-Hall, forthcoming).

2. Orley Ashenfelter, Statement before the Committee on the Budget, U.S., Congress, House, 6 February 1979.

3. Martin Neil Baily, "On the Theory of Layoffs and Unemployment," *Econometrica* (July 1977).

4. Martin Neil Baily and James Tobin, "Macroeconomic Effects of Selective Public Employment and Wage Subsidies," *Brookings Papers on Economic Activity*, Vol. 2 (1977).

5. Laurie Bassi and Alan Fechter, *The Implications for Fiscal Substitution and Occupational Displacement under an Expanded CETA Title VI*, Technical Analysis Paper No. 65, U.S. Department of Labor (March 1979).

6. Board of Governors of the Federal Reserve System, *Midyear Monetary Policy Report to Congress*, 17 July 1979.

7. Phillip Cagan, "The Reduction of Inflation and the Magnitude of Unemployment," in *Contemporary Economic Problems, 1977*, ed., William Fellner (Washington, D.C.: American Enterprise Institute, 1977).

8. Robert W. Crandall, "Federal Government Initiatives to Reduce the Price Level," *Brookings Papers on Economic Activity*, Vol. 2 (1978).

9. Council of Economic Advisers, *1979 Annual Report*, submitted to the President on 24 January 1979.

10. Paul O. Flaim, "The Effect of Demographic Changes on the Nation's Jobless Rate," *Monthly Labor Review* (March 1979).

11. Milton Friedman, "The Role of Monetary Policy," *American Economic Review* (March 1968).

12. Full Employment and Balanced Growth Act of 1978, H.R. 50, signed by President Carter on 27 October 1978.

13. Robert J. Gordon, "Alternative Responses of Policy to External Supply Shocks," *Brookings Papers on Economic Activity*, Vol. 1 (1975).

14. Edward Gramlich, "Macro Policy Responses to Price Shocks," *Brookings Papers on Economic Activity*, Vol. 1 (1979).

15. Robert E. Hall, "Prospects for Shifting the Phillips Curve Through Manpower Policy," *Brookings Papers on Economic Activity*, Vol. 3 (1971).

16. Charles C. Holt, C. Duncan MacRae, Stuart O. Schweitzer, and Ralph E. Smith, "Manpower Proposals for Phase III," *Brookings Papers on Economic Activity*, Vol. 3 (1971).

17. George E. Johnson, Statement before the Joint Economic Committee, U.S. Congress, 9 February 1979.

18. George E. Johnson and Arthur Blakemore, "The Potential Impact of Employment Policy on the Unemployment Rate Consistent with Non-Accelerating Inflation," paper presented at the 91st Annual Meeting of the American Economic Association, 28 August 1978.

19. Sar A. Levitan, and Robert Taggart, *The Promise of Greatness*, (Cambridge, Mass.: Harvard University Press, 1976).

20. National Commission for Manpower Policy, *Demographic Trends and Full Employment*, Special Report No. 12, (December 1976).

21. National Commission for Manpower Policy, *The Need to Disaggregate the Full Employment Goal*, Special Report No. 17, (January 1978).

22. Donald Nichols, Statement before the Joint Economic Committee, U.S. Congress, 9 February 1979.

23. Arthur Okun, "Efficient Disinflationary Policies," *American Economic Review* (May 1978).

24. Arnold Packer, Statement before the Joint Economic Committee, U.S. Congress, 6 June 1978.

25. George Perry, "Slowing the Wage-Price Spiral: The Economic View," *Brookings Papers on Economic Activity*, Vol. 2 (1978).

26. A. W. Phillips, "The Relation Between Unemployment and the Rate of Change of Money Wage Rates in the United Kingdom, 1861-1957," *Economica* (November 1958).

27. A. J. Preston, "A Dynamic Generalization of Tinbergen's Theory of Policy," *A Review of Economic Studies* (January 1974).

28. Isabel V. Sawhill, "Labor Market Policies and Inflation," in *New Approaches to Fighting Inflation*, ed. Richard Cornwall and Michael Claudon (New York: Academic Press, forthcoming).

29. Isabel V. Sawhill, Testimony before the Joint Economic Committee, U.S. Congress, 21 February 1979.

30. Robert M. Solow, "Macro-policy and Full Employment," in *Jobs for Americans*, ed. Eli Ginzberg (New York: Prentice Hall, 1976).

31. J. Tinbergen, *On the Theory of Economic Policy* (Amsterdam: North-Holland Publishing Company, 1952).

32. James Tobin, "Inflation and Unemployment," *American Economic Review* (March 1972).

CONTRIBUTORS

ELI GINZBURG is Director, Conservation of Human Resources, Columbia University and Chairman of the National Commission for Employment Policy.

MICHAEL E. BORUS is Director of the Center for Human Resource Research, The Ohio State University.

BERNARD E. ANDERSON is Director of the Social Sciences Division, The Rockefeller Foundation.

RICHARD P. NATHAN is Professor of Public and International Affairs, Woodrow Wilson School, Princeton University.

JUDITH M. GUERON is Executive Vice President, Manpower Demonstration Research Corporation.

LESTER C. THUROW is Professor of Economics, Massachusetts Institute of Technology.

JOHN PALMER is Assistant Secretary for Planning and Evaluation, Department of Health, Education and Welfare.

ROBERT M. SOLOW is Institute Professor of Economics at the Massachusetts Institute of Technology.

ROBERT H. HAVEMAN is Professor of Economics, University of Wisconsin.

ISABEL V. SAWHILL is Program Director, Employment and Labor Policy, Urban Institute.

LAURIE J. BASSI is a Ph.D. candidate in Labor Economics at Princeton University.

202

INDEX

Index

Index

Index

Shultz, George, 6, 7
single heads of households, 16
skills: and demand for labor, 180; in neoclassical economics, 104; surpluses of, 100
Smith, Adam, *Wealth of Nations, The*, 26
Social Security, 115, 175; "earnings test," 115
Social Security Act of 1935, 112
Social Security Act of 1967, 47
Solow, Robert M., 163, 169
Somers, Gerald G., 34
South (rural), 130
South Carolina: traininng-fund use, 19
Spanish-speaking people; *see* Hispanics
Special Imapct, 28
SPEDY Program, 123
SSI, *see* Supplemental Security Income
state employment service, 172; *see also* United States Employment Service
state governments: and CETA, 11; emergency programs of, 111; public-service employment and, 62–71
stress, graduated: in supported-work experiment, 76
Stromsdorfer, Ernst W., 33, 34
structurally unemployed people, 8; CETA and PSE jobs targeted for, 15, 23–24, 144; as client group, 182, 183; direct job creation for, 143; employment programs for, 123, 125–26; and Full Employment Act, 161, 163; macroeconomics, 171, 172; in manpower policies, 190; programs to aid, 28; in public-service employment, 60–62, 65, 70–72; subsidized-employment programs, 118–19, 121; costs of, 152–53; direct job creation in, 143, 145, 148–50; employee-based, 156–57; and inflation, 138–41; for low-income two-parent families, 124–25; for structurally unemployed, 126; supported-work, 73–93; training in, 158–59
supervision: in SPEDY Program, 123–24; in supported-work experiment, 76
Supplemental Security Income (SSI), 115, 145
Supported-Work Experiment, 73–93, 153
Sweden: manpower investment, 12; marginal employment subsidy, 158

Taggart, Robert, 169
Targeted Jobs Tax Credit (TJTC), 139, 140, 145, 189; macroeconomic theory in, 171; *see also* New Jobs Tax Credit
targeting, 57; of CETA and PSE jobs for structurally unemployed, 15, 23–24, 144; of discrimination victims, 181; in employee-based employment subsidy programs, 157; in Full Employment Act, 163;

in manpower policies, 190; of public-service employment programs, 66; in supported-work experiment, 75, 83–84, 90, 91; in tax credits for job creation, 145
taxation: credits for working poor in, 124; incentives in, 8, 22; and investment tax credit, 107; job-creating credits in, 139–40, 144–45; and selective-employment policies, 135; tax credits for training in, 99; and WIN tax credits, 93
tax incentives, 22; *see also* specific programs
Thurow, Lester C., 169
TJTC, *see* Target Jobs Tax Credit
Tobin, James, 166
training programs: budgets for, 99; distribution of earnings not altered by, 104; impact assessment of, 25–40, 119; impact on income distribution of, 100–1; and job-creation programs, 158–59; macroeconomics of, 172, 173; in manpower policies, 187; in public-service employment, 66
transition planning, 66

undocument workers, 185
unemployment: among blacks, 96; differential rates of, 105–7; direct job creation for, 143, 149–50; and earnings distribution, 104; Federal Reserve System on, 164–65; and Full Employment Act, 160–63, 174–77; during Great Depression, 111–12; among Hispanics, 97–98; impact of training on, 100–1; as impetus for federal legislation, 26–27, 41; income transfer programs for, 116, 122–23; and inflation, 43, 130, 136–38, 181, 190; during Kennedy-Johnson administrations, 4; among low-skill workers, 148; in macroeconomics, 165–74; manpower programs' effects on, 7; among middle class in 1970s, 114; of minorities and youth, 43, 51–52, 57; not related to posttraining earnings, 39; by occupation, 100; and Okun's Law, 154; structural, employment programs for, 125–26; after War on Poverty, 147; among women, 98–99; among youth, 99; *see also* structurally unemployed people
unemployment insurance, 3, 111, 112, 116, 123, 183, 188; as disincentive, 148; vs. employment programs, 125–26
USSR: wheat crop, effect on U.S. economy, 133
unions: support for manpower programs by, 192; unemployment protection plans of, 111
U.S. Chamber of Commerce, 18–19
U.S. Congress: commitment to full employment by, 184; Democratic majority, 6, 7;

208